The
VICTORIAN
NOVEL

Louis James

Blackwell
Publishing

BLACKWELL PUBLISHING
350 Main Street, Malden, MA 02148-5020, USA
9600 Garsington Road, Oxford OX4 2DQ, UK
550 Swanston Street, Carlton, Victoria 3053, Australia

First published 2006 by Blackwell Publishing Ltd

1 2006

Library of Congress Cataloging-in-Publication Data

James, Louis, Dr.
    The Victorian novel / Louis James.
        p.   cm.—(Blackwell guides to literature)
    Includes bibliographical references (p.) and index.
    ISBN-13: 978-0-631-22627-7 (hardcover : alk. paper)
    ISBN-10: 0-631-22627-3 (hardcover : alk. paper)
    ISBN-13: 978-0-631-22628-4 (pbk. : alk. paper)
    ISBN-10: 0-631-22628-1 (pbk. : alk. paper)   1. English fiction—19th century—
History and criticism.   2. Romanticism—Great Britain. I. Title. II. Series.
    PR871.J36 2006
    823'.809145—dc22

                                                                        2005012331

A catalogue record for this title is available from the British Library.

Set in 11/13.5 pt Dante
by SNP Best-set Typesetter Ltd, Hong Kong
Printed and bound in the United Kingdom
by T J International Ltd, Padstow, Cornwall

The publisher's policy is to use permanent paper from mills that operate a sustainable forestry policy, and which has been manufactured from pulp processed using acid-free and elementary chlorine-free practices. Furthermore, the publisher ensures that the text paper and cover board used have met acceptable environmental accreditation standards.

For further information on
Blackwell Publishing, visit our website:
www.blackwellpublishing.com

Contents

Key Texts   149

Major Presences

Main Texts

Illustrations

Acknowledgements

I would like particularly to acknowledge the kindness and assistance given me from the beginning of my interest in the nineteenth century by Geoffrey and Kathleen Tillotson, Humphry House, Philip Collins, Raphael Samuel and Robert Colby. More recently I have been indebted to Michael Slater, Sally Ledger, Rowan McWilliam, Joanne Shattock, Laurel Brake and, in particular, Hugh Cunningham and Anne Humpherys, both of whom nobly read the manuscript in whole or part in its final stages: they are not, however, responsible for the mistakes. Teaching is a learning experience, and over the years other insights have come from my students, particularly those in my classes on Dickens and on Melodrama. I would like also to thank the editors at Blackwell, Andrew McNeillie, who first proposed this project, and those who have seen it through the press, for their encouragement, assistance and patience. My greatest gratitude, however, goes to my wife Louise McConnell, without whose untiring encouragement and textual corrections this Guide would never have emerged into print.

How to Use This Book

This study is aimed at graduates and postgraduates, but it should be of interest also to members of reading groups, and to all who enjoy Victorian literature. It is intended to be a practical tool, concerned both with what to read and how to read. So, for instance, the section on melodrama and the novel gives the factual background, but also shows how the conventions of nineteenth-century drama shaped characters, *mise-en-scène* and plot in fiction. A discussion of the novels' 'implied readers' aims to give a better understanding of the way a work's style and approach were shaped by its intended audience. Context is there for its historical interest, but also to demonstrate the different ways novels were being read through the century, both for entertainment and in response to specific situations and events, and to show how this can affect their content.

The first section reveals the great diversity of the 'Victorian' period, and shows how novels became a means through which readers defined their social identity and formed their attitudes to such issues as nationalism, gender differences and the nature of the family. This leads to a consideration of how the novel emerged as a 'realist' form, closely linked to history and biography, responding to the religious and scientific controversies of the time. The study continues with a discussion of the way Victorian assumptions about society, ethics, and even time and space, can differ from our own.

Sections on 'key' authors, texts and topics are designed to help those looking for specific information about the Victorian novel. Because the field is so large, entries had to be selective. However, I have tried to strike a balance between novels distinguished as major literary achievements, and lesser works whose popularity makes them nevertheless important in the history of the novel. The 'topics' range widely, from the methods of novel publication to the significance of the 'sensation' novel and the issues raised by colonialism.

While this study aims to inform, it does not try to give definitive 'answers'. Its main purpose is to recover the fresh immediacy of literature too often dulled by familiarity or the routine of academic study, and to allow the reader the pleasure of recovering its power, not as a 'text', but as an original work of the creative imagination. If in the reading this book makes itself redundant, it will have performed its task.

Note: **Throughout this Guide, an asterisk (*) is used to indicate that an author or title is described in a separate main entry.**

Chronology

[P.] = poetry; [D.] = drama; [I.] = ideas

Date	Novels	Events
1830	Bulwer Lytton, *Paul Clifford*; Lyell, *Principles of Geology* (to 1833); Tennyson, *Poems Chiefly Lyrical* [P.]; *Fraser's Magazine* begun (to 1882); Comte, *Cours de philosophie positive* (France) [I.] prepares way for sociology	Accession of William IV; Reform Bill proposed; Manchester and Liverpool Railway opens; cholera epidemic (to 1832)
1831	Disraeli, *The Young Duke*; Gore, *Mothers and Daughters*; Peacock, *Crotchet Castle*; Surtees, *Jorrock's Jaunts and Jollities* (serial to 1832); Hugo, *Notre Dame de Paris* (France)	Reform Bill passed by House of Commons, vetoed by the Lords, followed by riots in Bristol and Nottingham; 'Swing' agricultural riots in southern England; Dickens (anonymously) reports debates for *Mirror of Parliaments*
1832	Bulwer Lytton, *Eugene Aram*; Scott, *Tales of My Landlord* (4th series); Byron, *Works and Letters* (to 1835) [P.]; Harriet Martineau, *Illustrations of Political Economy* (to 1834); Darwin, *Narrative of the Beagle* (to 1836) [I.]	Reform Bill forced through
1833	Dickens' short story, 'A Dinner at Poplar Walk', appears in *Monthly Magazine*; Newman, Pusey, Keble et al., *Tracts for the Times* (to 1841) starts the Oxford Movement; Bulwer Lytton, *England and the English* [I.]; Carlyle, *Sartor Resartus* in *Fraser's Magazine* (to 1834); Charles Knight, *Penny Cyclopedia* (to 1844)	Factory Acts restrict child labour; slavery abolished throughout British Empire

Date	Novels	Events
1834	Ainsworth, *Rookwood*; Bulwer Lytton, *Last Days of Pompeii*; Marryat, *Peter Simple*; Balzac, *Père Goriot* (France)	Old Houses of Parliament burn down; Poor Law Amendment act creates Union workhouses; abortive founding of Grand National Consolidated Trades Union; transportation of six 'Tolpuddle Martyrs' for taking illegal oaths to agricultural workers' union
1835	Bulwer Lytton, *Rienzi*; Clare, *The Rural Muse* [P.]	Municipal Reform Act
1836	Dickens, *Sketches by 'Boz'*; *Pickwick Papers* (in monthly parts to 1837); Marryat, *Mr Midshipman Easy*	Commercial boom (to 1836); early speculation in railways
1837	Dickens' *Pickwick Papers* in one volume; *Oliver Twist* serialized in *Bentley's Miscellany* (to 1838); Carlyle, *A History of the French Revolution*	William IV dies; accession of Queen Victoria
1838	Surtees, *Jorrocks* (volume edition); Dickens, *Nicholas Nickleby* (to 1839); Lyell, *Elements of Geology* [I.]	Anti-Corn Law League founded in Manchester; People's Charter founds the Chartist Movement (active to 1848); first Afghan War; Daguerre and Niépce pioneer commercial photography (Paris)
1839	Ainsworth, *Jack Sheppard*; Harriet Martineau, *Deerbrook*; Frances Trollope, *Michael Armstrong, the Factory Boy*; Thackeray, *Catherine* (to 1840)	Chartist riots; First Opium War in China

1840	Ainsworth, *The Tower of London*; Dickens' *The Old Curiosity Shop* published in *Master Humphrey's Clock*; Darwin, *Voyage of the Beagle*; Poe, *Tales of the Grotesque* (USA)	Marriage of Queen Victoria to Albert; penny post instituted; building of the new Houses of Parliament begun; Nelson's Column erected
1841	Dickens, *Barnaby Rudge* (in *Old Curiosity Shop*); Thackeray, *Samuel Titmarsh and the Great Hoggarty Diamond*; Lever, *Charles O'Malley*; Carlyle, *On Heroes, Hero-Worship and the Heroic in History*; *Punch* founded; Cooper, *The Deerslayer* (America)	
1842	Dickens, *American Notes*; Lover, *Handy Andy*; Tennyson, *Poems* [P.]	SS *Great Britain* launched; Wordsworth made poet laureate
1843	Dickens, *Christmas Carol*; *Martin Chuzzlewit* (to 1844); Carlyle, *Past and Present*; Ruskin, *Modern Painters*, vol. I (II, 1846; III-IV, 1856; V, 1860)	
1844	Dickens, *The Chimes*; Disraeli, *Coningsby*; Kinglake, *Eothen*; Jerrold, *Story of a Feather*; Thackeray, *Luck of Barry Lyndon*; Reynolds, *Mysteries of London* (with *Mysteries of the Court of London*, to 1856); Robert Chambers, *Vestiges of Creation* [I.]	Irish Potato Famine (to 1846); Marx meets Engels in Paris; railway speculation mania (to 1845); Turner paints *Rain, Steam and Speed*
1845	Dickens, *Cricket on the Hearth*; Disraeli, *Sybil*; Browning, *Dramatic Romances and Lyrics* [P.]; Poe, *Tales of Mystery and Imagination* (USA)	Newman joins Church of Rome
1846	Bulwer Lytton, *Lucretia*; Dickens, *Dombey and Son* (to 1848); Jerrold, *Chronicles of Clovernook*; Thackeray, *Snobs of England* (in *Punch*; afterwards published as *The Book of Snobs*); George Eliot's translation of Strauss' *Life of Jesus*	Repeal of the Corn Laws; first Christmas card printed

Date	Novels	Events
1847	Charlotte Brontë, *Jane Eyre*; Emily Brontë, *Wuthering Heights*; Disraeli, *Tancred*; Thackeray, *Vanity Fair* (to 1848); Trollope, *The Macdermots of Ballycloran*; Rymer, *Varney the Vampyre* (to 1848)	Factory Act restricts women and children to ten hours' work a day
1848	Gaskell, *Mary Barton*; Newman, *Loss and Gain*; Thackeray, *Pendennis* (to 1850); Marx and Engels, *Communist Manifesto* [I.]	Revolutions in Paris, Berlin, Vienna, Rome; cholera epidemic in London; Health Act; Pre-Raphaelite Brotherhood founded
1849	Charlotte Brontë, *Shirley*; Dickens, *David Copperfield* (to 1850); Bulwer Lytton, *The Caxtons*; Mayhew, *London Labour and the London Poor* (to 1850); Ruskin, *The Seven Lamps of Architecture*; Macaulay, *History of England* I–II (III–IV, 1855)	Bedford College London founded
1850	Kingsley, *Alton Locke*; Dickens starts *Household Words* (to 1859); Tennyson, *In Memoriam* [P.]; Wordsworth, *The Prelude* [P.]	Catholic hierarchy in England restored
1851	Gaskell, *Cranford* (to 1853); Carlyle, *Life of John Sterling*; Ruskin, *The Stones of Venice* (to 1853); Melville, *Moby Dick* (USA); Stowe, *Uncle Tom's Cabin* (USA)	The Great Exhibition, Hyde Park; Owens College, Manchester founded
1852	Dickens, *Bleak House* (to 1853); Thackeray, *Henry Esmond*	Second Burma War; Duke of Wellington dies

1853	Charlotte Brontë, *Villette*; Gaskell, *Ruth*; Surtees, *Mr Sponge's Sporting Tour*; Thackeray, *The Newcomes* (to 1855); Yonge, *Heir of Redclyffe*; Harriet Martineau's translation of Comte's *Positive Philosophy* [I.]	
1854	Dickens, *Hard Times*; Gaskell, *North and South* (to 1855); George Eliot translates Feuerbach's *Essence of Christianity*	Crimean War starts (ends 1856)
1855	Dickens, *Little Dorrit* (to 1857); Kingsley, *Westward Ho!*; Trollope, *The Warden*; Browning, *Men and Women* [P.]; Tennyson, *Maud* [P.]	Livingstone discovers Victoria Falls
1856	Reade, *It's Never Too Late to Mend*; Yonge, *The Daisy Chain*	
1857	Charlotte Brontë, *The Professor*; Eliot, *Scenes of Clerical Life* (in *Blackwood's*); Hughes, *Tom Brown's Schooldays*; Thackeray, *The Virginians*; Trollope, *Barchester Towers*; E. B. Browning, *Aurora Leigh* [P.]; Gaskell, *Life of Charlotte Brontë*; Flaubert, *Madame Bovary* (France)	Indian Mutiny (suppressed 1858); Second Opium War (to 1858); Matrimonial Causes Act allows divorce without Act of Parliament
1858	Macdonald, *Phantastes*; Trollope, *Dr Thorne*; Morris, *Defence of Guinevere* [P.]	Dickens begins public readings; Brunel's Great Eastern launched
1859	Dickens, *Tale of Two Cities*; Eliot, *Adam Bede*; Meredith, *Ordeal of Richard Feverel*; Darwin, *Origin of Species*; Mill, *On Liberty*; Smiles, *Self-Help*; Tennyson, *Idylls* (cont. 1869, 1872, 1873)	Franco-Austrian War (to 1861)
1860	Collins, *Woman in White*; Dickens, *Great Expectations* (to 1861); Eliot, *Mill on the Floss*; *Cornhill Magazine* (ed. Thackeray) leads a new wave of illustrated, fiction-carrying magazines	Huxley defeats Bishop Wilberforce in debate on evolution at British Association

Date	Novels	Events
1861	Eliot, *Silas Marner*; Henry Kingsley, *Ravenshoe* (to 1862); Reade, *Cloister and the Hearth*; Trollope, *Framley Parsonage*; Wood, *East Lynne*; Braddon, *Lady Audley's Secret* (to 1862)	Prince Albert dies; American Civil War (to 1865); the term 'sensation novel' appears
1862	Eliot, *Romola* (to 1863); Meredith, *Modern Love* [P.]; C. Rossetti, *Goblin Market* [P.]	
1863	Gaskell, *Sylvia's Lovers*; Kingsley, *Water-Babies*; Oliphant, *Salem Chapel*	Lincoln's Gettysburg Address; Thackeray dies
1864	Dickens, *Our Mutual Friend* (to 1865); Le Fanu, *Uncle Silas*; Trollope, *Can You Forgive Her?*; Gaskell, *Wives and Daughters* (to 1866); Newman, *Apologia pro Vita Sua*	First Socialist International meets in London
1865	Lewis Carroll, *Alice's Adventures in Wonderland*; Meredith, *Rhoda Fleming*; Arnold, *Essays in Criticism, First Series*; Swinburne, *Atalanta in Corydon* [P.]	Mrs Gaskell dies
1866	Collins, *Armadale*; Eliot, *Felix Holt*; Oliphant, *Miss Marjoribanks*; Yonge, *A Dove in the Eagle's Nest*	Cholera epidemic
1867	Ouida, *Under Two Flags*; Trollope, *Last Chronicle of Barset*; Marx, *Das Kapital*, vol. 1	Second Reform Act extends votes for urban electorate; typewriter invented; Dominion of Canada Act
1868	Alcott, *Little Women*; Eliot, *Spanish Gypsy* [P.]; Collins, *The Moonstone*; Trollope, *He Knew He Was Right*; Browning, *The Ring and the Book* [P.]	Last public execution; national telegraph system

1869	Reade, *Foul Play*; Trollope, *Phineas Finn*	
1870	Dickens, *Edwin Drood*; Disraeli, *Lothair*	Franco-Prussian War (to 1871); First Married Women's Property Act; Dickens dies
1871	Eliot, *Middlemarch* (to 1872); Lewis Carroll, *Through the Looking Glass*; Hardy, *Desperate Remedies*; Darwin, *Descent of Man* [I.]	Bank holidays introduced
1872	Hardy, *Under the Greenwood Tree*	Strike of agricultural labourers; secret ballots established
1873	Trollope, *Eustace Diamonds*; J. S. Mill, *Autobiography*; Pater, *Studies of the . . . Renaissance*	Mill dies
1874	Hardy, *Far from the Madding Crowd*; Trollope, *The Way We Live Now* (to 1875); Thomson, *City of Dreadful Night* [P.]	
1875		Public Health Act; Disraeli buys control of Suez Canal
1876	Eliot, *Daniel Deronda*	Queen Victoria Empress of India; Bell invents telephone
1877	James, *The American*; Zola, *L'Assommoir* (France); Meredith, 'The Idea of Comedy'	Russo-Turkish War
1878	Hardy, *Return of the Native*	Salvation Army founded; Congress of Berlin on Eastern Question; Swan demonstrates electric light bulb in UK

Date	Novels	Events
1879	Meredith, *The Egoist*; Stevenson, *Travels with a Donkey*; Ibsen's *A Doll's House* produced in Oslo, London première, 1890 [D.]	Zulu War
1880	Disraeli, *Endymion*; Gissing, *Workers in the Dawn*	First Anglo-Boer War (to 1881); Eliot dies
1881	James, *Portrait of a Lady*; Stevenson, *Treasure Island* (to 1882); Mark Rutherford, *Autobiography*	Death of Disraeli
1882	Hardy, *Two on a Tower*	Married Women's Property Act; Foundation of Society for Psychical Research; Britain occupies Egypt
1883	Schreiner, *Story of an African Farm*; Trollope, *Autobiography*	
1884	Twain, *Huckleberry Finn* (USA); James, 'The Art of Fiction'	Third Reform Act; Fabian Society founded
1885	Moore, *A Mummer's Wife*; Haggard, *King Solomon's Mines*; Pater, *Marius the Epicurean*	Death of Gordon in the Sudan; Third Burma War
1886	Hardy, *Mayor of Casterbridge*; Stevenson, *Dr Jekyll and Mr Hyde*; *Kidnapped*	Gold found in Transvaal; first Home Rule Bill for Ireland introduced
1887	Hardy, *The Woodlanders*; Haggard, *She*; Doyle, *A Study in Scarlet*	Queen's Golden Jubilee
1888	Kipling, *Plain Tales from the Hills*; Mrs Humphry Ward, *Robert Elsmere*; Rolf Boldrewood [T. A. Brown], *Robbery Under Arms* (Australia)	Jack the Ripper murders in London; accession of Kaiser Wilhelm II

1889	Gissing, *The Nether World*; Stevenson, *Master of Ballantrae*	London dockers' strike; national movement for woman's suffrage founded; Collins, Browning, Hopkins die
1890	William James, *Principles of Psychology*	Fall of Bismarck
1891	Morris, *News from Nowhere*; Gissing, *New Grub Street*; Hardy, *Tess of the D'Urbervilles*; Wilde, *Portrait of Dorian Gray*	
1892	Zangwill, *Children of the Ghetto*; Doyle, *The Adventures of Sherlock Holmes*	Tennyson dies
1893	Gissing, *The Odd Women*; Grand, *The Heavenly Twins*	Independent Labour Party founded
1894	Du Maurier, *Trilby*; Hope, *Prisoner of Zenda*; Kipling, *Jungle Book*; Moore, *Esther Waters*	
1895	Wells, *Time Machine*; Hardy, *Jude the Obscure*; Wilde, *The Importance of Being Earnest* [D.]	Trials of Oscar Wilde
1896	Wells, *Island of Dr Moreau*	Jamieson raid in South Africa; reconquest of Sudan (to 1896)
1897	Hardy, *The Well-Beloved*; Wells, *Invisible Man*; Bram Stoker, *Dracula*	Queen's Diamond Jubilee
1898	Wells, *War of the Worlds*; Hardy, *Wessex Poems* [P.]; Wilde, *Ballad of Reading Gaol* [P.]; Shaw, *Plays Pleasant and Unpleasant* [D.]	Death of Gladstone
1899	Kipling, *Stalky and Co.*; Mrs Oliphant, *Autobiography*	Second Anglo-Boer War (to 1902)
1900	Conrad, *Lord Jim*	Ruskin, Wilde die; Commonwealth of Australia Act
1901	Kipling, *Kim*	Queen Victoria dies

Introduction

The term 'Victorian novel' is at best an academic flag of convenience. Firstly, there is the problem of dates. Queen Victoria's death in 1901 comes too long after her coronation in 1837 for the term 'Victorian' to have much precise significance, either for history or for literature. The first major Victorian novel, Dickens' *Oliver Twist*, appeared conveniently in 1837, in time for the future queen to be reading it on the night before her coronation, but for a decade after this the novels of *Dickens stood largely alone among a sea of minor work. Raymond Williams and Kathleen Tillotson saw the 'true' Victorian novel as starting some ten years later, in the literary ferment of the years 1847–8.[1] In 1880 the death of *George Eliot coincided with changes in both the content and readership of fiction, and the genre's major phase ends around that period. But the novels that followed reflect back on the earlier period in important ways.

Then there is a question of the 'Victorian consciousness'. The first readers of Dickens and George Eliot did not think of themselves as living in the 'Victorian period'. 'Victorian' was first recorded in 1839, but it only gained general currency, largely as a term of disapproval, with the Edwardians. The British experienced the nineteenth century as a period of turbulent transition; although the term has been high-jacked by critics of the next era, they felt themselves to be inhabitants of the 'modern' period, a word that appears some six hundred times in the book titles listed in *The Nineteenth Century Short Title Catalogue* for 1816–70.[2] On the other hand,

---

[1] See Kathleen Tillotson, *Novels of the Eighteen-forties* (2nd edn, 1955); Raymond Williams, *The English Novel from Dickens to Lawrence* (1974).

[2] Raymond Williams, *Keywords* (1976), pp. 174–5; Andrew Sanders, *Dickens and the Spirit of the Age* (1999), p. 9.

the major writers of the era grew up in the earlier years of the Regency and William IV, and had their imaginations shaped by the age of English Romanticism. The 'nineteenth century' might be seen to begin in 1789, when the French Revolution opened up a fault line across the social, mental and religious structures of Europe, irreversibly changing ways of thinking and living, and laying the basis for the Romantic movement with its elevation of 'common' life, childhood and the emotions. The vision of Scott and Wordsworth lived on to culminate in the imaginative creations of George Eliot a decade after the mid-century. The creative tension within mid-Victorian literature comes from a cultural schizophrenia. If it was 'modern', materialist, factual, concerned with 'things as they are', it was also in many ways Romantic, fascinated with the 'savage' Gothic, melodramatic, idealistic.[3]

The 'novel' itself had little of the formal definition it has today. It was seen simply as a narrative form opposed to 'romance', a work of fiction dealing with the affairs of everyday life. As late as 1884 *Henry James could complain that, as a form, it 'had no air of having a theory, a conviction, a consciousness of itself behind it'.[4] Prose fiction was written, read and reviewed as part of a continuous spectrum of literature dealing with the humanities and science. No one would have debated where Scott the historian ended and Scott the novelist began, or thought the question relevant. Criticism of the novel genre goes back to the early eighteenth century, and was widely discussed during the Victorian period.[5] The subject of 'English literature' was included in the syllabus of the University of London when it was founded in 1851.[6] But studies of the novel were largely ethical, concerned with the 'truth' of literature, and Matthew Arnold's famous definition of poetry in 1888 as 'a criticism of life'[7] would have been applied equally to the novel. G. H. Lewes praised Charlotte Brontë's *Villette (1853), although it showed a 'contempt for conventions in all things, in style, in thought, even in the art of story-telling', because it had 'an astonishing power and passion . . . an influence

---

[3] See D. D. Stone, *The Romantic Impulse in Victorian Fiction* (1980).

[4] Henry James, 'The Art of the Novel', *Longman's Magazine* (1884).

[5] A useful, concise survey is still Miriam Allott, ed., *Novelists on the Novel* (1959). See also Further Reading.

[6] D. J. Palmer, *The Rise of English Studies* (1965); Franklin E. Court, *Institutionalizing English Literature: The Culture and Politics of Literary Study, 1750–1900* (1992).

[7] Matthew Arnold, 'The Study of Poetry', *Essays in Criticism, Second Series* (1888).

of truth as healthful as a mountain breeze'.[8] Literate readers were interested in the world in general, and even Dickens' populist *Household Words*
(1850–9) offered novels like *Hard Times* (1854) in a magazine that contained more non-fiction than fiction. In general, before about 1880, critics
saw form as a means of representing reality; in the later century, 'reality'
became increasingly the basis for artistic form.

David Lodge has remarked that 'novels burn facts as engines burn
fuel',[9] and Victorian fiction consumed whole forests of miscellaneous
information. But this brought with it a great diversity. By mid-century
David Masson could identify thirteen sub-genres of novel by type, objective and subject.[10] In the 1940s Leo J. Henkin summarized over 2,000
novels reviewed in *The Athenaeum* between 1860 and 1900, and placed
them in fifteen categories ranging from scientific discovery and religious
debate to politics and colonial settlement.[11] In an even more strenuous
exercise, the librarian Myron Brightfield drew on a lifetime of reading Victorian novels for a social history of the period, at his death leaving a dense
mosaic of extracts culled from some 2,000 novels, relating to over a
hundred main topics.[12]

There can be no accurate account of the number of novels issued
during this period, but a conservative estimate taken from *The Publisher's
Circular* between 1837 and 1901 suggests about 60,000 titles were published.[13] This, however, excluded novels published only in periodicals, and
most of those written for a mass readership appeared in ephemeral publications. There have been various attempts to map this vast sea. In *Fiction
with a Purpose* (1967), the late Robert A. Colby related eight key Victorian
titles to large clusters of contemporary fiction sharing the same interest.
In 1999 the greatly extended third edition of the *Cambridge Bibliography of
English Literature* included over 270 novelists writing between 1835 and

---

[8] Quoted in Miriam Allott, ed., *The Brontës: The Critical Heritage* (1947), p. 186.

[9] David Lodge in Michael Irwin et al., ed., *Tensions and Transitions* (1990), p. 191.

[10] David Masson, *British Novelists and their Styles* (1859), pp. 215ff. Hereafter Masson.

[11] Leo J. Henkin, 'Problems and Digressions in the Victorian Novel (1860–1900)', *The Bulletin
of Bibliography*, vol. 18, no. 2 (Sep–Dec 1943) to vol. 20, no. 1 (Jan–April 1950). Hereafter
Henkin.

[12] A selection was published in Myron F. Brightfield, *Victorian England in its Novels (1840–1870)*,
4 vols (1967–8). The full file occupies several filing cabinets in the UCLA library. Hereafter
Brightfield.

[13] John Sutherland, *The Longman Companion to Victorian Fiction* (1999), p. 1. Hereafter
Sutherland.

1900, but covered little 'popular' fiction. John Sutherland's invaluable *Longman Companion to Victorian Fiction* (1999) records nearly 900 novelists and gives brief synopses of nearly 500 works of fiction. But it makes no attempt to be comprehensive. Nor does this guide, which, with some exceptions, focuses on the writers who have selected themselves by their enduring literary quality, though these were not necessarily the most widely read novelists at the time.[14]

The 'classic' Victorian novel read and studied today was largely written by and for a specific, large but restricted middle-class readership, and consolidated middle-class cultural values. It is a myth that even Dickens was read by 'everyone' in the Victorian period. Sales of his early works were almost certainly exceeded by cheap plagiarisms recycling his fiction for popular consumption,[15] and if he was delighted that his pioneering venture into the popular market, the twopenny *Household Words*, sold 40,000 copies, this circulation was dwarfed by comparable lower-middle-class journals like *The Family Herald*, which had an estimated circulation of 300,000. When *Trollope boasted in 1870 that 'novels are in the hands of all: from the Prime Minister, Mr Gladstone, down to the last-appointed scullery maid', he omitted to say that the fiction pored over below stairs would have been very different to that found in the parlours of Downing Street. The amusing novel by the Mayhew brothers on *The Greatest Plague in Life* (i.e., the maidservant) featured the novel-reading Betsy, whose reading included the revealing titles *The Black Pirate*, *The Heads of the Headless*, *Ada the Betrayed* and *Amy, or Love and Madness*, all actual penny-issue works published by Edward Lloyd.[16] Betsy was reading in the late 1840s: average serving-girl literary tastes may have moved upwards by 1870, but not by that much.

Yet the middle-class Victorian novel was nevertheless related to the revolution in printing and reading that affected everyone in early nineteenth-century Britain. Print had played an important role in previous social and religious developments in earlier periods of change. But what happened in early nineteenth-century England was different. The Industrial Rev-

---

[14] A useful introduction to the distinction between 'original' and 'formulaic' literature is still John G. Cawelti's *Adventure, Mystery and Romance* (1976). Hereafter Cawelti.

[15] See Louis James, *Fiction for the Working Man, 1830–1850* (revised edn, 1974), ch. 4.

[16] Augustus and Henry Mayhew, *The Greatest Plague in Life* (1847), pp. 112ff.; Louis James, 'The Trouble with Betsy', in *The Victorian Press: Samplings and Soundings*, ed. Joanne Shattock and Michael Wolff (1982), pp. 349–66.

olution created cheap printing and papermaking, and rapid book distribution by rail, at a time when the reading population was rapidly expanding. As old social structures crumbled, new identities were forged through print. 'I can hardly describe to you the effect of these books. They produced on me an infinity of new images and feelings . . . Who was I? What was I? Whence did I come? What was my destination?'[17] The unlikely reader here is Frankenstein's Monster. By showing that its rational identity was created not in the laboratory, of which we know nothing, but in its reading, of which we know every title, Mary Shelley in 1818 was reflecting the revolutionary changes that were transforming the society of early nineteenth-century Britain, and at the same time recording her own creation of an independent identity through her reading and writing. William St Clair has documented in detail the unprecedented explosion in reading in England during this period, concluding that 'it is clear that the Romantic period marks the start of a continuing, self-sustaining, expansion, a take-off in the nation's reading equivalent to the take-off in manufacturing production which accelerated at about the same time'.[18]

At mid-century, the pottery worker Charles Shaw, although living in cramped back-to-back accommodation, kept a space exclusively for his books, and felt as if he 'entered into converse with presences who were living and breathing in that room'.[19] But it was not just autodidacts whose lives were changed by reading. George Eliot envisaged the middle-class Tertius Lydgate stumbling on a cyclopaedia article, and 'the world became new to him by a presentiment of endless processes filling the vast spaces planked out of his sight'.[20] Dickens recalled for Forster a summer evening in Chatham, 'the boys at play in the churchyard, and I sitting on my bed, reading *as for life*', the world of books more real to him than anything in his material surroundings.[21]

Reading, in ways we have lost in an electronic age, was a creative act. For the emerging lower middle classes it was political. Benjamin Franklin's dictum 'Knowledge is Power', above the woodcut of a hand press, became a Radical icon, and the extension of the vote in 1832 became inseparable from the fight against taxes on cheap periodical

---

[17] Mary Shelley, *Frankenstein* (1818, rev. 1831), ch. 15.

[18] William St Clair, *The Reading Nation in the Romantic Period* (2004), p. 13. Hereafter St Clair.

[19] Charles Shaw, *When I Was a Potter* (1903, facsimile by Caliban Books, Seaford, 1977), p. 224.

[20] George Eliot, *Middlemarch*, ch. 15.

[21] John Forster, *Life of Charles Dickens* (1872–4), bk 1, ch. 1 (my emphasis). Hereafter Forster.

literature.[22] Print still had 'weight' for the early nineteenth-century reader. Although this was to change after Applegarth developed the rotary press in the 1840s, for much of the century printed matter was still relatively rare and expensive, and even penny periodicals were costly for the class of readers that bought them. Names and inscriptions in careful copper-plate handwriting found today on the browning flysheets of nineteenth-century popular editions bear witness to the way books were treasured. For their readers, words on the page still vibrated with their associations from Shakespeare, Bunyan, and supremely, the King James English Bible.[23]

There was still the link with the human voice, and reading aloud was a popular pastime in families, workplaces and concert halls. Dickens was one of the performers who extended the written word into public readings. Without today's mental overload, untrammelled by academic boundaries, the printed word was savoured at a more leisurely pace. As the century developed John Stuart Mill deplored the effects of mass circulation news-papers on the reading public, and complained that this advance in literacy had brought 'no increase in ability, and a very marked decrease in vigour and energy' in mental activity.[24] Ruskin and Carlyle also looked with alarm at the rapid spread of cheap reading that they saw threatening public taste. Meanwhile the 'respectable' novel, in particular through the central role of women writers within it, became a potent force shaping the ways of life and ethos of the new middle classes in the Victorian period.[25]

Many of these readers came from a social group that had been tradi-tionally hostile to fiction, and for whom all reading apart from the Bible, *Pilgrim's Progress* (1678, 1684) and devotional literature was a trivial detraction from the serious purposes of reading.[26] 'Against the most per-nicious reading in the world, against novels, let me particularly warn you,' ran a late eighteenth-century manual for 'a young lady'; 'they poison the mind, they soften and pervert the understanding, and infuse a kind of false heroic sentiment, while they divest you of that which is really pure and virtuous.'[27] Where novels were allowed, they gave instruction for

[22] Patricia Hollis, *The Pauper Press* (1970).

[23] See, e.g., Michael Wheeler, *The Art of Allusion in the Victorian Novel* (1979).

[24] John Stuart Mill, 'Civilization', *London and Westminster Review* (April 1836), sec. 2.

[25] Ellen Moers, *Literary Women* (1972); Jane Spencer, *The Rise of the Woman Novelist* (1986).

[26] See, e.g., J. T. Taylor, *Early Opposition to the English Novel . . . 1760–1830* (1943).

[27] Anon, *Mental Improvement for a Young Lady on her Entrance into the World . . . A New Edition* (1796), pp. 97–8.

'real-life' situations, like those of Fanny Burney or Jane Austen.[28] That the middle-class readership came to accept a broader range of fiction was due above all to Sir Walter Scott, whose historical novels stood poised between fiction and chronicled fact. William St Clair has demonstrated that in the first decades of the century, more copies of Scott's novels were sold than those of all other novelists combined (St Clair, p. 221). Scott not only framed his stories in an accurate historical setting and so made them 'true', he also wrote from the historical viewpoint of the common people, making his stories relevant to the lives of his readers. Working-class libraries that banned fiction allowed Scott's novels. *Charlotte M. Yonge, tutored at home by her magistrate father, was allowed to read 'a chapter a day of the Waverley novels, once she had read a portion of Goldsmith's *Rome* or some equally solid book'.[29]

Scott prepared the way for the urban journalism of the 1830s, which discovered innumerable true histories swarming through the byways of the rapidly expanding cities. 'There is not a *street* in London, but what may be compared to a large or small volume of intelligence, abounding in anecdote, incident and peculiarities,' wrote the journalist Pierce Egan, Sr in *Life in London* (1820–1, p. 24). Dickens, who as newspaper reporter wrote the pieces collected as *Sketches by 'Boz'* (1836), moved seamlessly from observation of London streets into their dramas and human narrative for *Oliver Twist*, the first major Victorian novel.

But by 1870, when Trollope declared that the novel was a 'rational amusement',[30] reading with a moral purpose, he was already arguing against the tide. Novels had become ever cheaper, increasingly sold for their 'sensation' value and bought for casual recreation and railway reading. By the 1880s, writers like *George Meredith and *George Moore were challenging the censorship of lending libraries that selected only those novels they thought suitable for family reading. There would be a case for ending this study then. But as we have noted, as the main Victorian period was passing, debates about its values were central to the work of Henry James, *Thomas Hardy, *George Gissing, Oscar Wilde and *Robert Louis Stevenson, and to end this study about 1880 would be like

[28] See, e.g., David Vincent, *Bread, Knowledge and Freedom: A Study of Nineteenth-century Working-class Biography* (1981); Jonathan Rose, *The Intellectual Life of the British Working Classes* (2001).

[29] G. Battiscombe, *Charlotte Mary Yonge* (1943), p. 47.

[30] Anthony Trollope, 'On English Prose Fiction as a Rational Amusement', reprinted in *Four Lectures by Anthony Trollope*, ed. M. L. Parrish (1939), pp. 91–124.

leaving a good play before seeing the last act. The cycle begun by the movement away from the early Gothic of James Hogg's *Confessions of a Justified Sinner* (1824) and Mary Shelley's *Frankenstein (1818, revised 1831) to the serious 'social' novel ends with the return to sensational forms in Stevenson's *The Strange Case of Dr Jekyll and Mr Hyde* (1886), Rider Haggard's *She (1887) and H. G. Wells' *The War of the Worlds* (1898). There is both continuation and change. Old imaginings return, but now reinterpreted by new insights into psychology, evolution and sociology, marking the transition from the 'modern' of the Victorians into the 'Modernism' of the next century.

CONTEXT 1

Time Maps

Prelude: 1830–1846

'We live in an age of visible transition', declared Bulwer Lytton in 1833, '– an age of disquietude and doubt – of the removal of time-worn land-marks, and the breaking up of the hereditary elements of society – old opinions, feelings – ancestral customs and institutions are crumbling away, and both the spiritual and temporal worlds are darkened by the shadows of change.'[1] Popular millenarian movements preparing for the Second Coming and Radical Utopians looking for heaven on earth through reform shared a common concern with Thomas Carlyle's 'Signs of the Times' (1829), John Stuart Mill's 'The Spirit of the Age' (1831) and Bulwer Lytton's *England and the English* (1833). In 1825 the essays in Hazlitt's *Spirit of the Age* sought to understand the Romantic era: nine-teen years later, R. H. Horne's *The New Spirit of the Age* (1844) identified an emerging one. Britain was becoming the epicentre of interlinked revolutions in the expansion of its cities, its industrial development and the world of ideas.

We now know that the 'Industrial Revolution' is something of a mis-nomer, and that the transformation of Britain through industrial devel-opment was a gradual process that goes back to the eighteenth century and steadily changed the nation through the nineteenth. But by 1830 cotton mills and ironworks were forever changing northern England. Writing verse in the ledger books of his Sheffield iron foundry, Ebenezer Elliott marvelled at the 'tempestuous music of the giant, Steam', but noted ominously that its iron powers 'toil ceaseless, day and night, yet never tire, / or say to greedy man, "thou dost amiss"'. England had

---

[1] Edward Bulwer-Lytton, *England and the English* (1833), ed. Standish Mitcham (1970), p. 318.

become a divided nation. If the north was becoming increasingly indus-
trialized, the south was dominated by London, the centre of commerce.
With a population of over a million at the beginning of the century, it
contained more than a third of England's urban population, and topped
4 million by the end of the century. But all areas were affected by the
ethos of industry. 'It is an age of machinery', wrote Carlyle in 'Signs of
the Times' in 1829, 'in every inward and outward sense of the word.'

This was nowhere more apparent than in the expansion of the railways, our first focus for the changes of the era. 'Steam! Steam! Steam!'
Frances Trollope was to write in 1848:

> Steam has so changed the face of the country, from John o' Groats to the
> Land's end, that few persons of the present day who are basking on the
> sunny side of fifty either have, or can have, any accurate ideas of what
> England was, during the early part of the present century – and neverthe-
> less we have not yet reached the middle of it.[2]

The railways, carrying their first passengers in 1830, were by 1848
linking Britain from Aberdeen to Plymouth with 8,000 miles of metal
track. They transformed the English landscape, and altered the consciousness of space and time (see below, p. 97). In the world of publishing, over time they centralized the book market, rapidly distributing
books and periodicals across the nation and extending the circulating
libraries of Edward Mudie and W. H. Smith, which used rail to send boxes
to the provinces and overseas. With rapid circulation, periodicals catering
for every interest and occupation flourished, and it has been estimated
that the Victorians published over 25,000 journals, not counting hundreds
of reviews, magazines, weeklies and papers.[3] Books became part of
travelling, and railway station shops sold pocket-sized 'railway novels' for
passengers.

With rail and canals servicing its commerce, its overseas trade protected by naval supremacy, British industry was to expand at speed,
moving the nation into a period of unprecedented prosperity. But this was
in the future. For the masses surviving the economic depression and food
shortages that followed the Napoleonic Wars, the turbulence of the 1830s

[2] Frances Trollope, *Town and Country* (1848), p. 1.
[3] Walter E. Houghton, 'Periodical Literature and the Articulate Classes', in Joanne Shattock
and Michael Wolff, eds, *The Victorian Periodical Press* (1982), pp. 3–27.

was followed by continuing social distress in the 1840s. In rural areas, the effects of agricultural depression were intensified by draconian game laws and enclosures that drove cottagers to become exploited labourers, or to emigrate. The industrial population suffered cholera, unemployment, strikes and lockouts, and lived in the subhuman conditions Engels exposed in *The Condition of the Working Classes in England* (1845). Yet, remarkably, Britain remained free of the revolutions that devastated continental Europe in the 1840s. The excesses of the Reign of Terror, and patriotic opposition to the threat of invasion, cooled much public support for the French Revolution, although Napoleon remained a surprisingly popular hero with the working classes. Britain was moving towards a new social consensus. In the later eighteenth century popular religious movements, in particular that of Methodism, had created an upwardly mobile working and lower middle class, energized by self-discipline and the work ethic.

The Radicals Tom Paine and William Cobbett urged not revolution but constitutional reform, yet the methods of the reformers verged on violence. It was a fraught and dangerous time, with government spies infiltrating working-class groups, the imprisonment and execution of anyone considered a subversive, and sporadic riots and violence. The threat of mass revolution, underlined by the burning of an area of Bristol and Nottingham Castle, forced through the 1832 Reform Bill. The Bill itself brought a relatively small extension to the franchise, but it created a fracture line down the centre of the structure of political power. It recognized that at least in principle, Parliamentary power was based on individual rights, not on the privilege and wealth of Cobbett's detested 'Old Corruption'. In the new Parliament, evangelicals and secular Utilitarians united in a broad spirit of reform, defusing social discontent with legislated improvements to the penal code, factory conditions, public health and town planning. The Anti-Corn Law League (1834–46) campaigning for the removal of taxes on imported corn to bring down the price of bread, and the Chartist movement agitating for Parliamentary reform from 1838 into the 1850s, sought change within the legal process. But passions still ran high and threatened action that bordered on the illegal.

Shortly after the passing of the Reform Bill, St Stephen's Palace, which had previously housed Parliament, burnt down in 1834. If the enlargement of the franchise was one symbol of the new age, the building of the Palace of Westminster was another, for in a public competition the classical style was rejected in favour of the new Gothic form being introduced into England by A. W. N. Pugin. Looking back to the native European impulse of late medievalism, Pugin's *Contrasts* (1836) opposed the industrial ethos of the age with an aesthetic based on social and moral function, an organic form combining beauty, religion and the honesty of the builder's craft.[4] One cannot move far in the Victorian period without encountering the Gothic. It focused social debate. Carlyle's *Past and Present* of 1843 contrasted the aridity of industrial society with the creative humanity of medieval monastic communities: in the 1890s, it inspired William Morris' socialist vision. It entered the religious controversy as High Church movements looked back to pre-Reformation times. Ruskin's enthusiasm for the aesthetic and moral qualities of the Gothic influenced building design from railway stations to the acres of suburban villas spilling out from the city centres, over the countryside, housing the new urban middle classes. Although more popular in poetry than fiction (see below, p. 40), Gothic images pervaded literature and Pre-Raphaelite art.

The ferment of the period was reflected in a profusion of competing developments in the novel. Readers were entertained by the sea adventures of naval writers drawing on experiences in the Napoleonic Wars, of which the most popular was *Frederick Marryat. Concerns with Ireland were reflected in the *Irish novel, and its rural peoples received largely comic treatment in the picaresque fiction of William Carleton, Samuel Lover and Charles Lever, while in urban England, nostalgia for country ways was celebrated in the comedy of *Robert Surtees' cockney huntsmen. Mrs Gore and Lady Blessington drew on the sensational interest of fashionable London life with the 'silver-fork' novel. *Bulwer Lytton, who had pioneered this with *Falkland* (1827), ranged widely in the subjects of his writing, initiating the novel of highwayman adventure in *Paul Clifford* (1830), of psychopathology in *Eugene Aram* (1832), and developing the genre of historical romance in *The Last of the Barons* (1843). *Charles Dickens, too, never attempted to repeat the form of *Pickwick Papers* (1837–8), but restlessly experimented through the 1830s and 1840s, until he found a new form of social issue novel in *Dombey and Son* (1846–8).

---

[4] For the social significance of the Gothic movement, see Chris Brooks, *Signs of the Times: Symbolic Realism in the Mid-Victorian Novel* (1984). Hereafter *Signs*.

Although they were fascinated by the trivialities of high life, the 'silver-fork' novels of Bulwer Lytton and Mrs Gore, with their focus on a specific social group, laid the foundation of later domestic fiction, while the recreation of life in provincial communities in Mrs Trollope's *The Vicar of Wrexhill* (1837) and *Harriet Martineau's *Deerbrook* (1839) prepared the way for the *regional novel. The keyword of the 1840s was moral *earnestness*. The obituary of *Douglas Jerrold, a leading literary figure of the decade, declared that 'Jerrold and the age help to explain one another, and they found each other remarkably earnest in all their dealings'. Dickens, too, who was developing his own literary career through this period, gives as David Copperfield's credo for success as a writer, 'In great aims and in small, I have always been thoroughly in earnest'. *Benjamin Disraeli's *Sybil, or the Two Nations* (1845), with its warning of a nation divided between north and south, voiced a concern with social issues reflected in Douglas Jerrold's savage attack on wealth and poverty in London, *The History of St James's and St Giles* (1845–7). Popular literature was dominated by *G. W. M. Reynolds' inflammatory penny serial *The Mysteries of London* (1844–7), which also dramatized the inequalities between rich and poor. In a period of disruptive change, the novel was assuming a central role in contemporary debate.

Revolutions: 1847–1849

These three years had an importance out of all proportion to their duration. At the end of the 1840s, political unrest on the continent of Europe exploded into bloody revolutions in Sardinia, Italy, Austria, Hungary and Russia. In England, a nervous government gathered 8,000 troops, backed by police, special constables and heavy artillery in the Tower of London, prepared for a Chartist-led insurrection. But the labour leadership was divided and without middle-class support, and what might have become a major crisis petered out in a rowdy meeting on London's Kennington Common. In contrast to the bloody fighting and civil disruption that were taking place across the Channel, Britain moved towards a period of relative stability and rising standards of living.

What might be seen as the most significant revolution took place, not on a battleground in south London, but at a gathering of seven young artists (only three of whom were to be active in the movement) in the home of John Everett Millais, at 83 Gower Street on a corner near the British Museum. Like the radical cadres on the continent, the coterie adopted a secret name, 'P.R.B.' (the 'Pre-Raphaelite Brotherhood'), and drew up a manifesto. As artists they dedicated themselves to avoiding false conventions or ideas, to be absolutely true to nature, and, in the spirit of medieval craftsmen, to create only 'thoroughly good pictures and statues'.[5] For David Masson, a contemporary critic, the Pre-Raphaelite movement reflected the same spirit of social engagement that was to revolutionize the novel.

There was a growing demand for novels to supply middle-class family reading, a market that was to make the fortune of Charles Mudie with

[5] W. M. Rossetti, ed., *Gabriel Dante Rossetti: Family Letters* (1895), vol. 1, p. 135.

his Select Library of morally approved reading, opened in 1842 (see below, p. 73). Writers were turning from journalism and poetry towards the more lucrative field of novel writing. The *Brontë sisters' *Poems*, published in 1846, sold two copies in all: Charlotte Brontë's *Jane Eyre* (1847), helped by controversy, went through three editions in seven months. This was exceptional, but nevertheless *Jane Eyre* formed part of an extraordinary creative outburst in novel writing at this time. Three years also saw the publication of Emily Brontë's *Wuthering Heights* (1847), Anne Brontë's *The Tenant of Wildfell Hall* (1848), *William Thackeray's *Vanity Fair* (1847–8) and *Pendennis* (1848–50), and *Elizabeth Gaskell's *Mary Barton* (1848).

The outpouring was equally remarkable for its range of innovation. *Anthony Trollope published his two first (uncharacteristic) Irish novels, *The Macdermots of Ballycloran* (1847) and *The Kellys and O'Kellys* (1848). Disraeli's *Tancred* (1847) anticipated the Judaic themes of *George Eliot's *Daniel Deronda* (1876); Newman's *Loss and Gain* (1848) was the first in a long line of biographical religious fiction. These were shortly followed by Charlotte Brontë's *Shirley* (1849), Dickens' *David Copperfield* (1849–50) and *Charles Kingsley's *Alton Locke* (1850). In 1850 two major poems, Tennyson's *In Memoriam* and Wordsworth's *The Prelude*, showed the poetic vitality of the era. However, in the same year, a contributor to *The Prospective Review* had no doubts that now the predominant form was not poetry but the novel, a form as important to the age as 'the drama was in the reigns of Elizabeth and James I' (p. 495).

Equipoise: 1850–1870

The 'high Victorian' period lasted only some twenty years. Its opening coincided with the 1851 Great Exhibition in Hyde Park. Sir Joseph Paxton's soaring edifice of cast iron girders and a million panes of glass, a structure that Douglas Jerrold in *Punch* dubbed 'the Crystal Palace', contained some 13,000 exhibits from Britain, its empire and many other nations, and was attended by over 6 million visitors from Britain and abroad.[6] It is too simple to see the period as one of steady prosperity; it was, on the contrary, marked by years of both boom and slump. But it was a period characterized, overall, by economic growth. Britain was now the richest nation in Europe and a world leader in trade, with an ever-expanding empire. London was by far the largest city in the known world, and by 1870 Britain's exports exceeded those of France, Germany and Italy combined. England had become a country of town-dwellers, and the 1851 census showed that for the first time the urban population outnumbered the rural. The greatest population increases came in London and the northern manufacturing conurbations. The Coventry that George Eliot knew in 1832–5, when as Mary Ann Evans she attended a little private school run there, was a market town with a modest ribbon and cloth-weaving industry. By 1871, when as 'George Eliot' she drew on these memories as the model for *Middlemarch, Coventry had expanded into a booming industrial city, the future hub of the British bicycle industry. Although many slums persisted, the Town Improvement and Public Health Acts of 1847 and 1848 had brought improved street lighting and sanitation, and in cities like Leeds, Liverpool and Manchester,

---

[6] See Jeffrey A. Auerbach, *The Great Exhibition of 1851* (1999).

great town halls, libraries, public amenities and parks proclaimed a new civic pride.

English culture was no longer confined to England. There was massive emigration, mainly to the United States, but also to Canada, Australia and New Zealand. In 1860, 68,000 emigrated to the United States, 21,000 to Australia and 3,000 to Canada.[7] They established English institutions, culture and language around the globe. In fiction, Australia provided a setting for a model domestic life in Bulwer Lytton's popular *The Caxtons* (1849), and redemptive exile for Dickens' Little Em'ly and Magwitch, and for George Fielding in *Charles Reade's graphic *It's Never Too Late to Mend* (1856). The *colonial novel began to emerge. As the anti-slavery movement gained momentum, British attitudes to North America altered, and in 1852 Harriet Beecher Stowe's *Uncle Tom's Cabin* sold 150,000 copies in seven months, over four times the sale of Dickens' *Bleak House* (1852–3). The fiction of Edgar Allan Poe, Nathaniel Hawthorne and James Fenimore Cooper also had many readers.

Britain's social classes were becoming more integrated in the new cities. But the structure of society was changing. It was less industrially driven than in the early decades. Incomes of the skilled working classes increased by a third in thirty years, contributing to the evolution of an independent culture rooted in sport and music hall. But it was banking, insurance and the service industries that expanded most rapidly, bringing wealth to the upwardly mobile middle classes of small businessmen and white-collar workers. This class was earnest, and anxious to prove respectability through their moral purpose and self-discipline. Many attended chapel, and the 1851 census recorded nearly as many nonconformists as Anglicans. They voted Liberal, from 1846 to 1868 virtually excluding the old Tories from power.

It was the era of high Victorian morality. Readers borrowed the morally approved three-volume novels from the circulating libraries of Charles Edward Mudie and W. H. Smith. When in 1860 the success of *The Cornhill Magazine* boosted the popularity of novels serialized in monthly magazines, editors of 'respectable' serials were also anxious to censor anything likely to offend the respectable reader. Novelists resented this censorship, and Bohemian writers like *Wilkie Collins were careful to keep their private lives out of sight of their readers. But in general they

---

[7] I am indebted to Hugh Cunningham for these figures.

shared the common concern with decorum, and in 1859 Dickens was desperately anxious lest his separation from his wife should damage his popularity with his public. Arbiters of public taste looked nervously at the growing number of cheap periodicals for the working and lower middle classes, and Dickens launched his twopenny *Household Words* (1850–9) to counter their influence. But by today's standards, with the occasional exception of *Reynolds' Miscellany*, the penny magazines maintained a wholesome image: *The Family Herald*, which so massively outsold Dickens' publication, had no illustrations, and was as decorous in style and content as any three-volume novel in Mudie's stock. The topics were as diverse as the items in the news of the day, and novels directly reflected contemporary public events and scandals. As the middle-class audience consolidated in the mid-Victorian period, the divergent styles and genres of the earlier period merged into a more common form. *Charlotte Yonge's *The Heir of Redclyffe* (1853) contained religious, domestic and Gothic elements. 'Multiplot' novels contained several narratives, providing different perspectives on the story.[8] Sequences like Anthony Trollope's *Barsetshire Chronicles* (1855–67) and *Margaret Oliphant's *Chronicles of Carlingford* (1863–76) allowed character and place to continue across novels, moving in time with their readers. The intimate tone of the mid-Victorian novel was made possible by a social consensus among its readers.

But not everyone was complacent about the state of the nation. Dickens' *Bleak House*, whose first instalments appeared among the euphoria of the Great Exhibition, presented a dark image of Britain's moral, social and political confusion. In 1854 Britain embarked on two years of disastrous involvement in the Crimean War. In 1857 the savage Indian Mutiny was met with equally murderous suppression, and together with Britain's involvement in the Second Opium War of 1857–8, shook benign views of the country's acquisition of empire. If 1851 might be seen as one climactic of the Victorian period, 1859 might be seen as another. In that year the middle classes bought 50,000 copies of Samuel Smiles' *Self-Help*, the hagiography of autodidacts like George Stephenson, whose industry had laid the basis for Britain's prosperity. This coincided with one of Britain's most daring industrial ventures. Isambard Kingdom Brunel built the greatest ocean-going liner ever known, the *Great Eastern*, a double-hulled steel liner nearly 700 feet long, with a cargo capacity of 21,000 tons.

[8] See Peter K. Garrett, *The Victorian Multiplot Novel: Studies in Dialogical Form* (1980).

But the strains of supervising its construction hastened Brunel's death just before its maiden voyage, and the leviathan proved a financial disaster, too large for normal commercial use. Britain's engineering skills were over-reaching themselves. Also in 1859, Darwin's *Origin of Species* rocked religious belief (see below, pp. 60–1), and in the following year *Essays and Reviews*, a collection of seven essays by liberal churchmen and intellectuals, caused even greater controversy with its challenge to conservative Christian interpretations of the Bible and history.

The year 1860 brought a significant shift in the novel market. The *sensation novel was a response to the demand for a more entertaining form of fiction, in particular from middle-class women increasingly confined to household management. Its tales of bigamy, double identity and violence, located within domestic settings, reflected at one remove concern with married women's property rights and the inequalities of the divorce laws. But it also shocked respectable middle-class readers by confronting prevalent ideas of the proper subject for the novel, and its plots and characters directly subverted the accepted views of morality and the role of women in society. The romantic extravaganzas of *Ouida were more sensational still, looking forward to the more liberated fiction of the last decades of the century. There were other signs that the mid-century novel-reading consensus was fragmenting. While the middle-class novel was moving towards a wider audience, *George Meredith with *The Ordeal of Richard Feverel* (1859) began to write novels for a small literary elite whose form and content made no concessions to a popular readership he called the 'porkers'. When Dickens died in 1870, the scene was changing rapidly.

Turning the Tide: 1871–1880

This era marked a shift towards the *fin de siècle*. Throughout the 1870s most of the urban population enjoyed increasing prosperity, while agricultural depression continued to depopulate the countryside. Carlyle in *Shooting Niagara* (1867) had prophesied doom and disaster as electoral reform gave more power to the urban masses, and the Reform Acts of 1867 and 1884 trebled the number of males entitled to vote, enfranchising those in the expanding urban population. These helped Disraeli in 1874 win the first Tory election since 1841, and the Tories introduced a flurry of reforms, many of which had been in the Liberal government's pipeline, in public health, factory conditions and the recognition of trades unions. The Married Women's Property Act had been passed in 1870, giving women the right to own property within marriage, and this was extended in 1882, reinforcing the radical change of women's position in society that was to mark the closing decades of the century. Overseas, the Conservatives were committed to extending Britain's imperial influence, annexing some 4,750,000 square miles between 1874 and 1901, and drawing Britain into an increasingly costly burden of administration and conflict overseas.

The second challenge to the middle-class consensus came from the spread of literacy to include the poorer strata of society. In 1871 Forster's Education Act extended primary education to all under 10, although it was not free until 1891, accelerating a process that had continued steadily through the century, and dragging Britain into the new economic age. But it also had the effect Matthew Arnold forewarned of in *Culture and Anarchy* (1869), of creating a mass readership with little interest in traditional learning, breaking up the intellectual and moral consensus of the high Victorian middle classes. In the ensuing decades, it was to accentuate the split between 'high' and 'low' culture.

Other developments were changing the intellectual scene. Education and research were becoming more professional. Oxford and Cambridge Universities reformed, admitted nonconformists, and in the 1870s opened four women's colleges, although actual degrees for women only came later. Provincial city universities founded in the 1850s became autonomous. Research specialized, creating the independent disciplines of applied physics, anthropology, philology, theology, history and also of 'English literature', although as yet it contained little formal analysis. The Darwinians had largely won the battle against the biblical fundamentalists, and scientific interests increasingly shaped the development of the 'serious' novel (see below, pp. 59–61). While George Lewes applied experiments on animal reflexes to human behaviour in his massive work of research, *Problems of Life and Mind* (1874–9), his partner George Eliot put the organism of a small Midland town under the microscope of her imagination in the novel *Middlemarch*. Mainstream novels became increasingly dark. Trollope abandoned the gentle setting of Barsetshire in his late novels to portray an England driven by ambition, greed and cultural nihilism in *The Way We Live Now* (1874–5). *Thomas Hardy, an early disciple of Darwin, turned from the sunny orchards of *Under the Greenwood Tree* (1872) and, in *The Return of the Native* (1878), set doomed human passions against the impassive natural cycles of Egdon Heath. Two years earlier George Eliot's *Daniel Deronda* looked beyond England to the spiritual values preserved in the Judaic tradition.

The Last Decades: 1881–1901

If the Victorian era came in with the arrival of steam, it ended with electricity. In 1881 the D'Oyly Carte Theatre in London sensationally opened a season of Gilbert and Sullivan operas, staged in the first public building to be lit entirely by electric lighting. In the 1840s the first steam trains changed the face of Britain: forty years later, in 1882, electric trams began trundling through the streets of London. Where Victorian communications had depended on the penny post, the transatlantic cable had linked London to New York in 1866, and the first telephone exchange opened in 1879. Bicycles and early cars were invading the countryside. Britain was rapidly changing into a world that would be recognized today.

With the fall in prices and increasing competition from abroad, many of the middle classes felt they were moving into a period of depression. Nevertheless, cheaper prices and improving working conditions created a sustained rise in living standards for the working and lower middle classes. Trade unionism gathered force, and the founding of the Social Democrat Federation in 1881 and the Fabian Society in 1884 developed the modern ideology of socialism. In 1886 unemployed workers rioted in London. In 1884 William Morris established the short-lived Socialist League; combining politics with his skills as poet, designer and craftsman, he set out on the pursuit of the socialist vision evoked in his utopian novel *News from Nowhere* (1891). The national movement for woman's suffrage was founded in 1889, giving strength to the women's movement. Olive Schreiner's *Story of an African Farm* (1883) presaged the *'new woman' novel of the 1890s.

After Wilkie Collins died in 1889, Edmund Yates' obituary mourned the passing of 'almost the last of the great English novelists who made the middle of the nineteenth century remarkable in the history of fiction'. Collins' era 'was a time of straight speaking, when men wrote from their hearts in a way that would be scorned in these days of subtle intellectualism',[9] a reference to the writing of *Henry James, *George Gissing and *George Moore. Writers were becoming alienated from the mass of readers. Many of the leading intellectuals had come from outside England. George Moore, George Bernard Shaw and Oscar Wilde were born in Ireland; *Robert Louis Stevenson came from Scotland and retired to Samoa. Henry James was born in America, *Rudyard Kipling in India, Olive Schreiner in South Africa, Joseph Conrad in Poland. Gissing, raised in Yorkshire, was nevertheless alienated from mainline English culture, and died in France.

England was becoming an embattled nation. Against a background of Irish rural suffering, the Fenian movement agitated violently for home rule. Driven by evolutionary belief in British cultural and racial superiority, imperialist ambitions sparked conflicts in the Sudan, Egypt, Burma, China, and most disastrously in South Africa, provoking the Boer Wars of 1880–1 and 1899–1902. The popular reading of the era betrayed this underlying angst. Tales from *Rider Haggard's *King Solomon's Mines* (1885) to the novels of G. A. Henty, besides a score of penny magazines with titles like *Boys of the British Empire* (1882–5), romanticized adventures overseas, but did so with hectic excess. Extremes of religious belief and doubt made *Mrs Humphry Ward's *Robert Elsmere* (1888) the 'serious' bestseller of the century, and Gladstone and Queen Victoria were among the many thousands of readers who devoured *Marie Corelli's spiritual extravaganzas *Ardath, the Story of a Dead Self* (1889) and *The Sorrows of Satan* (1895). In a return to the Gothic mode, Robert Louis Stevenson's *The Strange Case of Dr Jekyll and Mr Hyde* (1886) and Oscar Wilde's *Portrait of Dorian Gray* (1891) dramatized the divided self, while Bram Stoker's *Dracula* (1897) presented the threat of psychic possession by the alien. *Utopias and dystopias, including *H. G. Wells' *The Time Machine* (1895) and *The War of the Worlds* (1898), cast a terrified gaze towards the future.

In 1884 Robert Louis Stevenson took part in a debate between *Walter Besant, the representative of earlier attitudes to the novel, and Henry

---

[9] [E. Yates], 'The Novels of Wilkie Collins', *Temple Bar* (August 1890), p. 528.

James, the critical spokesman for the new.[10] Against Besant, he argued that there is no division between 'realistic' and 'imaginative' fiction, for imagination is the essential element in all of creative literature. Against James' concern with the precision of form, he argued that the novel 'is not a transcript of reality, to be judged by exactitude, but a simplification of some side of life, to stand or fall by its significant simplicity' (quoted Regan, p. 100). For Stevenson, fiction was a selection from 'reality' consciously organized towards a creative end whose primary purpose, while it might have artistic and moral qualities, was to give pleasure. 'In anything fit to be called by the name of reading, the process itself should be absorbing and voluptuous.'[11] Cutting through the preoccupations of the previous century, Stevenson brought the novel into the clarity of a new era.

---

[10] Walter Besant, 'The Art of Fiction' (lecture given at the Royal Institution in 1884); Henry James, 'The Art of Fiction', *Longman's Magazine* (September 1884); Robert Louis Stevenson, 'A Humble Remonstrance' (1884). All three are reprinted in edited form in Stephen Regan, ed., *The Nineteenth-century Novel: A Critical Reader* (2001), pp. 61–100. Hereafter Regan.

[11] Stevenson, 'A Gossip on Romance', *Memories and Portraits* (1908), p. 151.

CONTEXT 2

Changing Perspectives

In this section, the changing intellectual climate of the period is examined to show how the imaginative world of the novel adapted to accommodate new attitudes to the meaning of the individual and society. It moves broadly from the questions posed by 'realism', through the formative influence of the developing disciplines of history and biography, before looking at the way the secular novel appropriated earlier ideas of Christian religion, and the new perspectives of science. It ends by taking the detective story as a trope for the movement into the era of postmodernism.

'Things As They Are'

'Art always aims at the Representation of Reality, i.e. of Truth,' declared G. H. Lewes in 1848.[1] 'Realism' was a central concern in the Victorian novel, and it reflected unprecedented interest in the scientific nature of the material world. The eighteenth-century Enlightenment had begun a shift from debates about religion and moral issues towards scientific observation of the natural universe, and by the early nineteenth century 'realism' in philosophy referred not to transcendent realities, such as the nature of good and evil, but to material phenomena defined through observation and experiment. In the arts, 'realism' referred to the belief that 'reality inheres in present fact' and that 'new doctrines of the physical world are independent of mind or spirit', 'a description of facing up to things as they *really* are, not as we imagine or would like them to be'.[2]

The novel was only one avenue of literature exploring new concepts of the world for the Victorian reader. Today, Charles Edward Mudie's Select Circulating Library is remembered as the institution that curiously kept the expensive three-volume novel going as a *publishing format throughout much of the century (see below, pp. 205–6). But in 1855 Mudie was assuring his clients that 'preference is given to works of History, Biography, Religion, Philosophy, and Travel', although noting that 'the *best* works of fiction are also freely added'. If the novel did emerge as a separate category of literature, it was the genre least capable of clear definition. *'Social problem' novels drew on journalism, biography, and Parliamentary reports; *historical novels shaded into history; and

---

[1] 'Realism in Art: Recent German Criticism', *Westminster Review*, n.s. 14 (Oct. 1858), p. 49.
[2] See Raymond Williams, 'Realism', in *Keywords* (1976), p. 217.

*religious novels played a lively part in theological debate. If the novel was concerned to represent life as it is, so were the visual arts, and these affected writers of fiction.

The Victorians felt driven by a moral imperative to understand their world. 'Go to nature,' Ruskin directed the young painter, 'having no thought but how to penetrate her meaning, rejecting nothing, selecting nothing, and scorning nothing.'[3] 'The truth of infinite value that [Ruskin] teaches is *realism*,' wrote *George Eliot, 'the doctrine that all truth and beauty are to be attained by a humble and faithful study of nature, and not by substituting vague forms, bred by imagination on the mess of feeling, in place of finite substantial reality.'[4] For Ruskin, even the act of drawing was ethical, not because it could be used for didactic purposes, but because the painstaking discipline of observation and technique was itself a moral activity, and led to a more perfect understanding of objective 'truth'. David Masson, writing in mid-century, associated the rise of the 'realistic' novel of the late 1840s with the political revolutions sweeping through Europe, and to the art revolution of the formation in 1848 of the Pre-Raphaelite Brotherhood. Politics, fiction and art all sought a new level of creative engagement with objective reality. For all their differences of content and style, from the late 1840s novelists showed a new 'resolute and careful attention . . . to facts and characters lying within their easy observation'. Writers now freed themselves from Romantic preconceptions, indicating a 'greater indifference to traditional ideas of beauty, and an increased willingness to accept, as worthy of study and representation, facts and objects accounted common, disagreeable, or even painful' (Masson, pp. 258–9).

But when Masson came to examine realism as it actually emerged in the novel, he distinguished between the 'Real' and the 'Ideal'. *Dickens, the writer most responsible for creating a sense of the period for subsequent generations, bitterly opposed the *factual* representation of reality in fiction. 'I have purposely dwelt upon the romantic side of familiar things,' he wrote in the 'Preface' to *Bleak House (1852–3), and developed this in a well-known passage quoted in Forster's *Life*.

> It does not seem to me to be enough to say of any description that it is the exact truth. The exact truth must be there; but the merit or art in the

[3] John Ruskin, *Pre-Raphaelitism*, 3, p. 623.
[4] George Eliot, *Westminster Review*, 66, p. 626.

narrator, is the manner of stating the truth. And in these times, when the tendency is to be frightfully literal and catalogue-like – to make the thing, in short, a sort of sum in reduction that any miserable creature can do in that way – I have an idea (really founded on the love of what I profess), that the very holding of popular literature through a kind of popular dark age, may depend on such fanciful treatment. (Bk 9)

In believing that the highest truths could only be reached through the imagination, Dickens' 'fanciful' approach of reality looked back to the Romantic movement. It also drew on a work that had been enthusi-astically discovered by the Romantics, and was the book most likely, after the Bible, to be found in Victorian households. Bunyan's *Pilgrim's Progress* (1676, 1684), secularized in the eighteenth century by William Hogarth in his *Harlot's Progress* (1732) and a succession of picture 'progresses' (see below, p. 199–200), transformed the objects and happenings of every-day life into moral allegory. Both reinforced the Victorian concern with understanding the 'truth' of the objective world in terms of moral 'truths' based in the Bible. As Chris Brooks put it, what separated the 'enterprise of realism' in the Victorian novel from the more conventional concept of the term was that it sought 'to capture what the *being* of the real world is . . . coextensive with an attempt to capture the *meaning* of the real world as well' (*Signs*, p. 3). By observing the 'scientific' progress of time as operating within a divine control, the Victorian novel embodied what Thomas Vargish has termed a 'providential aesthetic', again very different from the normal expectations of the 'realist' novel.[5] Bunyan's influence was particularly strong on Dickens' early work.[6] He called his first true novel *Oliver Twist; or the Parish Boy's Progress* (1837–8), and in the *Old Curiosity Shop* (1840), a novel shaped throughout by a subtext of Bunyan's work,[7] he describes Little Nell and her grandfather setting out on their travels, hand in hand, as two 'pilgrims'. Even Mrs Gamp in *Martin Chuzzlewit* (1843–4) speaks of living in 'this Piljin's projiss of a mortal wale'. But Bunyan's work had a seminal influ-ence on other fiction across the century. *Pilgrim's Progress* underpins the structure of Charlotte Brontë's *Jane Eyre* (1847) and *Villette* (1853),

[5] Thomas Vargish, *The Providential Aesthetic in Victorian Fiction* (1985).
[6] See Steven Marcus, *Dickens, from 'Pickwick' to 'Dombey'* (1965), pp. 73ff.
[7] The important difference is that Nell, unlike Pilgrim, is free from 'sin'. See Dennis Walder, *Dickens and Religion* (1981), p. 86.

and it was Maggie Tulliver's favourite book in Eliot's *The Mill on the Floss* (1860).

Masson identified Dickens as a 'Romantic', and contrasted him to *Thackeray, the artist of the 'Real'. But he claimed both were concerned with reflecting the same 'reality':

> The Ideal or Romantic artist must be true to nature as well as the Real artist, but he must be true in another fashion. He may take hints from Nature, her extremist moods, and make these hints the germ of creations fitted for a world projected imaginatively beyond the real one . . . Homer, Shakespeare and Cervantes, are said to be true to nature, and yet there is not one of their most pronounced characters exactly such as ever were to be found, or ever will be found in nature. (Masson, pp. 248, 50)

Others were less accommodating. 'I quarrel with [Dickens'] art in many respects, which I don't think represents Nature duly,' declared Thackeray himself, and he wrote to Masson:

> The Art of Novels *is* to represent nature: to convey as strongly as possible the sentiment of reality – in a tragedy or a poem or a lofty drama you aim at producing different emotions; the figures moving, and their words sounding, heroically: but in a drawingroom drama a coat is a coat and poker a poker; and must be nothing else according to my ethics, not an embroidered tunic, nor a great red-hot instrument like the Pantomime weapon.[8]

*Anthony Trollope, who satirized Dickens as 'Mr Popular Sentiment' in *The Warden* (1855), attacked Dickens' pathos as 'stagey and melodramatic', and his characters as static cut-outs. 'There is no real life in Smike,' he declared; 'Mrs Gamp, Micawber, Pecksniff and others have become household words in every house, as though they were human beings; but to my judgement they are not human beings, nor are any of the characters human which Dickens has portrayed.'[9] Trollope himself attempted to convey reality in the random happenings of everyday life, and praised Thackeray for creating characters based not on caricature or artistic effect, but on observation. The justification for creating Dobbin in *Vanity Fair*

---

[8] Quoted in John W. Dodds, *Thackeray: A Critical Portrait* (1941), p. 114.
[9] Anthony Trollope, *Autobiography* (1893), ch. 12.

(1847–8), Trollope insisted, was that 'Dobbins exist'. This sidesteps the issue. Trollope found Dobbin convincing not because the world was particularly peopled with Dobbins, but because Thackeray's portrayal of his ironic hero, honest and honourable but a deluded 'spooney', coincided with Trollope's own wry, tragicomic view of goodness in the world.

Masson saw the aims of realism coming closer with 'the advent of a new artist of the Real School, the author of *Adam Bede*' (Masson, p. 260). George Eliot brought a depth of knowledge in psychology, physiology, sociology and history to bear on the quest for objective reality, opening a new phase in realism. Her innovations coincided with the movements towards realism in the novel that were taking place in continental Europe. *Adam Bede* (1859) was published two years after Gustave Flaubert's *Madame Bovary*. But a comparison between the two texts only emphasizes the difference between French and English 'realism'. Where Flaubert sought to refine the author out of the text, George Eliot developed her authorial presence with greater subtlety, and where Flaubert aspired to emotional detachment, George Eliot made empathy central to the enlargement of the reader's understanding (see below, p. 69).

The divergence between the two realist traditions became even more pronounced in the novels of Emile Zola, works that provoked moral outrage in England. Zola's vast *Rougon-Macquart* series (1871–93) illustrated his theory of 'naturalism'. Although in practice the works' success owes much to their innovative narrative techniques, symbolism and the intensity of imaginative vision, Zola's professed object was to find a detached scientific understanding of the effects of heredity and social environment on family life.[10] The seventh novel in the series, *L'Assommoir* (1877), made a particular impact in England through the success of *Charles Reade's harrowing dramatization of the narrative, *Drink* (1879). The novels of Reade, *George Moore and *George Gissing, and Arthur Morrison's *A Child of the Jago (1896), were all influenced by Zola's powerful, unvarnished portrayal of the sufferings of the common people. But English readers generally rejected 'naturalism', in that it reduced humanity to its most basic elements, as bestial and 'un-natural'.

As a following section of this study will show, science, in particular evolutionary biology, was to increasingly inform the 'realism' of the

---

[10] Zola elaborated his ideal of 'naturalism' in *Le Roman experimental* (1880). See D. Baguley, *Naturalist Fiction: The Entropic Vision* (1990).

Victorian novel. But it will also demonstrate how the era's objective sense of external reality was also being shaped by developments in the study of history and biography, and that ways of seeing the world were mediated through theatre and the visual arts. These came together to create not a detached view of external reality, but a deeper sense of the challenges and responsibilities of the individual within this complex fabric. In her essay 'Against Dryness', Iris Murdoch looked back from an existential age to the Victorian sense of the density of its social reality, insisting that this created a literature of enduring importance to succeeding periods.

> We are not isolated free choosers, monarchs of all we survey, but benighted creatures sunk in a reality whose nature we are constantly and over-whelmingly tempted to deform by fantasy. Our current picture of freedom encourages a dream-like facility; whereas what we require is a renewed sense of the difficulty and complexity of the moral life and the opacity of persons. . . . We need a new vocabulary of attention. It is here that litera-ture is so important, especially since it has taken over some of the tasks performed by philosophy. Through literature we can rediscover a sense of the density of our lives.[11]

---

[11] Iris Murdoch, 'Against Dryness', *Encounter*, 88 (Jan. 1961), pp. 16–20.

History

'History,' Joyce's Stephen Daedalus famously declared at the beginning of the twentieth century, 'is a nightmare from which I am trying to wake up.'[12] But the Victorians were avidly interested in history, and historical works vied with novels in the interest of the general reader. While the first numbers of *David Copperfield* (1849–50) sold 25,000 copies, in 1855 the last two volumes of Macaulay's *History of England*, a more expensive investment, sold 26,000 in ten weeks, and the work's popularity was rivalled by sales of J. A. Froude's eleven-volume *History*, issued serially from 1856 to 1870. Readers bought 32,000 copies of J. R. Green's *A Short History of the English People* (1874) in the first year of publication, and the work went through numerous editions.

The interest in history was built into the stones of nineteenth-century British cities. John Nash placed England's naval victory over Napoleon at its centre when rebuilding central London. Trafalgar Square, completed in 1840, was dominated by Nelson, the architect of Britain's naval supremacy, looking out from his 76-foot column modelled on the tower of Mars in imperial Rome, dwarfing the statue of King Charles I riding his horse at the top of Whitehall. To the north of the square stood the National (Art) Gallery, backed by the National Portrait Gallery, containing a unique record on canvas of national personalities, one that was followed in print from 1888 by Lesley Stephen's *Dictionary of National Biography*. In Bloomsbury, the classical design of Robert Smirke's British Museum, finished in 1847, enclosed a great domed shrine to British literary scholarship, the British Library. In the north of England, civic

---

[12] James Joyce, *Ulysses* (1922), 'Proteus'.

buildings celebrated the achievements of the British Industrial Revolution, and the Gothic magnificence of Manchester town hall, if on a smaller scale, invited comparison with the Parliament of the metropolis.

This interest in history reflected the nation's search for identity in a changing age. As the Enlightenment questioned old religious certainties, history acquired a central importance. Peter Brooks has noted that as 'Voltaire announced and then the romantics confirmed, history replaces theology as the key discourse and central imagination, in that historical explanation becomes hereby a necessary factor for any thought about human society'.[13] Instead of looking for absolute truth, historians were conscious of interpreting the past from a particular political, ethical or religious viewpoint, making historical research not only a process of gathering data, but the study of the very nature of society. The factual groundwork of British history had been laid by David Hume's massive twelve-volume *History of England* (1754–62), a frame still being used in Charles Knight's *Popular History of England* (1855–66). But Hume was Scottish, Tory and a religious sceptic, and his views of history were constantly revised to accommodate different views of society throughout the century. One of the most important revisions was by a unique genius with interests in both history and creative literature, Sir Walter Scott.

Scott came to novel writing as the greatest editor of historical texts of his time, and as a brilliant social historian who based his work on local research into the lives of the Scottish communities around him. His antiquarian interests became fused with those in the contemporary world by his reading of German Romanticism. Writers like Goethe and Schiller based their vision of a new national culture on the folklore and oral traditions of the medieval period, leading to an impassioned recreation of the past that struck an immediate chord in Scott's imagination. Hazlitt was to write that in Scott's *Waverley novels 'all is fresh, as from the hand of nature: by going a century or two back and laying the scene in a remote and uncultivated district, all becomes new and startling in the present advanced period'.[14] Scott collected the ballads and folklore he remembered from his own childhood, and they became the inspiration for his own *The Lay of the Last Minstrel* (1805), a long narrative in ballad form set

---

[13] Peter Brooks, *Reading the Plot: Design and Intention in Narrative* (1984), p. 5. Hereafter *Plot*.
[14] William Hazlitt, 'Sir Walter Scott', in *The Spirit of the Age* (1825; Oxford World's Classics edition, 1954), p. 90.

in the mid-sixteenth century, *Marmion* (1808) and other verse. His verse made him the most popular poet of the day, to be rivalled only by Byron with 'Childe Harold' (1812–18) (St Clair, p. 217).

But Scott turned away from antiquarian verse towards the more immediate address of prose fiction. His identity was becoming divided. He was now wealthy from his legal practices and literary royalties, and building the great neo-Gothic country residence at Abbotsford on the Scottish borders where he could live as the local laird. Although his fortunes were to be devastated in 1826 by improvident publishing ventures, Scott the cultural nationalist of the Romantic period had now become a public British figure, unionist and Tory in politics. The transitions of Scott's own life gave him an acute sense of the individual's place in historical change. As Georg Lukács noted, 'what is lacking in the so-called historical novel before Sir Walter Scott is precisely the specifically historical, that is, derivations of the individuality of characters from the historical peculiarity of the age'.[15] Scott's genius was to base historical characters on their cultural identities at a particular time, rooted in a specific place, custom and language, and to see history in terms not of royalty and public figures, but of the experiences of the common people. In Scott's fiction it is the unheroic central figures who mediate historical processes, 'knocking at the door of the present . . . for whom the contemporary world is but a husk containing a different kernel from the old'.[16]

Contemporary critics marvelled at the range, diversity and vivacity of Scott's creations. *Henry James was to acknowledge the gap in sensibility between Scott's early readers and those of the late Victorian period: 'thoroughly to enjoy him, we must again become as credulous as children at twilight'. Nevertheless, declared James, it was Scott who had made the nineteenth-century novel possible. Scott 'was the first English prose storyteller. He was the first fictitious writer who addressed the public from its own level, without any preoccupation of place.'

> Before him no prose-writer had exhibited so vast and rich an imagination: it had not, indeed, been supposed that in prose the imaginative faculty was capable of such extended use. Since Shakespeare, no writer had created so immense a gallery of portraits, nor, on the whole, had any portraits been

---

[15] Georg Lukács, *The Historical Novel*, trans. Hannah and Stanley Mitchell (1962), p. 15.
[16] The phrase is Hegel's, quoted by Lukács, *Historical Novel*, p. 41.

so lifelike. Men and women, for almost the first time out of poetry, were presented in their habits as they lived. The Waverley characters were all instinct with something of the poetic fire.[17]

It was Scott who freed the novel to engage with all aspects and interests of life, opening the way for its extraordinary diversity in the nineteenth-century novel not only in Britain, but also in continental Europe, particularly in Germany and Russia. In the United States too, in particular through his influence on Fenimore Cooper, he contributed to the creation of a Native American literary tradition.

Scott helped create a new national consciousness in early nineteenth-century Britain. His novels coincided with the great hiatus in its history between the turmoil surrounding the French Revolution and the beginning of the Victorian era. Between 1814 and 1826 Scott wrote twenty-one works of fiction, covering every major era of British history, from the Crusades of *Ivanhoe* (1819), to the present of *Guy Mannering* (1815), *The Antiquary* (1816) and *St Ronan's Well* (1823). Peter Brooks has written that:

> it seems clear . . . that there have been some historical moments at which plot has assumed a greater importance than at others, moments in which cultures have seemed to develop an unquenchable thirst for plots and to seek the expression of central individual and collective meanings through narrative design. (*Plot*, p. 5)

Scott came at such a moment, and his narratives helped form a core of emergent national consciousness. If Scott brought the imagination to play on history, he made historians aware of the importance of the imagination. Macaulay attacked his contemporary historians for 'being seduced from truth, not by their imagination, but by their reason'.[18] Rational analysis by itself, he argued, could only create a catalogue of details, a theoretical reconstruction of the past with little relevance to the way human beings actually lived. He argued that 'the greatest and most momentous revolutions . . . are always the consequences of moral changes, which have gradually passed on the mass of the community.

[17] Henry James, unsigned review, *North American Review* (Oct. 1964), reprinted in John O'Hayden, ed., *Scott: The Critical Heritage* (1970), p. 429.

[18] Macaulay, Review of Neele, *The Romance of History* (*Edinburgh Review*, May 1828), reprinted in *Miscellaneous Writings*, new edn (1878), p. 153. Hereafter Macaulay.

... An intimate knowledge of the domestic history of nations is therefore absolutely necessary to the prognosis of political events.' He believed that 'instruction derived from history thus written would be a vivid and practical character. It would be received by the imagination as well as the reason. It would be not merely traced on the mind, but branded into it. Many truths, too, would be learned, which can be learned in no other manner' (Macaulay, p. 159).

Scott identified what was to be a central element in Victorian consciousness of 'Englishness', the Anglo-Saxons. This was a race 'distinguished by their plain, homely, blunt manners, and the free spirit infused by their ancient institutions and laws', surviving as a people through the imposition of the aristocratic 'Norman yoke'.[19] Dickens, whose ambivalent views of British history will be looked at below, enthusiastically embraced this ideal. *A Child's History of England* (1852–3) begins with:

> a handsome people. The men were proud of their long fair hair, parted on the forehead; their ample beards, their fresh complexions, and clear eyes. The beauty of the Saxon women filled all England with a new delight and grace.
>
> All the best of the English-Saxon character was first encouraged and shown under THE GREAT ALFRED. It has been the greatest character among the nations of the earth. Wherever the descendants of the Saxon race have gone ... even to the remotest regions of the world, they have been patient, persevering, never to be broken in spirit, never to be turned aside from enterprises on which they have resolved.

In *Bleak House* (1852–3) it is this yeoman stock in the person of the independent, resourceful Rouncewell that holds Britain's future; in *Great Expectations* (1860–1) its moral values persist in the honest blacksmith, Joe Gargery, and the practical country girl Biddy. Belief in Anglo-Saxon blood entered the English public school tradition in the Brown family, solid yeoman stock, in Thomas Hughes' *Tom Brown's Schooldays* (1857), a work that in turn shaped the outlook of the thousands of public school boys who went abroad as soldiers and civil servants to service the British Empire. Tractarian novelists with Roman Catholic (and so Norman) sympathies saw forthright Anglo-Saxon virtues ennobled by the chivalric ideals of the Norman invaders. In *The Lances of Lynwood* (1851) by the

---

[19] Sir Walter Scott, 1830 'Introduction' to *Ivanhoe* (1819).

High Church *Charlotte Yonge, the Catholic Lynwood family fight with the British under Edward the Black Prince to free France from exploitation by its aristocrats. At the climax, Sir Eustace saves his deadly enemy Fulke Clarenham from being stoned to death by enraged French villagers.

> 'Hold', he exclaimed in a clear full-toned voice that filled every ear. 'Hold! I am Eustace Lynwood, the Castellane of Chateau Norbelle!'

Awed, the villagers back off.

> 'Noble Knight!' [they whisper], 'flower of chivalry! how generous and Christian-like he bends over his enemy! Nay, if he revenge not himself, what right have we?' (Ch. 16)

Meanwhile, Kenelm Henry Digby's influential *The Broad Stone of Honour*, a work continually revised and enlarged between 1820 and 1877,[20] opened up a different vision of British history. Kenelm Digby looked back, not to Alfred, but to the pre-Saxon days of King Arthur and the Round Table, a world found in Thomas Malory's *Morte D'Arthur* (1485). The Arthurian legend rose in protest against the industrial world that Anglo-Saxon enterprise had created. Where the Anglo-Saxon view of history celebrated the populist achievements of the age, the Arthurian vision was concerned with the need to redefine the nature of the 'gentleman'. While Anglo-Saxons were heroes of prose fiction, the knights of the Round Table were celebrated in Victorian poetry and art, becoming the subject of Tennyson's *Idylls of the King* (1859–72), Pre-Raphaelite painting and Margaret Cameron's photography. *Bulwer Lytton wrote *The Last of the* [Norman] *Barons* (1843) in prose, but *King Arthur* (1848–9) in verse. Interest in history made the historical novel the most prestigious form of fiction for the Victorians. Almost all the major novelists tried their hand at writing it, and often considered these works to be their most important achievement: *Sir Arthur Conan Doyle was intensely annoyed that the public preferred his Sherlock Holmes stories to his historical romance *Micah Clarke* (1889).

As the nineteenth-century historical novel is little read today, it is examined separately (see below, pp. 197–8). Nevertheless, the Victorian historical consciousness permeated much of its life and literature. Dickens is an interesting case. He was temperamentally a reporter of the

---

[20] Mark Girouard, *The Return to Camelot: Chivalry and the English Gentleman* (1981), ch. 5.

present, not a novelist of the past. In *Barnaby Rudge* (1841), only violence and the theme of idiocy unite its complicated domestic plot to the history surrounding the 1780 Gordon riots, while in *A Tale of Two Cities* (1859), the French Reign of Terror serves as a backdrop to a timeless story of self-sacrifice and redemption. Dickens decorated his study at Gad's Hill with a set of false books labelled *The Wisdom of Our Ancestors* and individually titled 'Ignorance', 'Superstition', 'The Block', 'The Stake', 'The Rack', 'Dirt', 'Disease'.[21] He particularly disliked Royalist historians, and the genial but weak-minded Mr Dick in *David Copperfield*, with his obsession with 'King Charles' head', identifies them as kite-flying idiots.

In *The Old Curiosity Shop* the past becomes a world of looming shadows, and Dickens made a high-spirited sortie against the Victorian teaching of history in Mrs Jarley, proprietor of JARLEY'S WAX-WORK – 'One hundred figures the full size of life'. When Mrs Jarley wishes to impress the young ladies of local boarding schools, she makes the required adjustments (chs 27–9). Minor changes to the face and costume transformed Mr Grimaldi the clown into Mr Lindley Murray as he appeared when engaged in the composition of his English grammar, and a murderess of great renown became the moralizing bluestocking Mrs Hannah More. Both of these new likenesses were admitted as extraordinarily correct by Miss Monflathers, the head of the town's leading Boarding and Day Establishment. Mr Pitt in a nightcap and bed gown, and without his boots, represented the poet Cowper 'with perfect exactness'; and Mary Queen of Scots in a dark wig, white shirt-collar and male attire was such a complete image of Lord Byron that the young ladies 'quite screamed when they saw it', deeply disturbing the poise of Miss Monflathers. Mrs Jarley was perhaps in Lewis Carroll's mind when he created Alice's topsy-turvy schoolbook sense of history (see below, p. 101) – Carroll's Red Queen even squawks like her:

'I never saw any wax-work, ma'am,' said Nell. 'Is it funnier than Punch?' 'Funnier!' said Mrs Jarley in a shrill voice. 'It is not funny at all.' (Ch. 27)

'When you say "hill,"' the Queen interrupted, '*I* could show you hills, in comparison with which you'd call that a valley.'[22]

---

[21] Humphry House, *The Dickens World*, 2nd edn (1942), p. 35.
[22] *Alice Through the Looking Glass*, ch. 2. Miss Prickett, governess to the Liddell children, was traditionally held to be the model for the Red Queen.

But if Dickens is not much interested in the present in the past, he was acutely sensitive to the past in the present. He made a dutiful nod at writing historical romance, but actual history comes into focus most sharply not in *Barnaby Rudge* but in the largely contemporary novel *Bleak House*. Here mid-century Britain chokes under a foggy miasma of archaic legal impedimenta, a waste land littered with remainders of the past. History haunts Chesney Wold in the presence of a ghost from the seventeenth-century Civil War, a reminder of a divided English class sensibility that cripples Lady Dedlock. The recent past minces in the Regency manners of Turveydrop's School of Deportment, its degeneracy reflected in the feeble body of Prince; while contrasting values of Romantic egotism drive Harold Skimpole's self-serving, and Lawrence Boythorne's boisterous, independence. Even Trooper George with his seedy shooting gallery – significantly placed indeterminately north of Trafalgar Square off Leicester Square – is a relic of the Napoleonic battles of a bygone age.

George Eliot also dealt more interestingly with history in her rural idyll *Silas Marner* (1861) than in her major historical novel *Romola* (1862–3).[23] *Marner* tells how Silas escapes from the harsh industrial world of Lantern Yard into the Arcadian village of Raveloe. He buries his treasured guineas, lumber from his urban past, under the floor of his hut. When they are stolen, they become replaced in the gloom by the gleaming locks of the baby Eppie, ringlets which Silas' weak eyes first believe to be his returned gold. It is Christmas, and the parable of redemption through the coming of a child rings clear. But Sally Shuttleworth has suggested that, beneath the symbolism, the story explores current views of social development.[24] The innocence of the rural Raveloe community is undercut by the villagers' inability to see that 'they are pressed hard by primitive wants', and exploited by the feudal squirearchy of the Red House (ch. 6). Silas' past is both his weakness and his strength. If his soul has been withered by his life in Lantern Yard, the hardness of industrial living has created the sturdy independence that leads him to adopt and rear the child Eppie in defiance of village advice. Silas has been physically stunted by labour at the loom, yet in a (literally) touching scene, when Jane and Godfrey Cass come to

[23] For the ways historical consciousness shifted within George Eliot's successive novels, see Sally Shuttleworth, *George Eliot and Nineteenth-century Science* (1984). Hereafter Shuttleworth, *Eliot.*

[24] Sally Shuttleworth, 'Fairy Tale or Science? Physiological Psychology in *Silas Marner*', in Ludmilla Jordanova, ed., *Languages of Nature* (1986), pp. 244–88.

reclaim Eppie, Eppie can comfort and strengthen Silas because she knows the history of his weaver's hands, and understands that his craft has made them unusually responsive to her touch. 'She held Silas' hand in hers, and grasped it firmly – it was a weaver's hand, with palm and fingertips that were sensitive to such pressure' (ch. 19). By means of a human touch, history becomes alive in the domestic present.

Biography

'History is the essence of innumerable biographies,' declared Carlyle.[25] If Scott's historical fiction rooted the novel in time and place, and so fused the diverse strands of eighteenth-century fiction into the nineteenth-century 'realist' novel, the Romantic *Bildungsroman* (or 'self-development romance') grounded narrative in the experience of a unique and developing individual. Jean-Jacques Rousseau's autobiographical masterpiece, *Les Confessions*, published posthumously, frankly described the role of the emotions, including sexual desire, in his own development as a child, following themes in his *Emile, ou De l'éducation* (1862), a treatise on human nature in the form of a novel about a solitary boy being brought up by a wise tutor. Even more central to the genre was Goethe's *Wilhelm Meister's Lehrjahre* [Apprenticeship] (1796), a mystical and sometimes symbolic work, which portrayed the spiritual growth of a sensitive young dilettante with artistic ambitions to be an actor, coming through hard experience to discover happiness in engagement with life itself, and marriage to Natalie, the ideal woman. Romantic biography brought a change of emphasis rather than subject to the novel. Whereas earlier fiction was often concerned with the progress of the individual in the world, the *Bildungs-roman* focused minutely on the nature and meaning of human life itself. The shift was subtle but important. As Bakhtin was to note:

> The essential feature of the biographical novel [in the Romantic period] is the appearance of biographical time. As distinct from adventure and fairy-tale time, biographical time is quite realistic. All of its moments are

---

[25] Thomas Carlyle, 'On History' (1830), para. 5.

included in the total life process, and they describe this process as limited, irrepeatable, and irreversible. Each event is localized in the whole of this life process and there it ceases to be an adventure.[26]

The English *Bildungsroman* could not reproduce the mystical quality of Goethe's *Wilhelm Meister*, and was less frank on its sexual aspects, instead focusing on the practical and moral issues of youthful development. But the concept of early experience as an apprenticeship for active engagement with life itself found a strong affinity with the nonconformist conscience of early nineteenth-century Britain. David Masson declared that *Wilhelm Meister* was 'by far the greatest influence on [nineteenth-century English novels of art and culture] . . . and there can be no doubt that that work, since it was translated, has had some influence on the aims of British novel-writing' (Masson, p. 225). Scott wrote *Waverley* while under the spell of Goethe, and its direct impact has been traced on a range of novelists, including Disraeli and Bulwer Lytton.[27] Thomas Carlyle translated *Wilhelm Meister* into English in 1824, and it partly inspired his *Sartor Resartus* (1833–4) ('the tailor retailored'), although it is a very different work. Carlyle presented *Sartor* as a life edited out of six paper sacks stuffed with miscellaneous notes, jotting and documents by Professor Teufelsdröckh (Devil's-dung). Incoherent, dislocated, a bizarre, seriocomic mixture of styles and ideas, *Sartor* presents a fragmented universe of experience given a tentative meaning by the thread of biography deciphered by its green-spectacled editor. *Sartor* established the novelist's role as an editor selecting between the infinite possibilities of reality. So Charlotte Brontë subtitles her very different work *Jane Eyre*, in which Jane threads her way through conflicting views of a woman's duty, 'An Autobiography. Edited by Currer Bell'.

Carlyle proclaimed that 'Biography is by nature the most universally profitable, universally pleasant, of all things, especially the Biography of distinguished individuals'. He himself wrote brilliant lives of *John Sterling* (1851) and *Frederick the Great* (1858–65), among a flowering of biographies and autobiographies (see Further Reading, p. 237). The discoveries of the age were given human faces by journals and the personal narratives that accompanied them. David Livingstone's *Missionary Travels* (1856) sold out

---

[26] M. M. Bakhtin, *Speech Genres and Other Late Essays* (1986), pp. 17–18.

[27] See Susanne Howe, *Wilhelm Meister and his English Kinsmen* (1930). Hereafter Howe.

an edition of 12,000 before publication, and another 30,000 in five years. Charles Darwin's *Journal of Researches into the Geology and Natural History of the Various Countries Visited by HMS Beagle from 1832–6* (1839) paved the way for *The Origin of Species* (1859). The theological arguments of John Henry Newman's contributions to *Tracts for the Times* (1833–41), which launched the High Church movement, were rooted in personal experience by the autobiographical *Apologia pro Vita Sua* (1864); John Stuart Mill's philosophic *Utilitarianism* (1861) was put into context by his *Autobiography* (1873); while Ruskin's life of writing on art and society was consummated in the autobiographical *Praeterita* (1885–9).

J. G. Lockhart's monumental seven-volume *Memoirs of the Life of Sir Walter Scott* (1837–8) was the first of a succession of distinguished studies of lives in writing that was to include Elizabeth Gaskell's *Life of Charlotte Brontë* (1857), John Forster's *Life of Dickens* (1872–4), James Anthony Froude's *Thomas Carlyle* (1880, 1884), J. W. Cross' *George Eliot's Life* (1885) and Hallam Tennyson's *Memoir* (1897) of his father,[28] besides the autobiographies of Trollope (1883) and *Margaret Oliphant (1899). All these illuminated both the profession of letters and the creative process of authorship itself. The biographies of women authors in particular helped establish the central role of women writers, editors and reviewers in developing the Victorian novel, a task often only achieved in tandem with heavy domestic responsibilities, and contending with social prejudice against middle-class career women. More recently, Patrick Joyce's *Democratic Subjects* (1999) has brought a postmodern approach to language to examine the ways the narrative of biography constructed social identity in mid-Victorian Britain.

The biographical novel reflected the processes by which the fiction itself was written. The novel was seen as a form that turned the artist from introspection to engagement with life itself. In G. H. Lewes' semi-autobiographical *Bildungsroman, Ranthorpe* (1847), literary ambitions drive Ranthorpe to abandon a clerical career for a Bohemian life as a poet and dramatist, only to face spiritual despair. But he is saved from suicide by visiting Germany and by reading Goethe, whose inspiration leads him to return and find success in England as a writer of actual life (Howe, pp.

---

[28] See Christopher Ricks, 'Victorian Lives', in *Essays in Appreciation* (1996), pp. 114–234.

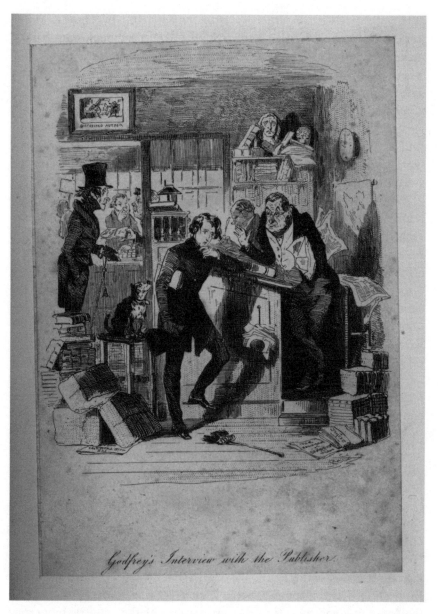

Plate 1 Hablôt K. Browne, 'Godfrey's Interview with the Publisher', from Thomas Miller, *Godfrey Malvern; or the Life of an Author* (2nd edn, 1844), p. 93.

The impoverished figure in the doorway intimates Godfrey's probable future.

221–5). *Godfrey Malvern, or the Life of an Author* (1843), by Thomas Miller, follows the author's career from writing verse as a Lincolnshire basket-maker in the 1830s to the search for fame and fortune as a London writer, where his divided cultural identity is embodied in loyalties to his country wife Emma, and love for the passionate, cosmopolitan Maria. He scrapes a pittance doing hackwork for periodicals, until a published volume of verse gains him access to the pretentious literary circle of 'Lady Smileall' (Miller himself had been patronized by Lady Blessington). But while writing verse leads him into social triviality, Godfrey finds success and personal fulfilment in writing a novel.

The work ends unsatisfactorily. Maria's death releases Godfrey to return to the country and Emma, where he discovers he is heir to an estate. (There was no release for Miller, who died in London as a literary hack in acute penury in 1874.) A minor, flawed novel, *Godfrey Malvern* nevertheless offers vivid glimpses of the way the novel emerged as a respectable form out of journalism and hack writing for magazines in the early century. It is the story of Thackeray's *Pendennis* (1848–50) and, by implication, Dickens' *David Copperfield*, of whose literary apprenticeship we are told nothing, but who presumably also begins authorship as a miscellaneous writer. Each work shows a development towards moral integrity, a progress underlined by love interest as the main protagonist makes the right choice of sexual partner. The point that when the author comes to moral maturity, he is able to write a successful novel, suggests that both processes are journeys towards a higher form of truth.

Biography, with its need to select from and interpret the life of its subject, is as creative an investigative process as constructing fiction. Bridging social reality and individual experience, biographical fiction became central to the realist agenda of the Victorian novel. It was a common strategy in industrial 'problem novels', including Elizabeth Gaskell's *Mary Barton* (1848), Charlotte Brontë's *Shirley* (1849) and *Charles Kingsley's *Alton Locke* (1850), and lay at the core of novels exploring issues of history, religion and Darwinian evolution. From Charlotte Brontë's *Jane Eyre* through George Eliot's *The Mill on the Floss* (1860) to the *'new woman' novels in the last decades of the century, biography was the mode through which women writers explored their gendered identity. The form's shared human experience emphasized the intimate relationship between the author and the reader typical of the mid-Victorian novel. Eliza Lynn Linton justified writing her fictionalized autobiography *Christopher Kirkland* on the grounds that her readers would recognize themselves in the narrative: for 'as no human being is absolutely unparalleled . . . it follows that no personal history can be without the interest that comes from sympathy and likeness.'[29]

[29] Eliza Lynn Linton, *The Autobiography of Christopher Kirkland* (1885), p. vi.

Religion and Morals

'At different times in our history,' wrote Trollope, 'the preacher, the dramatist, the essayist, the poet have been efficacious over others as moral arbiters – at one time the preacher, and at one the poet. Now it is the novelist.'[30] Religious issues underpin the Victorian novel, implicated in its concern with moral choice, its attitudes to scientific knowledge, to the childhood and family, to life and death, and its reverence for beauty.[31] Yet the titles read most today are essentially secular, with writers transferring religious instincts onto the material world. While specifically 'religious' novels are considered under a separate topic (see pp. 210–12), this section will look at the broader impact of religion on such fiction.

Religious institutions and clergy were a 'godsend' for the novelist looking for material. 'Especially within Britain,' noted Masson, 'there has been a determination to make representatives of all classes of clergyman and all religious creeds sit for their photographs in novels' (Masson, p. 262). The hierarchies and customs of church and chapel provided a microcosm of wider society in Trollope's *Barchester Chronicles* (see Key Texts, p. 168) and provided a background for Mrs Oliphant's *Chronicles of Carlingford* (see p. 134). In general, clergy and ministers come off poorly in Victorian fiction. Evangelical clergy, who emphasized personal holiness and an inward conviction of salvation, were particularly vulnerable to attack. Frances Trollope caused a scandal with her portrait of the repulsive Reverend William Cartwright in *The Vicar of Wrexhill* (1837), a novel that not only targeted a clergyman of the established

---

[30] Trollope, 'Novel-reading', *The Nineteenth Century* (Jan. 1879), p. 26. Hereafter 'Novel-reading'.
[31] Hilary Fraser, *Beauty and Belief* (1986).

Church, but also explicitly referred to his predatory philandering. But although he was careful never to identify them with specific sects or denominations, Dickens was the great progenitor of hostile stereotypes of ministers and clergy in Victorian fiction. The repellent appearance and inflated rhetoric of such figures as the red-nosed Reverend Mr Stiggins and the fat Shepherd in *Pickwick Papers* (1836–7), the Reverend Mr Melchisedech Howler (Mrs McStinger's spiritual guide) in *Dombey and Son* (1846–8), and the oily Mr Chadband in *Bleak House* declared open season on evangelical clergy. Fellow novelists followed, provoking a reproof from Margaret Oliphant that not all evangelical pastors were obnoxious hypocrites.[32]

Other accounts were more objective. Eliza Lynn Linton's *The Autobiography of Christopher Kirkland* (1885) is a moving, psychologically perceptive version of the life of its author, who, like 'Kirkland', grew up in Westmorland, leaving Keswick aged 21. In London Linton established her literary reputation with two historical novels, and as a reporter for the *Morning Chronicle* became Britain's first salaried woman journalist. Her reporter's eye directs in *Kirkland*, which explored a London crowded with competing ideologies and religions. In turn Kirkland encountered spiritualism, mesmerism, electrical magnetism, Owenism, High, Middle and Low Church, Catholicism, agnosticism and, like Linton herself, was drawn to Unitarianism. A Mrs Pratten is 'a kind of palimpsest of all the crazy faiths that float about the world . . . odd as she was in all this, [she] was not substantially insane' (vol. 2, pp. 112, 106). The novel moves from observation to increasingly austere self-searching as Kirkland refuses to find refuge from personal tragedy in religious faith, and he ends contemplating death with existentialist stoicism. As in novels like W. H. White's better-known *Mark Rutherford's Deliverance* (1888), fiction becomes a mask, giving Linton a greater freedom to explore personal crises than would 'real-life' autobiography.

If religion appeared in the Victorian novel in the outward costume of the age, it beat at the heart of its fiercely argued controversies of faith and doubt, creating the body of religious novels examined on pp. 210–12. But, as we have noted, religious consciousness affected Victorian fiction

[32] See Elizabeth Jay, *The Religion of the Heart: Anglican Evangelicism and the Nineteenth-century Novel* (1972); Valentine Cunningham, *Everywhere Spoken Against: Dissent in the Victorian Novel* (1975).

as a whole. This was particularly true of novelists like the *Brontë sisters, brought up in the isolation of Haworth rectory, their early lives dominated by both their Anglican father and their Wesleyan Methodist Aunt Branwell, who brought with her a complete file of *The Methodist Magazine*. Charlotte Brontë in *Shirley* described this reading as 'mad . . . full of miracles and apparitions, of preternatural warnings, ominous dreams, and frenzied fanaticisms'.[33] But it shaped the imaginative world of the sisters' fiction. The opening of Emily Brontë's *Wuthering Heights* (1847) invokes the oppressive atmosphere of dissenting religion in the Reverend Jabes Branderham's interminable chapel sermons, and the intolerable preaching of his semi-literate disciple Joseph. But while he is appalled by this world, the outsider Lockwood finds himself drawn into it, and he passes directly from the bad dream of Branderham's sermon into 'the intense horror of nightmare' of the child Cathy crying to enter through the window out of the storm. Lockwood adopts the impulsive cruelty of Heathcliff as he 'pulled [the child's] wrist on to the broken pane, and rubbed it to and fro till the blood ran down and soaked the bed-clothes'. The novel both rejects and perpetuates the overheated imaginative world of Methodist religious enthusiasm. As Margaret Maison has pointed out, Heathcliff can talk

> with all the rapture of a Methodist ecstatic: 'My soul's bliss kills my body,' he cries and the whole novel glows with an almost religious fervour. . . . Such strange and powerful enthusiasms are not uncommon in Methodist novels; some of John Ackworth's heroes behave in a similar way, rolling about and groaning when slighted by the lady of their choice and then, finding their love returned, falling on their knees sobbing and shrieking in an agony of bliss: 'Stay Thy Hand, O God! Stay Thy Hand! Thou wilt Kill me! Kill me with joy!'[34]

Yet nothing could be less 'Christian' than Heathcliff's violence and revenge, and Lockwood envisages the lovers reunited, not in a quiet grave, but released onto the freedom of the open moors.

It is interesting to compare Emily Brontë's *Wuthering Heights* with Charlotte Brontë's *Jane Eyre*. The latter owes much to the spiritual pro-

---

[33] *Shirley*, ch. 22. See also Winifred Gérin, *Charlotte Brontë* (1967), pp. 33–7.
[34] Margaret Maison, *Search Your Soul, Eustace* (1961), pp. 187–8. Hereafter Maison.

gresses recorded in evangelical novels (see Maison, ch. 5). The narrative progresses on two levels, a pilgrim's progress through the spiritual crises and moral dangers of the inner life, and the practical struggles of the single 'respectable' woman who had no alternative but to be a governess. The two journeys are both reflected in Jane's consciousness, which constantly shifts from actuality into dreams, divine intimations and waking visions. After the interrupted wedding ceremony,

> Self-abandoned, relaxed and effortless, I seemed to have laid me down in the dried-up bed of a great river; I heard a flood loosened in remote mountains, and felt the torrent come: to rise I had no will, to flee I had no strength. I lay faint; longing to be dead. One idea only throbbed life-like within me – a remembrance of God. (Ch. 26)

Both 'pilgrim's progress' and the wandering of the children of Israel in the Old Testament give her life significance. As George Landor points out, Jane finds that Rochester is usurping the place of God, and two chapters later on, discovering Bertha, she envisions herself in consequence suffering the fate of Pharaoh before Moses, declaring: 'My hopes were all dead – struck with a subtle doom, such as, in one night, fell on all the first-born in the land of Egypt' (ch. 26).[35]

But a reading of evangelical literature only emphasizes Charlotte Brontë's departure from previous models. The life and death of the saintly Helen Burns, which frames Jane's progress, echoes the Reverend Legh Richmond's *The Dairyman's Daughter* (1809), a religious tract that sold an estimated 2 million copies in English in eleven years, and has some claim to be the most popular tract ever written. Richmond gave the actual death of one Elizabeth Wallridge the cosmic significance Dickens was to bring to Little Nell's in *The Old Curiosity Shop*, and which is reflected in Helen's death in *Jane Eyre*. Compare Richmond:

> At length I said to Elizabeth, 'Do you experience any doubts or temptations on the subject of your eternal safety?'
>   'No, sir; the Lord deals very gently with me, and gives me peace.'[36]

---

[35] George P. Landow, *Victorian Types, Victorian Shows: Biblical Typology in Victorian Literature, Art and Thought* (1980), p. 97.

[36] Legh Richmond, *The Dairyman's Daughter* (in the *Christian Guardian*, 1809, republished in *Annals of the Poor*, 1814), part vii. Hereafter *Dairyman's Daughter*.

with Charlotte Brontë:

> 'But where are you going to, Helen? Can you see? Do you know?'
> 'I believe; I have faith: I am going to God.'
> 'Where is God? What is God?'
> 'My Maker and yours, who will never destroy what he has created.'
> (Ch. 9)

But Jane gives a pointed reply to the Reverend Brocklehurst's question, 'What must you do to avoid [hell fire]?': 'I must keep good health, and not die' (ch. 4). Legh Richmond himself refers to the Protestant doctrine that Heaven can also be won in life: 'when Divine grace renews the heart of the fallen sinner, Paradise is regained, and much of its beauty restored to the soul' (*Dairyman's Daughter*, part ii): *Jane Eyre* indeed tells of Paradise regained through faith and the resistance to temptation. Yet, as early hostile critics of the novel pointed out, it was not the orthodox Christian Paradise. Jane's career reflects Charlotte Brontë's passionate concern with the occupational needs of single women rather than religious duty, and in her rejection of a missionary life with St John Rivers, she flouts the conventional ending of evangelical novels, marriage to a clergyman.

The Unitarian Mrs Gaskell was careful to keep her religious principles from intruding onto social issues. But nevertheless, as the wife of a Unitarian minister, she instinctively interpreted contemporary events within a biblical framework. At the conclusion of *Mary Barton*, objective reportage of the sufferings of Manchester cotton workers elides poignantly into a secular *pietà*.

> Mr Carson stood in the door-way. In one instant he comprehended the case. He raised the powerless frame: and the departing soul looked out of the eyes with gratitude. He held the dying man propped in his arms. John Barton folded his hands as if in prayer.
>
> 'Pray for us,' said Mary, sinking on her knees, and forgetting in that solemn hour all that had divided her father and Mr Carson.
>
> No other words could suggest themselves than some of those he had read only a few hours before.
>
> 'God be merciful to us sinners. – Forgive our trespasses as we forgive them that trespass against us.' (Ch. 35)

John Barton, crucified by the economics of the mill industry, dies on a representative of that cross, the arms of the mill-owner, while his daughter doubles for another Mary in another place (Mark 15:39).

Dickens was also drawn to the Unitarian faith with its rejection of orthodox doctrine, and located New Testament commandments in social action, not in a code of belief. In *Bleak House*, Dickens lampoons Mr Chadband preaching on the 'slumbering Heathen' figure of Jo. But when the crossing sweeper actually dies, it is Dickens himself who takes the pulpit to give the sermon as it should be given: 'Dead men and women, born with Heavenly compassion in your hearts. And dying thus around us every day.' Christmas, a time when a benevolent spirit could make all society one family,[37] lay at the heart of Dickens' social philosophy. Louis Cazamian subtitled his chapter on Dickens in *The Social Novel in England*, 'The Philosophy of Christmas', claiming that its 'social altruism . . . exhibits the best qualities of Dickens' heart, and all the limitations of his head'.[38] But Dickens' belief in the need for a changed heart recurs through his early work, in the redemption of Dick Swiveller in *The Old Curiosity Shop*, of Martin Chuzzlewit, and of Pip in *Great Expectations*. In each of these cases it is associated with a Pavlovian crisis of shock or illness. The most dramatic example is Scrooge in *A Christmas Carol* (1843), who goes through all the stages of the typical evangelical conversion narrative – revelation, repentance, the experience of a 'warmed heart' and the changed life. Although there is no rebirth in Christ, reborn into a new sense of social responsibility Scrooge babbles like any evangelical convert as he enters his new life as a model of social affection:

> 'I don't know how long I have been among the spirits. I don't know anything. I'm quite a baby. Never mind. I don't care. I'd rather be a baby. Hallo! Whoop! Hallo here!' ('Stave Five')

Trollope took a very different approach. Ten years after the publication of Dickens' *A Christmas Carol* he was moved by the experience of a midsummer evening in the precincts of Salisbury Cathedral to write *The*

---

[37] This idea appears as early as 'Christmas Festivities' in *Sketches by 'Boz'* (1835).

[38] Louis Cazamian, *The Social Novel in England 1830–1850*, trans. Martin Fido (1903, 1973), p. 137.

Warden (1855). The story is simple. Mr Harding, a gentle, kindly, retiring man with a love of music, is approaching 60 and living with his only daughter as warden of Hiram's Hospital. The almshouse was founded in 1435 to care for twelve Barchester indigents. Over the years the warden's keep has improved. Now Harding receives £800 a year and a house, and the men, one and sixpence a day and their care. It is a happy arrangement until the prevalent spirit of reform leads a young doctor, Mr Bold, to demand the trust's funds go to the beadsmen. Bold soon discovers that changing centuries of tradition on a point of principle is not so simple. Without the warden's salary Harding and his daughter, whom Bold loves, face penury, while reforms will bring the pensioners nothing. His challenge involves spiralling lawyers' fees and the national press, battening on the story, blowing it into a national scandal. Bold, appalled by what he has started, at great personal expense halts the legal action. But Harding's conscience has been touched, and he resigns as warden, disregarding the consequences for him and his daughter, rather than live with the possibility of causing injustice.

Bold's action and Harding's resignation leave everyone worse off, including the old men who greedily supported Bold's action. But Trollope shows no sympathy for corrupt church practices either, and condemns the Reverend Vesey Stanhope who lives off three sinecures in an Italian villa. Originally, Trollope makes clear, the moneys of Hiram's Hospital were intended for its inmates, and on these grounds Bold is historically justified in his challenge. The first readers found the moral issues of the book unclear, and *Geraldine Jewsbury in *The Athenaeum*[39] thought Trollope showed 'too much indifference as to the rights of the case'. But the point is that there are no absolute 'rights'. The morality concerns Harding's private conscience, and whatever the wider issues, he can only find peace of mind through a courageous personal action.

Although the novel contains Dickensian characters and descriptions, Trollope contrasts his own approach to moral debate against that of Dickens. In a set piece (ch. 15), the case of Hiram's legacy is taken up in the muckraking London press by the ranting mystic Dr Anticant (Thomas Carlyle), and in 'The Almshouse' by Mr Popular Sentiment (Dickens), transformed into an emotional horror story about starving paupers. Trol-

---

[39] (Anon.), 27 Jan. 1855, quoted in R. C. Terry, ed., *The Oxford Reader's Companion to Trollope* (1999), p. 561.

lope, although a staunch churchgoer, believed that in real life moral issues arose from the gradual working out of the individual conscience within the complexities of social reality at a particular historical moment. As M. A. Goldberg has argued,[40] Harding's morality is not based on the ethical principles current in earlier eras, on benevolence, radical insight or utilitarian practicality, 'but rather [on] the essence of tranquillity, quietude and compromise', ideals located specifically in the social equipoise and balance of the 1850s.

But as faith came under pressure, the interest in the spiritual did not disappear. Exiting out of the front door in the novels of doubt that made *Mrs Humphry Ward's *Robert Elsmere* the bestseller of 1888, religious interest returned through the back in a flood of fantasy, ghost stories, scientific romance and novels of the occult. The mystical extravaganzas of *Marie Corelli sold even more than *Elsmere*, and Margaret Oliphant turned from realism to find a new popularity with a succession of effective ghost narratives. One of her most popular, a novella entitled *A Beleaguered City: A Story of the Seen and Unseen* (1880), recounts the supernatural experiences of Sémur, in Haute Bourgogne, France, in an unspecified period of the past through the witness of various inhabitants. The community is settling into self-centred materialism. One citizen, Jacques Richard, loudly proclaims, 'There is no *bon Dieu* but money', provoking a woman in the street to cry out, 'It is enough to make the dead rise out of their graves'. And rise out of their graves they do. For three days invisible angelic forces drive out the inhabitants, separating the men from the women and children, and possessing the town. The mayor, Martin Dupin, is summoned back into the ghostly city. He finds his house unchanged, save for his wife's room, which is free from the haunted atmosphere. A veil has been drawn away from a little shrine to their lost daughter, Marie, and the child looks lovingly out at him from her picture, an olive branch poised above the frame. Dupin falls to his knees. Nothing much else happens in the story. The spirits leave, the town's visionary dies, the inhabitants return, and their reformation proves temporary. But Dupin keeps the olive branch with its intimation of immortality, and has a new tender understanding of his wife and her nurturing womanhood. The story

---

[40] M. A. Goldberg, 'Trollope's *The Warden*: A Commentary on the "Age of Equipoise"', *Nineteenth-century Fiction*, 27, no. 5, reprinted in Ian Watt, ed., *The Victorian Novel: Modern Essays in Criticism* (1971), pp. 337–46.

looks back to Oliphant's own grief at the death of her beloved daughter Maggie in Rome in 1864, when she identified her mixed despair and hope as at one with 'the spirit of the age'. She was living, she declared, in a period 'which believes and does not believe, and *perhaps*, I think, carries the human yearning and longing farther than it was ever carried before'.[41] It is a poignant note re-echoed in much religious literature in the later nineteenth century.

[41] Margaret Oliphant, *Autobiography* (1899), p. 93.

Evolution

The astounding innovation of Mary Shelley's *Frankenstein* (1818, revised 1831) was the absence of God. Milton's *Paradise Lost* was one model for the story, and was cited as such in the text; but the story held no Heaven or Hell, no divine judgement, no damnation or redemption. Orthodox polarities of good and evil were confused in the tangled relationship of man to monster. The moral universe hung precariously over an abyss, suspended between a vision of humanity's innate divinity and contemporary scientific debates about the nature of life itself. It reflected a ferment of contemporary scientific debate. Over half a century before his better-known grandson, Erasmus Darwin, grandfather of Charles, was already speculating about life evolving by natural means in the verse epics of *Loves of the Plants* (1789). In *Zoonomia* (1794) he wrote:

> all animals undergo perpetual transformations; which are in part produced by their own exertion in consequence of their desires and aversions; their pleasures and their pains, or of irritations, or of associations, and many of these acquired forms or propensities are transmitted to their posterity.[42]

On this basis, Frankenstein erred not in assuming the role of God, but in bypassing the natural sexual processes of evolution. When Mary Shelley wrote, other investigations were threatening established views of a divinely created universe. In 1798 the clergyman scholar Thomas Robert Malthus, an important influence on Charles Darwin, published *On the Principle of Population* (1798), a work that applied evolutionary principles

---

[42] *Zoonomia* (1794), I, sec. 39, ch. 4, p. 550.

to the human species by suggesting that it was controlled by food supply. Sir Charles Lyell's *The Principles of Geology* (1830–3) established that rock strata were created over millennia, not in the seven days of the account in Genesis, and even more controversially, Robert Chambers' (anonymous) *The Vestiges of the Natural History of Creation* (1844), a hugely popular work written for the lay reader, argued that all aspects of creation, including life itself, could be explained by natural causes.

Early reactions to evolutionary theory were mocking. In Thomas Love Peacock's *Melincourt* (1817), the simian Sir Oran Hut-ton (ourang-outang) satirized the eccentric eighteenth-century philosopher Lord Monboddo, who believed the great apes were 'wild' human beings. Later *Benjamin Disraeli, a persistent opponent of evolution, in *Tancred* (1847) lampooned Chambers' *Vestiges* as *The Revelations of Chaos*, a work proving that humans could be related to either crows or fish. Such baiting looked forward to W. H. Mallock's *The New Paul and Virginia* (1878), which featured a Professor Darnley who wrote *The Origin of Life* out of long research into fermenting hay and cheese. Shipwrecked on a desert island, he meets the 'missing link' of human evolution, only to find later that it is an escaped pet monkey (see Henkin, pp. 93–4). But decades before the publication of *The Origin of Species* in 1859, evolutionary concepts were shaping the mental frameworks of the novel. Industrial conflicts focused current economic and social debate on what Carlyle called 'the Condition-of-England' problem, and the 'social problem' novel came into being to consider the organic changes taking place in society. From the late 1840s John Stuart Mill, G. H. Lewes and subsequently George Eliot popularized the 'positivism' of Auguste Comte, the atheistic study of social evolution according to observable scientific principles that was to form the basis of sociology. Christian belief blended with evolutionary views in Kingsley's *Alton Locke*, in which its Chartist protagonist experiences an extraordinary dream of human evolution from the primeval slime, and in the remarkable combination of fantasy, polemic and social theory, Kingsley's *The Water-Babies* (1863).

The studies of Leo Henkin, Sally Shuttleworth, George Levine and Gillian Beer (see Further Reading, p. 237) have shown in some detail the ways in which evolutionary ideas also shaped the fiction of writers like the Brontë sisters, George Eliot and *Thomas Hardy. But the impact of Darwin's *Origin of Species* and *The Descent of Man* (1871) and their forebears went beyond the conscious application of scientific ideas to the novel. As George Levine declared, they 'revolutionized the ways we imagine ourselves within the natural world and have raised fundamental questions about the nature of self, society, history, and religion'.

> Obviously, Darwin's revolution was not single-handed, but he can be taken as the figure through whom the full implications of the developing authority of scientific thought began to be felt by modern non-scientific culture. Darwin's theory thrust the human into nature and time, and subjected it to the same dispassionate and material investigation hitherto reserved for rocks and stars.[43]

Like the impact of Freud's psychoanalysis on the next generation, Darwinism had an influence independent of Darwin's actual writing. Levine has noted that the conservative writer Trollope had little interest in scientific developments. 'Yet Trollope's whole narrative method (as he describes it) is to achieve a kind of Darwinian position in relation to his materials, to see how they will evolve, to observe meticulously, to let the accumulated evidence provide the primary authority.'[44] Darwinism shaped the fiction of writers who had never read a page of Darwin.

Recent critical debates have turned to examine the search for an appropriate language, organization and imagery common to both creative fiction and science in the nineteenth century. In 1948 Wylie Sypher declared that Darwin's theories of evolution were as much melodrama as science, and later scholars have demonstrated that scientists had to find literary structures through which to communicate their material as much as did the novelists of the period. If Hardy constructed his plots around Darwinian concepts, on what basis did Darwin create narrative out of the independent data gathered by objective observation? As the title of Gillian Beer's seminal study asks, what were Darwin's 'plots'?

---

[43] George Levine, *Darwin and the Novelists: Patterns of Science in Victorian Fiction* (1988), p. 1.
[44] George Levine, ed., *One Culture: Essays in Science and Literature* (1987); Levine, *Darwin and the Novelists*, p. 183.

Detectives

Among the young Dickens' favourite reading was a novel little known today, but widely popular in the early nineteenth century: Alain-René Le Sage's *The Devil Upon Two Sticks* (1707). The story tells of the lame devil Ashmodeus imprisoned in a bottle who rewards his liberator with a flight over Madrid. Le Sage's work was still being cheaply reprinted in the 1830s, when it inspired an ephemeral penny journal *The Devil in London* (1832), whose editor promised similar revelations: 'One whisk of our tail, and *hey presto*, away went the roofs of the houses, and with them too, the artificial covering of every human breast.' Dickens in *Dombey* cries: 'Oh for a good spirit who would take the roof-tops off, with a more potent and benignant hand than the lamed demon in the tale' (ch. 47), and Le Sage's novel has been seen as an inspiration for the panoptic vision of London that recurs in Scrooge's flight over the city in *A Christmas Carol*, and the opening to *Bleak House*. Its process goes to the root meaning of 'detection' – to expose by 'unroofing'. It embodied the new urban gaze. The journey through the framing perspectives of the Victorian novel leads finally on to the detective story.

William Godwin's *Adventures of Caleb Williams* (1794) has been seen as a precursor of the form. But Caleb's detection of his master Falkland's dark secret was obsessive and passionate: the detective story method is detached. Between 1841 and 1843 Edgar Allan Poe invented the modern genre with three stories featuring the analytic detachment of C. Auguste Dupin, 'The Murders in the Rue Morgue', 'The Mystery of Marie Rôget' and 'The Purloined Letter', tales written as Poe's conscious exercise in controlling his own dangerously disordered emotions at the time. Although 'Marie Rôget' was based on an actual New York crime, he distanced the stories by setting them in Paris, and created the six-point formula that was to provide a typical basis for the detective genre: the introduction of the detective; the crime and clues; investigation; announcement of the solution; explanation of the solution; dénouement (Cawelti, pp. 8–2).

Monsieur Dupin was the creation of Poe's imagination. But the reorganization of the police forces in London and Paris was also producing a new breed of professional investigators, and the word 'detective' (for the previous term 'spy') was first recorded in 1843. Detective activities had been anticipated by the French criminal-turned-police chief François-Eugène Vidocq, whose ghosted *Memoirs* (1828) were the probable model for Balzac's Vautrin in *La Comédie humaine* (1842–7). In England, Charles Dickens reported on the activities of the newly formed Detective Branch of Scotland Yard in articles in *Household Words*, and later used the actual Detective Inspector Charles Frederick Field as a model for Inspector Bucket of *Bleak House*. Bucket (whose name suggests simply a container, and who wore a prominent ring 'more setting than stone') is an innovation in function as well as character. He is an unostentatious omnipresence, genial in behaviour but impervious to compassion. Under a bluff exterior, he is the unbending, ambivalent incarnation of the modern legal process.

What Bucket intimates becomes startlingly embodied in Sergeant Cuff, in what T. S. Eliot claimed as the greatest Victorian detective story, *Wilkie Collins' The Moonstone (1868). Grizzled, elderly, dressed in black, yet with disturbingly sharp light grey eyes, 'he might have been a parson, or an undertaker, or anything you like, except what he really was'. Cuff was enigmatic and changeable, a hardened law enforcer with a hobby of growing roses – as he tells Mr Betteredge, 'when I *have* a moment's fondness to bestow, the roses get it'. As Ian Ousby has noted,[45] Cuff's persona focuses and intensifies the mysteries he works to solve, making fallible deciphering by the detective an organic part of Collins' novelistic strategy. 'Serious' novelists like Mrs Oliphant were ambivalent about detective fiction, believing that with lesser writers than Dickens and Collins the focus on plot would impoverish the novel's human concerns. But the detective figure was now a fact of fiction, and sleuths multiply in the crime-fraught novels of the 1870s.

[45] Ian Ousby, *Bloodhounds of Heaven: The Detective in English Fiction from Godwin to Doyle* (1976), pp. 121–5.

The private detective in fiction, who had arrived with Mr Bozzle in Trollope's *He Knew He Was Right* (1868), came fully into his own with Conan Doyle's Sherlock Holmes. Holmes first appeared in *A Study in Scarlet* (1887) and, after an uncertain start, became established in the public imagination as an Olympian figure inheriting the infallibility earlier assumed by the authority of religion. The Sherlock Holmes stories were written simply as a form of intellectual entertainment, and Doyle himself became annoyed that they eclipsed his own more 'serious' historical fiction. But Holmes personified a new moral order emerging at the end of the century, and could not be denied. As W. H. Auden wrote:

> Holmes is the exceptional individual who is in a state of grace because he is a genius in whom scientific curiosity is raised to the status of a heroic passion. . . . [His] motive for being a detective is, positively, a love of the neutral truth (he has no interest in the feelings of the guilty or the innocent), and negatively, a need to escape from his own feelings of melancholy.[46]

The Holmes stories in effect created the detective story in the form that was to dominate light reading in the last decade of the century. Arthur Morrison, E. W. Hornung and B. L. Farjeon were among a growing host of detective story writers who supplied cheap periodicals like *The Strand Magazine* (1891–), which catered for a continuously expanding reading public. They marked the passing of the moral content and earnest readership that had sustained the main phase of the Victorian novel.

---

[46] W. H. Auden, 'The Guilty Vicarage', in *The Dyer's Hand* (1963), p. 155.

CONTEXT 3

Foundations

This section examines some basic elements in the Victorian reading experience that have changed for the modern reader.

The Truth of the Heart

'One writes with his head,' wrote Flaubert in 1852. 'If the heart warms it, so much the better, but it doesn't pay to say so. It ought to an invisible fire.'[1] Most modern academics would agree. Contemporary criticism, with its interest in 'meanings', has no vocabulary for states of feeling, and tries to avoid emotion as the clouding of intellectual clarity. This reverses the Romantic attitude, which rejects the socially conditioned intellect as an obstacle to engagement with the true reality of innate and universal human feeling. Barbara Hardy, in her excellent *Forms of Feeling in Victorian Fiction* (1985), reminds us that the novel has always been 'an affective form', and that feeling takes new and refined roles in the nineteenth century in ways distinct from sentimentality or emotional indulgence. There are several reasons for this. Some are to do with rhetoric and aesthetics of the melodramatic genre, examined separately below. Another is religious. The Methodist movement began when John Wesley felt 'his heart strangely warmed' in Aldergate Chapel, London, on the evening of 24 May 1738; and the conviction that God reveals his presence through a sensed experience remained a central tenet of evangelicals both within and outside the established Church. Even the prosaic *Harriet Martineau was moved to declare that 'our great duties are *written with a sunbeam*' on the heart.[2] Later Ludwig Feuerbach, seeking to find 'the essence of Christianity', argued that the suffering of Jesus made Christianity uniquely a religion of feeling: in other faiths 'the heart and the imagination are

---

[1] Flaubert to Louise Colet, 6 Nov. 1852.
[2] Harriet Martineau, *Practical Piety; of the Influence of the Religion of the Heart on the Conduct of Life*, 5th edn (1811), vol. 2, p. 121; my emphasis.

divided, in Christianity they coincide. Here the imagination does not wander, left to itself; it describes a circle, whose centre is feeling.'[3]

The Romantic movement also focused on feeling, beginning with the sensations that first formed the germinating self in childhood. As Donald Stone[4] has shown, the impact of Romanticism in England went through different stages. The rebellious passion of Byron and Shelley dominated the first Radical phase of popular English Romanticism. But after Byron's death in 1824 this interest in the disruptive energy of individual passion rapidly diffused, living on in the Victorian fascination with melodramatic villains and the divided self. It was replaced as a social force by the reverence for the enduring, profoundly human feelings of the common people, in the child and in simple domestic affairs. These were typically embodied in the social Wordsworth of *Lyrical Ballads* (1798, 1800) and *The Excursion* (1810) – *The Prelude* was published only in 1850. Coinciding with evangelical belief in the virtue of Christian suffering, this reinforced in particular the sacrificial ideal of Victorian womanhood, and its advocacy of 'wise passivity' in harmony with nature provided a healing counter to a doubting age for intellectuals from Arnold and John Stuart Mill to William Hale White.

There was nothing generalized about these forms of feeling, which were precisely located in time and place, and were particular to the individual situation. Hazlitt, arguing that human identity can only exist in the felt moment of immediate experience, declared, 'I am what I am in spite of the future'.[5] In contrast to philosophy that sees emotion as clouding the intellect, for the Romantics feeling was central to the cognitive process. Keats famously wrote, 'Axioms of philosophy are not axioms until they have been proved upon our pulses'.[6] The strength of feeling formed a basis for aesthetics. To again quote Keats: 'the excellence of every art is its intensity, capable of making all disagreeables evaporate, through their being in close relationship with beauty and truth'.[7] Hazlitt used the term 'gusto' for this aesthetic intensity, a force that expressed the

---

[3] Ludwig Feuerbach, *The Essence of Christianity*, trans. George Eliot (1957), pp. 148–5.

[4] Donald D. Stone, *The Romantic Impulse in Victorian Fiction* (1980), ch. 4.

[5] William Hazlitt, 'On the Principles of Human Action' (1806, 1835), in *Complete Works*, ed. P. P. Howe (1930), vol. 1, pp. 48–9. Hereafter 'Principles'.

[6] Letter to J. H. Reynolds, 3 May 1818. See also Anthony Hatzimoysis, ed., *Philosophy and the Emotions* (2005).

[7] Letter to G. and T. Keats, 21 Dec. 1817.

'truth of character from the truth of feeling'.[8] He declared that the sensations gave direction to social relationships, since human action was driven by the 'liveliness and force' of feeling for others that was aroused through the power of the imagination ('Principles', pp. 48–9).

All this passed into the Victorian novel. The task of the novelist is 'to awaken the sense of pity – in the words of the poet, to melt the heart', wrote Anne Marsh Caldwell in *Emilia Wyndham* (1852, p. ix). *George Eliot declared that 'the greatest benefit we owe to the artist, whether painter, or poet, or novelist, is the extension of our sympathies'.[9] She praised the creative art of Scott and Wordsworth for enabling the reader more precisely to empathize with the experience of others in the past, and so extend 'our contact with our fellow men beyond the bounds of our personal lot' (*Essays*, p. 271). Even *Anthony Trollope, who satirized *Dickens as Mr Popular Sentiment in *The Warden* (1855), and was wary of loose emotion, accepted that feeling was central to the artistic process. The fiction of *Wilkie Collins, he argued, in spite of its contrived plots, was 'real' because Collins makes us '*feel* that men and women with flesh and blood, creatures with whom we can sympathize, are struggling amidst their woes' (*Autobiography*, ch. 12). For G. H. Lewes 'the joys and sorrows of affection, the incidents of domestic life aspirations and the fluctuations of emotional life, assume typical forms in the novel'. Therefore the novel was the particular province of the woman writer, who 'by her greater affectionate needs, her greater range and depth of emotional experience, is well fitted to give expression to the emotional facts of life'.[10]

Although it is peculiarly difficult to define and analyse, feeling provides the complex and inner texture of the finest nineteenth-century fiction. Raymond Williams noted that each era has its particular registers of sensitivity and ways of experiencing reality that are as distinctive to that period as are the current fashions in dress or in architecture. He coined the phrase 'structures of feeling' to describe the way this emotional receptivity is precisely located in time and place,[11] describing a state of feeling

---

[8] William Hazlitt, 'On Gusto', in *The Round Table* (1817).

[9] George Eliot, 'The Natural History of German Life', *Westminster Review* (July 1856), reprinted in George Eliot, *Essays*, ed. Thomas Pinney (1958), p. 271 (hereafter *Essays*). For George Eliot's view of the relationship between sympathy and the imagination, see Forest Pyle, *The Ideology of Imagination* (1995).

[10] [G. H. Lewes] 'The Lady Novelists', *Westminster Review* (July 1852), p. 133.

[11] Raymond Williams, *Marxism and Literature* (1977), vol. 2, p. 9.

as the unique human response to a life situation at the instant when a new sense of reality is emerging into consciousness. At this point, human reception is tuned to a pitch unique to that moment. Later, memory will interpret and 'set' that experience, and so change it from its original structure. Nevertheless, the imagination of the writer can recreate the way feeling transformed awareness at the moment of crisis and communicate it to the attentive reader. The inadequacy of plot summaries of major Victorian novels arises partly because their essence lies not in *what* happens, but in the complex structure of emotions that the story evokes in the reader at specific key moments. These are states of feeling often prepared for by previous scenes. Just how this happens is different with every novelist and in each novel, but the process occurs both in relatively simple melodramatic examples, such as the final despair and suicide of Ralph Nickleby in *Nicholas Nickleby* (1838–9, ch. 62), and in complex psychological moments like Dorothea Brooke's experience of transcendent peace after despair towards the end of *Middlemarch* (1871–2, bk 8, ch. 80).

'Structures of feeling' changed continuously over the Victorian period, and were to some extent class specific. When *The Old Curiosity Shop* first appeared as a separate volume in 1841, Little Nell's death at the end of the novel affected even hard-headed middle-class intellectuals like Richard Jeffrey, Walter Landor and Thomas Carlyle: the politician Daniel O'Connor even burst into tears and threw the book out of a train window in his dismay. But by the time of Dickens' death in 1870, readers were finding it sentimental, and the indulged emotion of Dickens' early work was falling out of favour.[12] Dickens himself continuously reassessed the nature and significance of 'feeling' in his novels, and made an examination of 'the undisciplined heart'[13] a central concern of *David Copperfield* (1849–50). Framed within a work that breaks new ground in the subtlety of its evocation of childhood emotions, the novel explores the consequences of uncontrolled feelings in the process of advancing into adulthood. David observes a gallery of models of 'feeling'. The vulnerable emotionality of his mother; the undisciplined passions of Steerforth and Little Em'ly; Rosa Dartle's insatiable anger; Uriah Heep's cold-hearted calculation; Micawber's theatrical attitudes; and Aunt Betsy's practical benevolence – all these are lessons of the heart David must observe and learn from in

[12] G. H. Ford, *Dickens and His Readers* (1965), ch. 4.
[13] The phrase occurs in ch. 43.

order to understand and control his own feelings as he enters the realities of responsible adulthood. In the end he finds, in the words of T. S. Eliot, 'the end of all our exploring/Will be to arrive where we started/And know the place for the first time'. Achieving emotional fulfilment with Agnes, he finds himself back in the affective simplicity of his childhood. Even the kinds of flowers in their home are the same.

> 'I have found a pleasure,' returned Agnes, smiling, 'while you have been absent, in keeping everything as it is used to be when we were children. For we were very happy then, I think.' (Ch. 60)

Few areas of experience had stronger connections with feeling for the Victorians than childhood and home, and this will form the subject of the next section.

Affairs of the Heart(h)[14]

Much has been written of why the Victorians made the family such a central institution of their society (see Further Reading, p. 237). The investment in the home came partly as a reaction against the moral laxity of the late eighteenth century and the Regency period, and the structured family unit reflected the self-discipline and organization of a new era. It embodied current ideals of childhood associated with the Romantic movement, of the father as a figure of authority, and the self-discipline of the virtuous life. As middle-class families became wealthier, larger houses and the employment of servants demanded a new degree of family management. The rapidly expanding acres of suburban Victorian villas became the outward evidence of inward domesticity and prosperity. Pressures of business and work increased, and the home became a refuge from public life. Within a home the family's 'lives would be ordered, their memories coherent'.[15] Dickens famously represented Wemmick in *Great Expectations* (1860–1) retreating from Jagger's city office into the mock Gothic castle of his home in suburban Walworth, which was reached by a plank across a four-foot ditch. 'Then look here,' says Wemmick. 'After I have crossed the bridge, I hoist it up – so – and cut off the communication.'

The domestic ethos of the Victorian family directed the nature of its reading. 'We aspire to live in the Household Affections, and to be numbered among the household thoughts of our reader,' declared Dickens in

---

[14] This title is indebted to Rod Edmond's (relevant) study of Victorian domestic poetry, *Affairs of the Hearth* (1988). Hereafter Edmond.

[15] V. S. Naipaul, *A House for Mr Biswas* (1969), p. 581 – a very 'Victorian' modern novel.

his first editorial to his venture into popular journalism, *Household Words* (1850–9). In choosing his title he was following serials such as *The Family Herald* and popular series such as *Murray's Family Library, Burns' Fireside Library* and *Clarke's Home Library*.[16] Reading was a family affair. From Jane Austen's family at the beginning of the century to Dean Liddell's in the 1860s, family members read aloud to each other, in the way they watch television today. Publishers' readers kept in mind what *George Meredith contemptuously called 'the republic of the fireside' when accepting or rejecting manuscripts, and Edward Mudie made his fortune by stocking his circulating library with books suitable for family consumption. The writer of *Emilia Wyndham* painted a sentimentalized but familiar scene:

> It is a beautiful sight to behold the blazing fire, the happy circle assembled, the embroidery-frames, or the poor-clothes basket, or the drawing mate-rials brought out; while father rests in his arm-chair, and the brother, or perhaps the mother, or maybe one of the fair creatures themselves, pro-duces to the bright eyes beaming with pleasure the new novel of the day.

Reading aloud brought the novel into the heart of the family, and the process replicated the novel's dialogue between the authorial voice and the reader in the narrative itself. The world of the domestic novel came alive in a domestic setting:

> But the perfect illusion, the feeling of absolute reality, of sympathy – as beings who like ourselves have actually enjoyed and suffered – is, I believe, more intense when the novel, from the voice of a really good reader, gives life and interest to the winter fireside.[17]

The domestic concerns of the novel mirrored those of the readers. They encouraged novelists to envisage their fictions in terms of different age groups and personalities, to widen their range of interest, and to write in a style accessible to younger readers. This did not mean the exclusion of adult interests. The recurrence of the governess in the novel reflected contemporary educational debates as well as concerns with the available prospects for single women. Sir Joseph Kay-Shuttleworth's *The Social*

---

[16] Examples given in Robert Colby, *Fiction with a Purpose* (1967), p. 21. Hereafter Colby.
[17] Mrs Annie Marsh-Caldwell, *Emilia Wyndham* (1852), p. xii.

Condition and Education of the People in England and Europe (1850) influenced Charlotte Brontë's **Villette* (1853),[18] while Dorothea's story in George Eliot's *Middlemarch* originally gained from the interest aroused by the recent founding of Girton College for women (Colby, pp. 179–83). Current religious and social controversies imposed themselves on *historical fiction about another age (see above, p. 36). Closer to home, domestic novels like those of *Ellen Wood and *Charlotte M. Yonge described ways the family should respond to bereavement, debt and the conflicting temperaments within the family group.

Long novels stayed with the family a considerable time.[19] 'Whether I shall turn out to be the hero of my own life, or whether that station will be held by anybody else, these pages must show,' ran the opening sentence of *David Copperfield*, and readers of the original monthly parts had to pursue the question for over two years before they concluded the answer. Meanwhile the plot, characters and moral dilemma became lodged within a shared consciousness. Trollope claimed that:

> Our girls become wives and our wives mothers, and then old women, under the inspiration of novels. Our boys grow into manhood, either nobly or ignobly partly as novels teach, and in accordance with such teaching will continue to bear their burdens gallantly, or repudiate them with cowardly sloth. ('Novel-reading', p. 25)

Just how far this was actually true is perhaps less important than the fact that both novelists and middle-class readers in mid-Victorian England believed it to be so.

As noted, the family reflected the new attitudes to children associated with the Romantic movement. These rejected the concept of original sin, and asserted that 'the child was father to the man', possessed of insight and emotional spontaneity inaccessible to the adult. But recent research has gone beyond romantic stereotyping, divided, as Hugh Cunningham has observed, between those whose prime interest is in the history of ideas about childhood, and those who try to recall what it was like to be

---

[18] Charlotte Brontë knew Kay-Shuttleworth personally.
[19] See Graham Clarke, 'Bound in Moss and Cloth: Reading a Long Victorian Novel' and Ian Gregor, 'Reading a Story: Sequence, Pace and Recollection', in Ian Gregor, ed., *Reading the Victorian Novel: Detail into Form* (1980).

a child at a particular time and place.[20] Cunningham points out that by penetrating into the immediate experience of children, the issues cannot be seen as specifically 'Victorian'. Nevertheless, contemporary debates about the nature of childhood experience, and the effects of discipline and education, can be seen in its fiction, from Dickens' account of Paul Dombey at Dr Blimber's academy in Dombey and Son (1846–8) to Samuel Butler's intimate exposure of Ernest Pontifex's parental oppression in *The Way of All Flesh (1902).

The new reverence for childhood was double-edged, for it also made children in the Victorian period the subject of close and often restrictive observation. Domestic novels reflected the constrained but intense emotions of family activities. Overtly, sex was a taboo subject, but, as Foucault observed,[21] this could have the effect of intensifying interest in sexual matters. This was particularly true of boys' masturbation. Discussion of the erotically charged subjects of tight-lacing and the flagellation of servants brought brief notoriety even to the respectable The Englishwoman's Domestic Magazine (1852–80).[22] Behind the façade of respectability lay the largely hidden world of prostitution and pornography explored by Steven Marcus' The Other Victorians (1964), and for much of the century the stability of the middle-class family was achieved on the back of a massive sex industry and repressive male-orientated marriage laws.[23]

Yet, if in some ways the Victorians were more obsessed with sex than modern society, in other ways they were less so. They were often more practical and less prurient about its social consequences. Prostitution was seen as a social problem that, without scandal, could attract the concern of public figures such as Dickens and Gladstone. Victorian society was also clear-eyed about the effects of sexual infidelity in a period where there were few safety nets for middle-class women who strayed outside the family circle. The fruit on the Freudian tree of sexual knowledge was still unpicked. At least until the last decades of the century, the

[20] Hugh Cunningham, 'Childhood Histories,' Journal of Victorian Culture, 9.1 (Spring 2004), pp. 90–6.

[21] Michel Foucault, The History of Sexuality, trans. Robert Hurley (1979), vol. 1, pp. 44–5.

[22] See Margaret Beetham, A Magazine of Their Own? Domesticity and Desire in the Woman's Magazine, 1800–1914 (1996), ch. 6.

[23] The standard studies of the subject are Michael Mason, The Making of Victorian Sexuality and The Making of Victorian Sexual Attitudes (both 1994).

Victorians were not only less knowing but also, more crucially, less self-conscious about sex. Neither Tennyson's elegy to young male friendship, *In Memoriam* (1850), nor Lewis Carroll's exploration of the imagination of a pre-pubescent girl in the *Alice* books (1865, 1871), could have been written in the form they were in a later era.

In general, while they chafed at the absurd pruderies of literary censorship that grew more intrusive, not less, as the century progressed, novel writers shared their readers' reticence about exposing the private intimacies of sex in the public world of family books. Sexual relationships are in fact central to the plots and concerns of the Victorian novel, but their physical aspects were implicit, leaving tantalizing silences for the modern reader: in *Middlemarch*, for example, how one would have liked to know more of Dorothea Brooke's expectations on her wedding night. But reticence in expression could intensify literary effect. Erotic feeling flashed in a brief eye contact, the colour of a woman's hair, in the shape of a lover's handwriting. Lady Dedlock in *Bleak House* (1852–3) only has to recognize a scrap of 'Nemo's' manuscript for her voice to change (ch. 2). In *The Mill on the Floss* (1860), when Stephen Guest observes Maggie Tulliver's bare arm, George Eliot empathizes with his erotic feelings:

> Who has not felt the beauty of a woman's arm – the unspeakable sugges-
> tions of tenderness that lie in the dimpled elbow, and all the varied gently
> lessening curves down to the delicate wrist, with its tiniest, almost imper-
> ceptible nick in the firm softness? (Bk 5, ch. 10)

Thornton in Mrs Gaskell's *North and South* (1854–5) seems indifferent to Margaret Hale's personality as a woman, until we glimpse him watching her moving hand, and he 'almost longed to ask her to do for him what he saw her compelled to do with her father, who took her little finger and thumb in his masculine hand, and made them serve as sugar tongs' (ch. 10).

If sex is often a silent area of the Victorian novel, home is privileged as a circle of vivid emotions and poignant recollection, a point of security in a rapidly changing world. In a moving moment in *Villette*, Lucy Snowe wakes up in Belgium after a nervous collapse and finds herself emotionally restored by recognized objects transported from her childhood Bretton, each detail caressed by her eyes:

There were two oval miniatures over the mantelpiece, of which I knew by heart the pearls about the high and powdered 'heads'; the velvets circling the white throats; the swell of the full muslin kerchiefs; the pattern of the lace sleeve-ruffles. Above the mantel-shelf there were two china vases, some relics of a diminutive tea service . . . (Ch. 16)

From 1823 home had its own theme song: 'Home Sweet Home' from John Howard Payne's sentimental melodrama *Clari, the Maid of Milan*, and later in the century Coventry Patmore wrote his poem to woman as 'The Angel in the House' (1874). Poems and parlour songs celebrated the sanctifying power of home, investing its hearth, furniture and pictures with iconographic significance. In Eliza Cook's widely popular poem, recited and sung in thousands of homes, 'The Old Armchair' was endowed with the sacredness of a fetish:

> I love it, I love it; and who shall dare
> To chide me for loving that old Arm-chair? . . .
> I've bedewed it with tears, and embalmed it with sighs
> 'Tis bound by a thousand bands to my heart . . .
> Would you learn the spell? – a mother sat there
> And a sacred thing is that old Arm-chair.[24]

Conventions of stage gesture placed tableaux of family life at the core of narrative art, melodramas, poetry and fiction. A particularly vivid early example appears in W. T. Moncreiff's *The Lear of Private Life* (1820). The second scene is set in the 'favourite apartment of the widowed Fitzarden' as his only daughter Agnes sings an aria from Handel's *Deborah*, accompanying herself on the harp. The villain Alvanley lures her away, seduces and deserts her, leaving her to carry their child. The betrayal drives Fitzarden insane, and meeting Agnes and her child wandering in the snow, he tries to kill them. As Sally Shuttleworth has noted, his insanity would have had a wider social significance for its original audience:

The association between the mental and social economy in Victorian rhetoric was not merely one of analogy. The life of the mind was believed to be linked to that of the social body in one unified system of force:

---

[24] Eliza Cook, *Poetical Works . . . Complete Edition* (1859), pp. 31–2; frequently reprinted.

irregularities in the body's circulation system would produce insanity which would in turn undermine the health of the social economy.[25]

Later Alvanley repents and marries Agnes. To heal Fitzarden, his keeper rebuilds the earlier scene of Agnes singing, held within a frame above the stage. Fitzarden sees the restored tableau of domestic bliss, and his sanity returns. Other tableaux embodied domestic happiness by its opposites, dramatizing childhood death and expulsion from the home by drunkenness, rape or seduction.[26] The happy families in Dickens' novels are far outnumbered by the orphans, lonely children and oppressive parents.

The home, like sexual intimacy in the century that followed, became the sensitive medium through which the novel engaged with the broader issues of society. When *Elizabeth Gaskell came to explore the industrial situation in Mary Barton (1848), she did so through the crises in the Barton family; Dickens' industrial novel Hard Times (1854) is more explicit on the domestic trials of the Gradgrind family and Stephen Blackpool's inability to divorce his drunken wife than on the factory situation; and Charlotte Yonge evangelized the virtues of her High Church faith through such family sagas as The Daisy Chain (1856). But by the 1860s family reading was declining as more specifically *children's fiction was written, and as prosperity created an increasing audience of women with time on their hands to read on their own.

At this point the celebration of the family went into sudden and dramatic reverse in the vogue for the *sensation novel.[27] Lucy Graham, in *Mary Elizabeth Braddon's *Lady Audley's Secret (1861–2), appears everything the domestic heroine should be. Like Jane Eyre, she is a governess who has worked her way up from poverty, and her marriage to the 56-year-old Sir Michael Audley, like Jane's to the blinded Rochester, promises to demonstrate a woman's nurturing devotion. She has all the signifiers of innocence, fair hair and blue eyes, and is a beacon of social responsibility. 'Wherever she went she seemed to take joy and brightness with her. In the cottages of the poor she shone like a sunbeam' (ch. 1). Yet her

---

[25] Sally Shuttleworth, Charlotte Brontë and Victorian Psychology (1996), p. 47 (hereafter Shuttleworth, Brontë). Performance of Moncreiff's play was forbidden until after the death of the insane George III.

[26] Sacheverell Sitwell, Narrative Pictures (1937), ch. 4 (hereafter Sitwell); Christopher Wood, Victorian Panorama (1976); Edmond, pp. 17–18.

[27] See Winifred Hughes, The Maniac in the Cellar (1980), pp. 42ff.

portrait, hidden in her room, tells of another identity, 'her fair head peeping out of the lurid mass of colour as if out of a raging furnace' (ch. 8). The novel reveals not 'a secret' but secrets, deception, a lost child and bigamy leading to two attempts at murder.

Braddon confuses the moral issues still further. While we see nothing of Lady Audley's inner life, she is driven by passions with which many readers would have sympathized. While Fitzarden in *The Lear of Private Life* goes mad when he loses his family order, Lucy Graham is driven to murder and possible madness by the prospect of returning to routine family life with Talboys. Earlier in the book Braddon railed against 'this cruel hardness in our life – this unflinching regularity in the smaller wheels and meaner mechanisms of the human machine, which knows no stoppages or cessation':

> Who has not felt, in the first madness of sorrow, an unreasonable rage against the mute propriety of chairs and tables, the stiff squareness of Turkey carpets, the unending obstinacy of the outward apparatus of existence? We want to root up gigantic trees in a primeval forest, and to tear their huge branches asunder in our convulsive grasp; and the utmost we can do for the relief of our passion is to knock over an easy-chair, or smash a few shillings' worth of Mr Copeland's manufacture. (Ch. 24)

In the sensation novel, the protected circle of home can become the bars of a madhouse.

Ways of Seeing

The eyes of a time traveller to mid-nineteenth-century Britain would be confronted by an extravagance of variety, eccentricity and colour. Gothic redundancy decorated building from railway stations and suburban cottages. In the streets, multicoloured advertisements shouted from walls and hoardings. Spectacle ruled in the theatre. Playbills featured the name of the stage designer in larger print than that of the playwright, and whole dramas were constructed around the sensational scenic effects made possible by inventions in stage lighting and machinery. Londoners crowded into panoramas and slide shows. Women's dress glowed in the colours that live on in the painted scenes of William Powell Frith, George Elgar Hicks and Ford Madox Brown.[28] The Pre-Raphaelite movement sought a new visual intensity to art, experimenting with the different effects of light and tone. Innovations in printing techniques brought an explosion in the production of *illustrated books, newspapers and magazines, and introduced colour printing. From the 1850s the ever-expanding popularity of photography brought still new ways of seeing.[29]

The eye confirmed factual reality, and the visual had a particular importance for the realist novel. Even a writer like Trollope, who uses relatively little description in his actual fiction, first conceived his characters in visual terms. 'There is a gallery of them,' he wrote, 'and of all in that gallery I may say that I know the tone of the voice, and the colour of the hair, every flame of the eye, and the very clothes they wear' (*Autobiography*, ch. 12). But the methods by which the writer transferred the visual

[28] See Further Reading, pp. 239–40.
[29] Alan Thomas, *The Expanding Eye* (1876).

into words, and the significance of that imagery, were as complex and various as the nature of Victorian realism itself. Dickens' *Pickwick Papers* (1836–7), the first best-selling novel of Victoria's reign, began as text to comic sketches in the style of the eighteenth-century tradition of caricature:[30]

> What a study for the artist did that exciting scene present! The eloquent Pickwick, with one hand gracefully concealed behind his coat tails. (Ch. 1)

For the beginning of *Oliver Twist* (1837–8), however, Dickens turns to a nineteenth-century perspective, drawing on Thomas Carlyle's reflection on the symbolic reality of clothes in *Sartor Resartus* (1833–4):

> What an excellent example of the power of dress, young Oliver Twist was! . . . [E]nveloped in the old calico robes which had grown yellow in the same service, he was badged and ticketed, and fell into his place at once – a parish child . . . (Ch. 1; see pp. 44, 155)

Both were preceded by the work of William Hogarth. Hogarth had pioneered the art of 'visual narrative' in the early eighteenth century. *The Harlot's Progress* (1732) told the story in six hugely popular plates of the rise and ruin of a country girl who comes up to London in search of her fortune, and predated the 'rise of the novel' in the fiction of Samuel Richardson and Henry Fielding in the next decade. With *The Rake's Progress* (1735), *Marriage à la Mode* (1745) and *Industry and Idleness* (1747), Hogarth's series established a new form of visual narrative that made a significant impact on both the drama and the novel into the nineteenth century.[31] As the title indicates, Hogarth domesticated John Bunyan's *Pilgrim's Progress* (1676, 1684) for a bourgeois, materialist age. Where Bunyan saw Heaven and Hell in the towns and byways of his native Bedfordshire, Hogarth viewed the streets of London peopled with parables and dense with symbolism: when a miser soles his shoe, it is with leather from the cover of the family Bible; cobwebs cover the poor box in the church where the Rake gets married (plates 1 and 5). Lamb declared that 'Hogarth's pictures we read', and they created a form continued in Hablôt

---

[30] 'Caricature' comes from the Italian word 'to overload'. The caricaturist exaggerated distinguishing eccentricities.

[31] See Martin Meisel, *Realizations* (1983), ch. 7. Hereafter Meisel.

K. Browne's book illustrations to Dickens and Victorian narrative paint-ings.[32] There was more of 'reading' than art criticism in Ruskin's inter-pretation of the harlot's boudoir in Holman Hunt's *The Awakening Conscience*:

> there is not a single object in all that room – common, modern, vulgar (in the vulgar sense, as it may be), but it becomes tragical, if rightly read. The furniture so carefully painted, even to the last vein of the rosewood – is there nothing to be learnt from the terrible lustre of it, from its fatal newness; nothing there that has the old thoughts of home upon it, or is ever to become part of a home? Those embossed books, vain and useless – they also new – marked with no happy wearing of beloved leaves . . .[33]

In Dickens' fiction visualized objects rarely have concealed meanings. In *David Copperfield* the contents of Barkis' box, kept until his death at the bottom of his horse's hay bag, offer tantalizing indications of a world of which the reader knows nothing: 'a silver tobacco-stopper, in the form of a leg . . . a piece of camphor, and an oyster shell' (ch. 31). But more typ-ically, 'things' take on a life of their own, dramatically visible. 'There was the man's full life written legibly on those clothes, as if we had his auto-biography engrossed on parchment before us,' runs Dickens' 'Meditation on Monmouth Street', and the clothes and shoes begin to dance before his (and our) eyes (*Sketches by 'Boz'* [1836], 'Scenes', ch. 6). Images focus violence, like the effigy that Quilp mindlessly beats in his Thames-side warehouse. Dickens' contemporaries were disturbed by the extraordinary detail of his observation, and the way inanimate objects existed in the nar-rative independent of the viewer (*Signs*, pp. 25ff.), their lack of life making them a terrifying presence, like the eyes of Mrs Jarley's waxworks, which 'stare in extraordinary earnestness at nothing'. They fragment, like the bizarre eyes and body parts in the shop of Mr Venus, taxidermist.[34] Objects morph with their possessors. In *David Copperfield* Miss Murd-stone's 'hard steel purse' was kept 'in a very jail of a bag, which hung upon her arm by a heavy chain, and shut up like a bite' (ch. 4). In *Our Mutual Friend* the parvenu Veneerings' furniture gleams with a 'fatal fresh-

---

[32] See Sitwell; J. H. Harvey, *Victorian Novelists and Their Illustrators* (1970).

[33] John Ruskin, *Works*, ed. E. T. Cook and Alexander Wedderburn (1904), vol. 12, p. 354.

[34] Quilp and Mrs Jarley are in *The Old Curiosity Shop* (1840), Mr Venus in *Our Mutual Friend* (1864–5). See also John Carey, *The Violent Effigy* (1973), passim.

ness', while the self-important Podsnap's monstrous silverware gloatingly demands, 'wouldn't you like to melt me down?'

While the reader is constantly drawn to the visual dimension in Victorian fiction, each novelist peoples it with his or her perspective on the world. 'Things' in *Thackeray lack the energy of objects in Dickens, but are more sharply observed signifiers of class and fashion. Hats, clothes and furniture, carriages and house interiors, are assessed with the cultural discrimination of a writer who made his name with *The Book of Snobs*. Dickens uses food as an indicator of heartiness and natural appetite or its opposite: in *David Copperfield*, Micawber's goodness is immediately established when he shares a feast of griddled mutton (ch. 28). Thackeray betrays the taste of a gourmand: one of Becky Sharp's weapons in *Vanity Fair* (1847–8) is her Parisian skill in *haute cuisine*. Elizabeth Gaskell's interest is in the socially significant object of household management. The Bartons' basement sitting room in *Mary Barton* is described in a detail that could have come out of a journalistic report. Yet the account also embodies working-class qualities of industry, thrift and family affection, and Mrs Barton's stabilizing influence in the family (ch. 2). When she dies, 'by degrees the house was stripped of its little ornaments', and loss of domestic order is a macrocosm of John Barton's moral disintegration (ch. 10). In Gaskell's observation, even dress colours had significance. 'Most fine people tire my eyes out wi' their colours,' the invalid mill girl Bessy tells the cultured southerner Margaret Hale in *North and South*; 'but somehow yours rest me. Where did ye get this frock?' (ch. 13).

For Trollope, too, although he was interested less in things than in people, objects gained a patina of significance through usage. In *Barchester Towers* (1857):

[The archdeacon] had always been accustomed to a goodly board of decent length, comfortably elongating itself according to the number of the guests, nearly black with perpetual rubbing, and bright as a mirror. Now round dinner tables are generally of oak, or else of such new construction not to have acquired the peculiar hue which was so pleasing to him. He connected them with what he called the nasty new-fangled method of leaving a cloth on the table, as though to warn people that they were not to sit long. In his eyes there was something democratic and parvenu in a round table. He imagined that dissenters and calico-printers chiefly used them. (Ch. 21)

Dickens was widely influential in creating a visual typology of London. 'A strange place is Leicester Square,' runs a line in a novel of 1845, '– now for a description à la Dickens,' and a catalogue of local detail follows: the 'quaint lamp-posts', 'its policewomen and apple women', the 'moustachioed Frenchmen and Germans'.[35] 'Dickens?' asked another novelist. 'Why he has transformed London. He is as great a magician as the fog . . . he has made common streets and alleys as rich in poetic interest.'[36] As in Hogarth, buildings in Dickens' fiction took on personalities of their own – 'old deserted broken-windowed houses grow crazed with staring each other out of countenance, and crook-backed chimney-pots in cowls turn slowly round with a witch-like mutter'.[37] Places become characters in the narrative. Dombey's mansion decays with his declining fortunes. In *Little Dorrit* (1855–7) Mrs Clennam's self-imposed isolation is at one with the house that imprisons her, creaking and echoing, both waiting to collapse. Outside London, when the cryogenic Miss Havisham bursts into flames in *Great Expectations*, her glacial wedding parlour disintegrates about her: 'I looked round,' said Pip, 'and saw the disturbed beetles and spiders running away over the floor' (ch. 49).

Objects give density to the imagined world. Outside Mr Dombey's office street vendors sell 'slippers, pocket-books, sponges, dog's collars, and Windsor-soap, and sometimes a pointer or an oil-painting' (*Dombey and Son*, ch. 12). This chaotic vitality contrasts with the submarine gloom of Dombey's office, but has nothing to do with the story. Roland Barthes has argued that such superfluity of detail, rather than giving it a sense of solidity, reduces its significance.[38] This would have puzzled the Victorian reader. Novelists described objective reality because it was *there*, fascinating in its own right.

The visual world of fiction also drew on iconographies lost to the modern writer. Melodrama, which is examined more fully below (see pp. 88–96), provided Dickens with immediately recognizable codes of appearance and gesture. No one could mistake the wickedness of Sir Mulberry Hawk in *Nicholas Nickleby*, with his insolent stare, monocle, toothpick and

---

[35] William North in *The Impostor* (1845), vol. 1, p. 115, quoted in Brightfield, vol. 1, p. 177.

[36] Colburn Mayne, *Which Does She Love?* (1862), vol. 2, p. 73, quoted in Brightfield, vol. 1, p. 178.

[37] H. Horne, 'Charles Dickens', in *A New Spirit of the Age* (1844), vol. 1.

[38] Roland Barthes, 'The Reality Effect', reprinted in Dennis Walder, ed., *The Realist Novel* (1981), pp. 141–8.

dandled claret glass, or confuse villain and heroine in the confrontation of Carker and Edith in *Dombey and Son*:

> He stood before her muttering and menacing, and scowling round as if for something that would help him to conquer her; but at the same time with the same indomitable spirit she opposed him, without faltering.

But Dickens' use of melodramatic stereotypes was rarely simple. More complex than the conventional stage villain, Ralph Nickleby is repressing the memory of the son who, finally acknowledged, will drive him to suicide. This is suggested on his first description through details of his dress. 'The corner of a small-plaited shirt-frill struggled out, as if insisting to show itself, from between his chin and the top button of his spencer' (a short double-breasted overcoat), intimating suppression. Below it 'two little keys: one belonging to the watch itself, and the other to some patent padlock' hang on a watch-chain, hinting at time-locked secrets (*Nicholas Nickleby*, ch. 2). The stereotypes of melodrama feed into Dickens' journalistic observation of real life. In *Oliver Twist*, the eyes of a ruffian from the London streets glare through the mask of a stage villain in the face of Bill Sikes:

> [He wore] a brown hat on his head, and dirty belcher handkerchief round his neck: with the long frayed ends of which he smeared the beer from his face as he spoke. He disclosed, when he had done so, a broad heavy countenance with a beard of three days' growth, and two scowling eyes; one of which displayed various part-coloured symptoms of having been recently damaged by a blow. (Ch. 13)

If melodrama provided one visual code, phrenology, the art of telling character from the face and the shape of the head, is another.[39] In *Jane Eyre* (1847) Rochester challenges Jane to assess him by his face – 'Criticise me: does my forehead not please you?' (ch. 14). In *Villette* both M. Paul and Dr John scrutinize Lucy's identity in her face. 'We know your skill in physiognomy,' Madame Beck tells M. Paul; 'use it now. Read that countenance' (ch. 6). While phrenology surfaces in the novel unusually

[39] George Combe's *The Constitution of Man* (1821), a textbook on phrenology, sold 90,000 copies in England in a little over twenty years. See Shuttleworth, *Brontë*, p. 57.

clearly in the work of *Charlotte Brontë, the early Victorian public's wide acceptance of the 'science' reinforced their interest in the moral significance of physical appearance.

By the mid-century the sensation novel was introducing multiple narrators to provide different perspectives on a single action, and authors used what was seen to reveal the character of the seer. From the opening of *Great Expectations*, where the terrifying apparition of Magwitch permanently changes Pip's consciousness of his world, the use of pictorial detail tells us as much about Pip as about what he sees. Mrs Joe's black eyes and hair and her reddened skin are recalled in close detail by the physically threatened Pip, while our picture of Joe is distanced by Pip's patronizing attitude to him. Contempt sharpens Pip's view of Pumblechook into caricature: 'a large, hard-breathing middle-aged slow man, with a mouth like a fish, dull staring eyes, and sandy hair standing upright on his head'. But the masterstroke is what Pip does not see. Compeyson originates the tragedies of Miss Havisham, Magwitch and, consequently, the story of Pip. He is logically a central figure in the book. Yet he remains virtually unseen to Pip, a fleeting form in the graveyard, a shadow in the theatre, a face of white terror disappearing into the water under the weight of the avenging Magwitch, a figure as evanescent as the nature of evil itself.

Description moved towards the objective clarity of Pre-Raphaelite art and of photography. George Eliot began her first work of fiction, *Scenes from Clerical Life* (1858), with luminous word painting: 'Look at [Amos Barton] as he winds through the little churchyard! The silver light that falls aslant on church and tombs enables you to see his slim black figure, made all the slimmer by tight pantaloons, as it flits past the pale gravestones' (ch. 2). In *Adam Bede* (1859) she wrote of the artist's responsibility to represent only the objective truth: 'my strongest effort is . . . to give a faithful account of men and things as they have mirrored themselves on my mind' (bk 2, ch. 17). The 'truth' is visual. The novel opens with a carefully composed picture of a workshop set precisely in place, the Midland village of Hayslope, and in time, the eighteenth of June, 1799. George Eliot recreates the light, warmth and even the scents of the summer afternoon: 'A scent of pine-wood from a tent-like pile of planks outside the open door mingled itself with the scent of the elder-bushes which were spreading their summer snow close to the open window opposite.'

Yet even as this was written, other factors were deconstructing the visual aspects of the novel. The sensation novel dramatized the mysteries and fallibility of the individual vision. Science, relating sight in the working of the brain, discovered the unreliability of the physical eye.[40] 'There are frequent occasions of conflict between the receptive faculties of the senses and the reflective faculties of the intellect,' wrote S. P. Thompson, 'occasions on which the mind, prejudging the sensation received, assigns it to a non-existent cause.'[41] In her wide-ranging survey *The Victorians and the Visual Imagination* (2000), Kate Flint moves from the 'fascination with the legibility of Victorian surfaces and the apparent transparency of signifying systems' to the era's interest in blindness and visual illusion. In a novel written at the beginning of the Victorian period, Jane Eyre came to see the hidden secret of the attic of Thornfield Hall. At the ending of the period, another fictional governess, in Henry James' *The Turn of the Screw* (1898), is confronted with the mystery – is what she sees really there at all?

[40] C. Bell, *Idea of a New Anatomy of the Brain* (privately printed, 1810); Johannes Müller, *Elements of Physiology*, trans. W. Baly (1838–42).

[41] Silvanus Phillips Thompson, 'Optical Illusions of Motion', *Brain* (1880), 3, p. 289.

The Modality of Melodrama

Apart from pantomime and the circus, few respectable families attended public playhouses in early nineteenth-century England. Theatres had the seedy associations vividly evoked in the early chapters of Thackeray's *Pendennis* (1848–50), prostitutes frequented them, and long, noisy performances deterred family playgoing. Many of those belonging to dissenting congregations disapproved of plays. Only in the 1850s and 1860s did a new generation of smart playhouses, offering shorter, more coherent programmes, draw in the mass of the middle classes, pushing the working classes out into music halls. But a dramatic age was instinct with theatre. Queen Victoria built a private playhouse in Windsor. The middle classes organized family and private theatricals, bought toy theatres in their thousands for their children to re-enact the latest plays in the sitting room, and some, like the young Dickens, slipped into small local theatres to see touring productions. If English drama was considered by the respectable public to be in a decadent state, novelists like *Bulwer Lytton and dramatists like William Macready were working to reform it. Lytton, Wilkie Collins and *Charles Reade doubled as successful novelists and playwrights, and even 'intellectual' writers like Trollope, George Eliot and *Henry James had an enthusiastic interest in the theatre, and dramatic situations and characters give vitality to their fiction.

The Victorian interest in 'picturing' was shared by both the novel and the theatre. By the early nineteenth century, performances were viewed as front-lit pictures carefully composed within a gilded frame. Some plays 'realized' on the stage meticulously recreated popular prints (see

Meisel).[42] This was reinforced by current acting conventions. These go back at least to Charles le Brun, *Conférence . . . sur l'expression générale et particulière* (1689), a work based on classical art and sculpture that graphically illustrated the way the human passions, their variations and graduations, should be represented by the actor. Le Brun's was the first of many handbooks used by artists and actors across Europe in the ensuing centuries. Cheap acting handbooks like Leman Thomas Rede's *The Road to the Stage* (1827) placed a compendium of codified gestures for every character and situation in the rucksack of every travelling actor. It is important to note that these codified gestures were primarily concerned with emotion and passion. Although they could signify class and morality, identifying the villain, the hero or the comic figure, gestures did this primarily through the graduation of the emotions they signified.

Melodrama is the theatre of emotional excess, of extremes of passion, whether of fear, compassion or delight. Music, as the term indicates, is essential to its effect. The earliest play designated a 'mélodrame' was Rousseau's *Pygmalion* (first produced in 1770), a monodrama in which music and mime, which Rousseau believed was more basic to humanity than words, were used to intensify the feeling and go beyond the significance of words (see Further Reading, p. 238). By mid-century the music of melodrama was becoming codified into 'bars of agit', a repertoire of musical motifs that choreographed the action, intensified emotion, and signified the moral status of the actor with the reinforcement of codes of gesture and movement.[43] Taken together, gesture and music were used to create tableaux, held momentarily on the stage and sometimes repeated after a curtain drop at the end of a scene, that focused and embodied the action of the play in a pictorial form.

As a popular genre, melodrama came to England from France in the plays of Gilbert Giles de Pixérécourt, a prolific dramatist and producer who wrote simplified, intensely physical and highly moral dramas for the mass audiences of post-revolutionary Paris. Its early popularity in England has been attributed to its exclusion from the Licensing Acts that limited the production of 'legitimate' drama in London to Covent Garden

---

[42] The earliest nineteenth-century example I have found, one not mentioned by Meisel, recreated illustrations by the Cruikshank brothers for Pierce Egan, Sr's *Life in London* (1821).

[43] See David Meyer, 'The Music of Melodrama', in David Bradby et al., eds, *Performance and Politics in Popular Drama* (1980), pp. 49–63.

and Drury Lane. But the first English melodrama, *A Tale of Mystery*, adapted by Thomas Holcroft from Pixérécourt's *Coelina*, premiered at the licensed theatre of Covent Garden in 1802, and melodrama enjoyed a broad appeal along with opera and ballet, whose conventions it largely shared.

In its many transmutations, melodrama became the unlikely bedfellow of bourgeois realism. Michael Booth traces the form of domestic drama in England back to James Kenney's *Ellen Rosenberg* of 1807, which combines a Gothic tale with the cottage setting in the story of a wife rescued from villainy by the Elector of Hanover. But a new engagement with actuality came with *Douglas Jerrold's *The Rent Day* of 1832, the play G. H. Lewes selected to represent 'Domestic Drama' in *Selections of Modern British Dramatists* (1867).[44] In the plot the avaricious agent Crumbs schemes to dispossess and evict the honest farmer Martin Heywood, while Crumbs' highwaymen cronies Silver Jack and Hyssop plan to rob the local Squire. Complicated by a subplot concerning Heywood's wife Rachel, who is wrongly accused of infidelity, the story does not sound a promising basis for theatrical realism. But in two key scenes the scene painter Clarkson Stanfield 'realized' on stage David Wilkie's pictures of rural domestic life, *The Rent Day* (1806) and *Distraining for Rent* (1807), scenes that caught the life of common people in a way that had inspired Wilkie's compatriot Sir Walter Scott. Engraved by Abraham Raimbach, they hung in innumerable parlours and sitting rooms and were well known (Meisel, ch. 8). Jerrold, writing the play at the time of the 1830 Reform Bill agitation, used the conventions of melodrama to turn Wilkie's realistic representation of the poor into contemporary radical protest.

Melodrama partly became central to the turbulent Victorian age because it is the modality of crisis. Holcroft modified Pixérécourt's original for English tastes, and its formula – stereotyped plot and character, codified moral message and emotion intensified by music – proved infinitely adaptable in an era of restless change. There were Gothic and eastern melodramas, naval melodramas, military melodramas, industrial melodramas, domestic melodramas, criminal melodramas, 'sensation' melodramas, and hybrid forms combining more than one

---

[44] See Michael Slater, *Douglas Jerrold* (2002), pp. 88–90.

sub-genre.[45] Emerging from the social upheaval surrounding the French Revolution, melodrama articulated a cry from the heart of the oppressed, a form that gave passionate voice to the inarticulate poor. Its climactic resolutions expressed a desire, not for the conservative status quo, but for a redemptive restoration of justice and harmony. It embodied the conflict between the wealthy aristocrat and the dispossessed. This could lead to distortion. Anna Clarke has shown how melodramatic conventions reshaped historical events into Radical myth.[46] So Maria Marten, a loose village girl with illegitimate children who was murdered in dubious circumstances, emerged onto the stage as a spotless maid seduced and done away with by the wicked squire, and avenged by God, who revealed the truth in her mother's dream. But, equally, melodrama was the expressive form protesting against the actual sufferings of the underprivileged in Victorian society, in particular as it became modified to deal with the concerns of the common people. As Martha Vicinus has argued in an important article, 'domestic melodrama, situated at the emotional and moral centre of life, is the most important type of melodrama; it is here that we see primal fears clothed in everyday dress'.[47]

Dickens pioneered the use of melodrama in the novel. He was enjoying moderate success as a playwright before *Pickwick Papers* diverted his energies to the novel. As the Royal Shakespeare Company demonstrated in its 1981 stage show, an early work like *Nicholas Nickleby* is virtually a theatrical scenario awaiting production. But even here the use of melodrama is complex. Crummles' troupe, with its jealousies and petty posturing, parodies melodramatic acting. This throws into relief the 'serious' melodrama in the story, the villainy of Sir Mulberry Hawk and the actions of Ralph Nickleby, who exposes Kate to the threat of rape by Sir Mulberry and his son Smike to probable death in a Yorkshire school. Smike is comic when acting on Crummles' stage, but serious in his prolonged and pathetic death. Squeers is both comic and villainous. Different

---

[45] Several of these genres are discussed in Michael Booth, *English Melodrama* (1965); see also Kurtz Tetzeli von Rosador, 'Victorian Theories of Melodrama', *Anglia*, 95, pp. 1–2 and 'Myth and Victorian Melodrama', *Essays and Studies*, 32, n.s. (1979).

[46] Anna Clarke, 'The Politics of Seduction in English Popular Culture, 1748–1848', in Jean Radford, ed., *The Progress of Romance* (1986), pp. 47–70.

[47] Martha Vicinus, ' "Helpless and Unbefriended": Nineteenth-century Domestic Melodrama', *New Literary History*, 13 (1981), p. 128.

attitudes to melodrama are held together by the protean Nicholas, 'heroic' when he thrashes Squeers and Sir Mulberry, 'humorous' when inveigled by Fanny Squeers or subject to the petty jealousies of Crummles' troupe, 'tragic' as he consoles the dying Smike, and 'Romantic' when he rescues and marries Madeline Bray. Melodrama, often criticized as simplistic and rigid, was in fact varied and fluid. One (false) Victorian etymology traced the meaning of the term back to 'mélange' or mixture.

As he developed his novelistic skills, Dickens continued to experiment with the prose use of theatrical conventions. In *Hard Times*, Dickens was writing short instalments for his weekly magazine *Household Words* instead of his usual more leisurely monthly numbers, and his dramatic method becomes particularly concentrated. The second book ends with a tableau in which Gradgrind attempts to hold his daughter Louisa in his arms, but she falls senseless at his feet. The next chapter is a reprise of this, only now Louisa embraces Sissy Jupe:

> In the innocence of her brave affection, and the brimming up of her old devoted spirit, the once deserted girl shone like a beautiful light upon the darkness of the other.
>
> Louisa raised the hand that it might clasp her neck and join its fellow there. She fell upon her knees, and clinging to this stroller's child looked up at her almost with veneration.
>
> 'Forgive me, pity me, help me! Have compassion on my great need, and let me lay this head of mine upon a loving heart.'
>
> 'O lay it here!' cried Sissy. 'Lay it here, my dear.' (Bk 3, ch. 1)

The scene shows a simple physical embrace. Yet its theatricality invests each detail with iconographic meaning. A moral spotlight ('shone like a beautiful light') haloes Sissy for Louisa as she, once paralysed by Utilitarian logic, sinks to her knees and places her head on Sissy's warm heart.[48]

For the Victorians, the conventions of melodrama, which now appear the height of artificiality, had their base in the actual. In *Oliver Twist* Dickens argued that its violent transitions only appeared artificial when they were represented on the stage, but passed without remark when they occurred in common life (ch. 17). He believed melodramatic plots, with their coincidences and intricate intrigues, were validated by experience,

---

[48] See Peter Brooks, *The Melodramatic Imagination* (1976), ch. 3. Hereafter *Melodramatic Imagination*.

and revealed the workings of divine providence. Dramatic theorists like Henry Siddons related codified stage gesture and speech to innate human behaviour and to current social conventions. Charles Darwin's *The Expression of Emotions in Man and Animals* (1872) used photographs to claim that the codified expression of feeling was common to both humanity and the animal world.

This does not mean that melodrama on the stage or in the novel exactly represented 'real life'. The formulae of melodrama codified and heightened reality, and gave it the form required for artistic expression. A few novels like *Jane Eyre* or *Nicholas Nickleby* were written with a melodramatic intensity throughout, but melodrama was more characteristically used in fiction to intensify a 'realistic' narrative, in the way Turner used a brilliant red buoy to focus the muted blues and greys of the seascape into dramatic energy in his painting *Helvoetsluys*.[49] So Thackeray focuses the casual progress of *Vanity Fair* with sudden *coups de théâtre*:

'Oh, sir Pitt!' [Becky] said. 'Oh, Sir – I – I am married already.' (Ch. 14)

or:

Amelia was praying for George, who was lying on his face, dead, with a bullet through his heart. (Ch. 32)

In George Eliot's *Middlemarch*, slow developments of character become intensified and interpreted in theatrical tableaux: Dorothea and Casaubon; Dorothea and Ladislaw; or Dorothea, after her desolating night vigil, looking out onto a morning world transfigured. Scenes transcend speech into gesture. Bulstrode and his wife Harriet sit side by side, sharing a truth they cannot speak. 'She could not say, "How much is only slander and false suspicion?" and he did not say, "I am innocent" ' (ch. 74).

As early as 1948 Wylie Sypher argued that melodrama reflected the pervasive vision of the nineteenth century. While the eighteenth century interpreted the world in terms of balance and order, and the twentieth saw all truth as relative:

---

[49] I am indebted to Michael Irwin for this example. See his 'Readings in Melodrama', in Gregor, ed., *Reading the Victorian Novel*, pp. 22–3.

Plate 2 'Horror', from Henry Siddons, *Practical Illustrations of Rhetorical Gesture and Action* (1822), plate 24.

'Then, with averted face, she holds forth her face and throws back her body, whilst revolted nature makes her breathe a sudden cry from the bottom of her heart.' The illustration shows how an actress should act Medea when contemplating murdering her children. Compare with H. K. Browne's illustration to *Dombey and Son* (below, p. 201).

for the nineteenth century the modality is melodrama, the oversimplifica-
tion into polarities and opposition that may be animated by emphatic
instances. To the nineteenth-century mind the very iron laws of science
operate with melodramatic fatalism – the pressure of population against
subsistence, the dynamics of supply and demand and the wages fund, the
struggle for existence in nature red in tooth and claw, the unalterable
majestic course of matter and force mythologized by Hardy and the biol-
ogist Haekel . . . all this is melodrama, not tragedy, and certainly not
science.[50]

Since then studies have applied the principles of melodrama to many
aspects of Victorian life and culture, from imperialism to the temperance
movement, from family life to political theory.[51] It has no longer been seen
as exclusively popular culture. Juliet John has analysed Dickens' villains
to argue that Dickens developed a melodramatic aesthetic in opposition
to the intellectual tradition.[52] But Peter Brooks has made claims for the
genre's relevance to elitist literature. In *The Melodramatic Imagination*
(1976), he identified melodramatic aesthetics as those of 'astonishment',
'muteness', 'excess' and 'Romantic dramatization', and applied them to
the novels of Balzac and Henry James. Brooks argued that while there
was no 'direct influence of melodrama proper' on these writers, 'melodrama is the reductive, literalist version of the mode to which they
belong. The world of melodrama . . . offers a complete set of attitudes,
phrases, gestures coherently conceived towards dramatization of essential spiritual conflict.' As in melodrama, the novels of Balzac and James
operate through codified actions and characters that heighten and illu-
minate the moral issues, transcending words in a startling climax in which
morality is clarified and resolved, melodrama's 'text of muteness'. Thus
in Milly Theale's heroic death at the climax of James' *The Wings of a Dove*
(1902): 'Life has been dramatized, the abyss has been sounded, to produce
finally the pure emblem of the dove' (*Melodramatic Imagination*, p. 192).

The province of melodrama has been extended to the development
of psychology. Eric Bentley has noted how the imagery of Gothic

---

[50] Wylie Sypher, 'The Aesthetic of Revolution', *Kenyon Review*, 10.3 (Summer 1948), pp. 431–44.
[51] For example, Anthea Trodd, 'Resistance to the Haunted House: A Perspective on Melodrama', *Journal of Victorian Culture*, 4.2 (Autumn 1999), pp. 292–304. See also John W. Frick,
Theatre, Culture and Temperance Reform in Nineteenth-century America (2003), pp. 1–18.
[52] Juliet John, *Dickens' Villains* (2003).

melodrama passed over into Freudian psychology, where imprisonment in the castle dungeon becomes transposed into the concept of the 'ego' and the 'id'. Melodrama, claimed Bentley, was the articulation of the sub-conscious, realized in sleep. 'That we are all ham actors in our dreams, means that melodramatic acting, with its large gestures and grimaces and its declamatory style of speech, is not an exaggeration of our dreams, but a duplication of them. In that respect *melodrama is the Naturalism of the dream life.*'[53] And indeed, in the unsettling years of the *fin de siècle*, melo-drama on both the stage and in the novel did turn inwards to the dramas of the psyche in parallel to the nascent science of psychology. Nine years before Samuel Butler published *Unconscious Memory* (1880), a little-known actor named Henry Irving startled London with his performance in Leopold Lewis' melodrama *The Bells* (1871) as Matthias the burgomaster of an Alsatian village. An exceptionally severe winter arouses associations of similar cold fifteen years earlier, a time when poverty drove Matthias to murder an itinerant Polish Jew for his gold. As his repressed self takes over his present identity, he hallucinates the sound of his victim's sleigh bells: in a particularly effective device, the bells are inaudible to other char-acters on the stage, but piercingly clear in the ears of the audience. In a dream Matthias is hypnotized into re-enacting his crime, and on waking is strangled to death mid-stage in an invisible noose.

The Bells preceded the emergence of the doppelgänger in the novel. The suppressed alter ego emerged in *Robert Louis Stevenson's *The Strange Case of Dr Jekyll and Mr Hyde* (1886) as the beast; in Oscar Wilde's *The Portrait of Dorian Gray* (1891), in the decadence of painted art. As melodrama moved inwards, its polarities of good and evil became the empty conventions that lived on in the stereotypes of hero and heroine in popular theatre and romance. Lady Frances Horner, nursing her mother in 1896, was startled to find her revelling in *Ouida's morally dubious but undoubtedly melodramatic romances. When she read how the hero leapt over the crowd to reach the heroine, and 'gazed with a hungry glare on the snowy loveliness of her form palpitating beneath the shimmering gauze', Horner looked up to see her mother's eyes wet with tears. 'It's all very noble dear,' the dowager explained. 'What I admire in Ouida is that Vice is Vice, and Virtue is Virtue.'[54]

[53] Eric Bentley, *The Life of the Drama* (1965), p. 205.
[54] Lady Frances Horner, *Time Remembered* (1933), pp. 183–4.

The White Rabbit's Watch

'Oh dear! Oh dear! I will be too late!' exclaimed the White Rabbit, anxiously consulting his pocket watch at the beginning of *Alice's Adventures in Wonderland*, voicing a frequent Victorian complaint against the pressure and hurry of the age. Through the century, revolutions in technology changed common concepts of time and space. It was gaslight, significantly used first in 1800 to increase working hours in factories, that first broke time away from the natural cycles of seasonal change. Clock time itself was becoming set with ever-increasing precision. From 1792 meridian time superseded that of the sundial across England, and clocks were set to a standard according to the longitude. Bristol time was ten minutes before London, a difference maintained into the mid-century. In 1852, however, the electric telegraph brought uniform time across Britain, set from Greenwich. In the meanwhile the railway, by cutting travel times between London and remote locations in the country from days to hours, revolutionized time's relation to space, and its regulated timetables had the effect of standardizing distance. Bradshaw published his first Railway Map of Britain in 1838, and it was the needs of the railways that launched the project of accurate, comprehensive ordinance survey mapping in 1841.

Space and time had shaped the novel since Fielding wrote *Tom Jones* (1749) with a map and an almanac at his elbow, but both gained a new importance in the nineteenth-century novel. Scientific method, which saw an accurate awareness of time as fundamental to the understanding of the material universe, and sociology, which applied organic principles to the evolution of human communities, emphasized immutable progression. Auguste Comte, the father of sociology, above all 'expressed the truth, that the past rules the present, lives in it, and that we are but the outgrowth and outcome of the past'.[55]

In the 'realist' Victorian novel, too, narrative was framed within strict chronology. Novels were typically set back in time, not to evade temporal reality, but to fix it in an objective distance. 'The magic reel, which, rolling on before, had led the chronicler thus far, now slackens in its pace, and stops,' wrote Dickens at the conclusion to *The Old Curiosity Shop*, and most Victorian novels were attached firmly to their chronological bobbins. In an imaginative universe overseen by the nonconformist conscience, misdeeds waited in the wings to reappear, in a flash of judgemental lightning, in the present. In popular sensation fiction and the 'serious' novel alike, the past re-enters with an unexpected door-knock, the silent witness of a forgotten letter. A hidden baby's shoe and lock of hair trap Braddon's Lady Audley as securely as the reappearance of the forgotten roué Raffles dooms his old crony Bulstrode in George Eliot's *Middlemarch*. As religious awareness faded before secular science in the later century, divine judgement was replaced by the evolutionary processes that ruin Hardy's tragic figures, or by the burden of irredeemable choice that binds Isobel Archer to Osmond in Italy in Henry James' *Portrait of a Lady* (1881). There were exceptions. A work like George Eliot's *Daniel Deronda* (1876) began at a point well into the story, and moved outside Gwendoline Harleth's narrative to the timeless verities of Judaism. The new genre of *science fantasy gazed into futurity, and the popularity of the *supernatural moved into alternate dimensions. But these gained point from being set against an unbending chronological structure.

The Victorian concept of time was related to its sense of space. Franco Moretti's *Atlas of the European Novel 1800–1900* (1998) cites Bakhtin's suggestive claim that Sir Walter Scott's historical sense gave him an 'ability to read time in space'.[56] By setting narrative within a specific locale, he created a 'completely *new sense of space and time* in the artistic work':

> Typical for Sir Walter Scott is a striving after precisely local folklore. He covered every inch of his native Scotland on foot. . . . For him, each clump

[55] Lewes, quoted in Shuttleworth, *Eliot*, p. 11.

[56] Mikhail Bakhtin, 'The *Bildungsroman* and its Significance in the History of Realism', in *Speech Genres and Other Late Essays* (1986), p. 53 (hereafter Bakhtin). Quoted by Franco Moretti, *Atlas of the European Novel 1800–1900* (1998), p. 38 (hereafter *Atlas*).

of land was saturated with certain events from local legends, was profoundly intensified in legend time, [while] on the other hand, each event was strictly localized, confined, condensed in spatial markers. (Bakhtin, pp. 52, 47)

Jane Austen related geography to fiction with great subtlety by writing about a small, virtually closed circle of provincial communities. But it was the rapid growth of the Victorian city, and in particular London, that was the seminal influence on the emergence of the Victorian novel, for it bound an infinite range of human possibilities within finite limits of time and space. In the 1830s the fashionable squares and mansions of the West End of London provided a coherent geography for the 'silver fork' novel of Bulwer Lytton's *Pelham* (1828) and the novels of Lady Blessington and Mrs Gore, but it was Dickens' journalism in the next decades that embraced the huge diversity of London life. 'This great metropolis,' wrote Jerrold in the Preface to *Martha Willis* (1831), 'teems with persons and events, which, considered with reference to their dramatic capabilities, beggar invention.'[57] Dickens began an early short story with a paragraph composed in a curious but significant mixture of styles. 'Once upon a time there dwelt, in a narrow street on the Surrey side of the water within three minutes' walk of the Old London Bridge, Mr Joseph Tuggs.'[58] The prose combines fantasy ('once upon a time'), realism ('a narrow street on the Surrey side of the water') and the physical presence of the observer ('within three minutes' *walk*'). These conflicting narrative perspectives mark the evolution of a new form of urban fiction, at once fanciful and located in the actuality of the city streets.

If the *regional novel offered alternative imaginative worlds to that of city life, London was seminal to the emergence of the Victorian novel. The rapid pace, variety and restless movement of the city became reflected in its literature. Its streets offered a changing panorama of contrasting dress, class, occupation and physical appearance. In its alien settings, individual characteristics stood out with a new clarity, and personal dramas gained poignancy by being played out against the indifferent

[57] Douglas Jerrold, *Martha Willis, the Servant Maid* (Lacy's Acting Edition, n.d.), p. 2. I am grateful to Kate Newey for this quotation.
[58] 'The Tuggses at Ramsgate', *Sketches by 'Boz'*, 3rd series (1837); first published in *The Library of Fiction*, 1.1 (April 1836).

urban background. With its contrasts of wealth and poverty, London provided a social and moral map for the novelist. Starting south of Bloomsbury, a line running roughly down Charing Cross Road to Trafalgar Square marked the borders of 'respectable' London. Areas east of Farringdon Road down to London Bridge were 'low' and probably criminal. Douglas Jerrold's savage social protest novel, *The History of St Giles and St James* (1845–7), actually names his two contrasting protagonists after their origins in different areas of London: the warren of thieves' kitchens around Seven Dials, and the fashionable mansions west of Piccadilly. In a city of contrasts, Oliver Twist could have trotted in ten minutes from the respectability of Mr Brownlow's Bloomsbury residence to the dark alleyways of Saffron Hill where Dickens placed Fagin's den, just below the present Holborn Viaduct.

But London was also complex and evolving. Moretti plots the homes and movements of Dickens' characters against a map of London to relate different areas and what they signify. He 'shows us London as an archipelago of autonomous "villages" . . . where the various novelistic threads remain largely unconnected' (*Atlas*, p. 130). Locations in between Charing Cross and Farringdon roads, including Covent Garden, the Inns of Court and the Monument, the site of 'Todgers',[59] had mixed associations, and significantly predominate in Dickens' fiction. The city's kaleidoscope of place and class provided a brilliant theatre for a London cognoscente like Dickens. Its rapid expansion in the nineteenth century left its history trapped in a mosaic of individual communities, like Bleeding House Yard off Hatton Garden in *Little Dorrit*, which was so hidden that 'you got into it down a flight of steps . . . and got out of it by a low gateway into a maze of shabby streets' (bk 1, ch. 12). In *Great Expectations*, Pip, newly arrived in London, wanders out of the Little Britain of Jagger's office, with its macabre mementoes of human crime and execution, and finds himself in the answering animal shambles of Smithfield: 'the shameful place, being all asmear with filth and fat and blood and foam, seemed to stick to me' (ch. 20). Such atmospheric *coups de théâtre* became less available as urban renewal and increasing pollution dimmed London in fact and in the novel into a greyer uniformity, forcing novelists like *George Gissing, *Walter Besant and Arthur Morrison, author of *Child of the Jago*

---

[59] In *Martin Chuzzlewit* (1843–4): Dorothy van Ghent made this the starting point for her important essay, 'The View from Todgers', *Sewanee Review*, 58 (1950).

(1896), to look to the working-class ghettoes of the East End for the drama of 'Dickensian' London.

As 'realist' novelists moved into an ever-closer engagement with the harsher realities of urban life, writers like *George Macdonald and Lewis Carroll were engaging with the realities of time and place from quite different perspectives. We have noted that at the beginning of *Alice's Adventures in Wonderland*, the White Rabbit, in Tenniel's illustration complete with check jacket, wing collar, waistcoat and umbrella, looks anxiously at his watch like any city gentleman awaiting an appointment. But following him down the hole, Alice finds time and place disintegrating in the nightmare of Victorian uncertainty and doubt. 'I wonder what Latitude or Longitude I've got to?' she wondered, although neither makes sense to her. Swimming though a sea of tears, she is surrounded by a noisy crowd of crustaceans, animals and birds, including the 'extinct' dodo, who conduct a mad parody of Victorian history lessons. This jumbles together Anglo-Saxon chronicles, geology and theories of evolution, until narrative time itself withers into the disappearing 'tale' of a mouse. Another pocket watch appears at the Mad Hatter's tea party. But by now, even larded with the '*best* butter', it has lost all chronological meaning.

In the sequel, *Through the Looking Glass*, where time moves into reverse, and space is alienated into white and black chessboard squares, the White Knight stumbles along on a horse with spikes around its hooves to repel the 'sharks'. Only older readers would see that the spikes were a joke with reference to geological time, in which, as Tennyson meditated gloomily, 'There where the long street roars, hath been, / The silence of the central sea' (*In Memoriam*, stanza 123). Abandoning the security of mid-Victorian childhood and adolescence, in Carroll's inverted world Alice races backwards down terrifying vistas of relative time. 'Now here, you see, it takes all the running *you* can do to, to keep in the same place,' the Black Queen tells Alice. 'If you want to get somewhere else, you must run at least twice as fast as that' (ch. 2) Einstein, quantum theory and the time warps of modern science fiction stand waiting in the wings.

Key Authors

William Harrison Ainsworth (1805–82)

Ainsworth was one of the most popular historical novelists of the 1840s. He was born in Manchester and intended for the law, but his wealthy father's death in 1824 allowed him, a youth with handsome looks and dashing manners, to live a fast life in the literary circles of Regency London. From 1830 he became associated with the lively new Tory-orientated periodical, *Fraser's Magazine*. *Rookwood* (1834), a romantic and largely invented life of highwayman Dick Turpin, spiced up with flash songs and racy thieves' slang, became a literary sensation and made his name. By the 1840s his Kensal Manor House residence hosted a literary circle that included *William Makepeace Thackeray, Thomas Carlyle, George Cruikshank and, in particular, the young *Charles Dickens. *Jack Sheppard* (1839), which again combined the historical genre with criminal appeal, began his creative partnership with Cruikshank. It followed Dickens' *Oliver Twist* (1837–8) in *Bentley's Miscellany*, briefly eclipsing the popularity of Dickens' work. Stung by accusations that his novels romanticized crime, Ainsworth turned to a current antiquarian interest in London's buildings, using them as historical backdrops to *The Tower of London* (1840), *Old St Paul's* (1841) and *Windsor Castle* (1843). Although Ainsworth went on to write forty novels, his reputation declined and his literary energies were channelled into editing *Ainsworth's Magazine* (1842–54), as well as supervising *Bentley's Miscellany* (1854–68) and *The New Monthly Magazine* (1845–70), which he owned. In his heyday, Ainsworth was compared to Scott, Dumas and Hugo, but although accurate in historical detail, he was weak on plot, characterization and dialogue. His gift for narrative is, however, shown in the fact that his fictional account of Turpin's ride from London to York is often taken as fact, and his novel *Jack Sheppard* elevated a petty eighteenth-century criminal into an urban hero.

Walter Besant (1836–1910)

Besant, although a prolific and varied author, is now remembered for his novels of London slum life. Between 1872 and 1882 he published nine popular novels in collaboration with James Rice, notably *The Golden*

Butterfly (1876), a satire on a philistine American oil millionaire with pretensions to British culture, and *The Chaplain of the Fleet* (1881), depicting a feisty heroine's social progress through eighteenth-century society. His own fiction of London's East End life combined extravagant romantic plots with exposés of slum squalor, and showed an extensive knowledge of the city. His plea for social reform in *All Sorts and Conditions of Men* (1882) led to the formation of a cultural working-class centre, the People's Palace, in Stepney; while the grim revelations of Hoxton life in *Children of Gibeon* (1886), a novel describing two girls of contrasting parentage, brought the area to the notice of social workers.

Modest and self-effacing, Besant conducted a lifelong campaign for the rights of authors, founding the Society of Authors in 1883. His essay, 'The Art of Fiction' (1884), provoked a famous critical debate with *Henry James and *Robert Louis Stevenson.

Mary Elizabeth Braddon [later Maxwell] (1835–1915)

Elizabeth Braddon, one of the most successful and prolific writers of the *sensation novel, lived an early life worthy of her own melodramatic fiction. Deserted by her father, a feckless and philandering London solicitor, in 1840, she supported her family by the then disreputable profession of touring actress. Here she became fascinated by popular melodrama, and the form directed her first attempt at fiction, *Three Times Dead* (1860), one of the first English detective novels. She met the publisher John Maxwell while revising the work for republication as *The Trail of the Serpent*, and moved in with him and his children, although she was unable to marry him until his first wife died, confined in an asylum, in 1874. In 1862 her *Lady Audley's Secret appeared in *The Sixpenny Magazine*, a work that sold nearly a million copies in her lifetime. This success was rivalled by *Aurora Floyd* (1862–3), a novel whose tempestuous, sexually aware heroine caused an even greater scandal than Lady Audley. Writing rapidly to support the demands of a large family, Elizabeth Braddon became the 'Queen of the Circulating Libraries', publishing over eighty novels besides short stories, plays and poems. The best of these were *John Marchmont's Legacy* (1863), *The Doctor's Wife* (1864) (a work indebted to Gustave

Flaubert's *Madame Bovary* [1857]), and *Birds of Prey* (1867). In her later work she moved away from sensational writing to more serious engagement with social issues, and to satire. From 1864 she edited and wrote for *Belgravia* and *Temple Bar*.

Her fiction combines the sensational plots of *working-class fiction, refined by the skilful models of *Wilkie Collins' novels, with the settings of middle-class respectability. In her lifetime the craft, human interest and sheer readability of her stories brought her the admiration of Tennyson, Gladstone, *Bulwer Lytton and the young *Henry James, while her concern for the situation of women has increasingly attracted the interest of feminist critics.

Charlotte Brontë, 'Currer Bell' (1816–55)

Emily [Jane] Brontë, 'Ellis Bell' (1818–48)

Anne Brontë, 'Acton Bell' (1820–49)

The wild isolation of the Yorkshire moors impressed itself indelibly on the novels and poetry of the Yorkshire sisters. But only four miles of stone-paved tracks separated their father's austere stone parsonage in the eastern Pennines from the rapidly expanding mill town of Keighley and the library of its Mechanics' Institute. Recent scholarship has demonstrated the depth of the sisters' interest in contemporary science, philosophy and literature, and their extraordinary skill and originality as writers.

From childhood the sisters and their younger brother Branwell, with barely four years between them, were driven to seek comfort in their own company and resources. With the early death of their mother, they were dominated by their Irish-born father, who brooded darkly on a disappointed academic career, and, after a traumatic education at a local school for the girls of clergy, by their intensely Calvinist Aunt Branwell. They read avidly, in particular Scott and Byron, raiding works of fiction, philosophy and natural sciences in their father's library and seizing on issues of *Fraser's Magazine* and *Blackwood's* for developments in literature and science. They painted and sketched, fascinated by the reproductions of the cataclysmic panoramas of John Martin. In 1826 their father's gift of a set of wooden soldiers inspired their creation of the complex imaginary worlds of Angria and Gondal, which filled tiny handmade books with accounts of their cities, geography, societies and histories, and interwove myth with such actuality as the Duke of Wellington and the Ashantee wars of West Africa. Ultimately Charlotte and Branwell continued with the kingdom of Angria, while Emily and Anne created a separate world of Gondal.

In adulthood, the imaginative vistas of this violent, anarchic juvenilia collided with the hard experience of the external world. Outside marriage, there were few outlets for middle-class young women other than teaching. Attempts to set up schools led Charlotte and Emily to study languages in Brussels, where Charlotte's obsessive attachment to the charismatic Latin professor and husband of the proprietor, M. Constantin Heger, was to become imprinted on the plots of *The Professor, Jane Eyre* and *Villette*. The school project failed. With their father blind, and their brother Branwell a disintegrating alcoholic, life took a new turn when Charlotte discovered Emily's poetry. The sisters began a joint writing venture under the pseudonyms Currer (Charlotte), Ellis (Emily) and Acton (Anne) Bell. A joint verse anthology failed, but Charlotte's novel **Jane Eyre*, published in 1847, was an immediate success and rapidly went through three editions; Emily's **Wuthering Heights* followed, published together with Anne's *Agnes Grey*, but only received popular recognition in a corrected edition with a biographical notice by Charlotte, in 1850. Anne Brontë's *The Tenant of Wildfell Hall* was published in 1848.

Only Charlotte Brontë survived beyond May 1849, publishing *Shirley*, a historical novel of the Yorkshire mill life and Luddite disturbances, at the end of that year. In 1853 she published her masterpiece, **Villette*. The following year she overcame her father's opposition to marry his curate, the Reverend Bell Nicholls. But she died the following year in pregnancy, aged 38. *The Professor*, her first-written novel, was published posthumously in 1857.

Rhoda Broughton (1840–1920)

When *Cometh up as Flower* appeared in 1867, becoming an immediate best-seller, Broughton was recognized as bringing a new voice into the mid-Victorian novel. A tragic tale enlivened by the provocative, lively personality of the first-person narrator, it told of a passionate, romantic young woman, in love with a penniless soldier. But she is entrapped by her love for a doting but oppressive father, and by her cold, manipulative sister, into a loveless marriage with an older man with money that she hopes will pay medical fees to save her father's life. Its account of a girl's sexual awakening, and her feisty questioning of religious faith and family loyalties, caused a scandal on its first appearance, but the story, which ends with her awaiting her release from marriage through an early death from consumption, was itself morally impeccable.

Broughton was a fast, prolific writer. The best of her novels, which became less provocative in her later work, included *Red as a Rose is She* (1870) and *Belinda* (1888), which again return to the theme of a young woman marrying an older man. Her novels established a line of young, vivacious heroines, usually speaking in the first person, intellectually questing, and combining breathless conversational style with a web of literary references. They vigorously challenge the social attitudes and conventions of the period, comment on the economic restrictions of women, and dramatize the strains between romantic yearning and domestic responsibility. Writing into the twentieth century, Broughton's later works were less controversial, in part because public taste had caught up with her liberated perspective.

[William] Wilkie Collins (1824–89)

Collins began with careers in law and painting. Neither was successful, but they sharpened his eye for visual effect and gave him knowledge of crime and the law, which, combined with a lifelong love of the stage, were to shape his *'sensation' fiction. His first novel, *Antonina* (1850), drawing on childhood experiences of Italy and written under the influence of *Bulwer Lytton, was a spectacular panorama of the fall of fifteenth-century Rome before the Goths. *Basil* (1852), in contrast, was an introspective, violent tale of sexual passion, duplicity and revenge. It was attacked for its 'vicious atmosphere' and amorality, but its dark intensity attracted *Dickens, and the two writers began a long, mutually creative relationship.

Collins contributed *Hide and Seek* (1854) and *The Dead Secret* (1857) to Dickens' *Household Words*. In 1857, while acting together in Collins' melodrama *The Frozen Deep*, Dickens conceived of *A Tale of Two Cities* (1859). This was followed in *All the Year Round* by Collins' greatest success, *The Woman in White* (1860). *No Name* (1862), one of Collins' most entertaining novels, featured an ingenious and morally ambivalent heroine, Magdalene Vanstone, who, teamed up with a colourful rogue named Captain Wragg, uses disguise and impersonation to outwit an evil housekeeper and the police to win an inheritance denied her and her sister. *Armadale* (1866) is Collins' most complex psychological work. An exploration of guilt, intuition and destiny, it centres on two friends, both named 'Allan Armadale' (though one calls himself Ozias Midwinter). They are contrasted in temperament, but bonded together by a plot of murder and of contested inheritance, both manipulated by a demonic *femme fatale*, Lydia Gwylt.

In spite of constant ill health, Collins remained creative for over thirty years. Social concerns dominate *Man and Wife* (1870), an attack on women's inequalities under the English and Scottish marriage laws. *The New Magdalene* (1873), which he turned into his most successful play, features a 'fallen woman' who finds a new identity when, having escaped from society as a nurse, she is believed dead on the battlefield. Collins' later work showed his increasing interest in the occult, telepathy and science. A master of ingenious plotting, he successfully adapted his novels for the stage, declaring, in the Preface to *Basil*, that 'the Novel and the Play are twin-sisters in the family of Fiction'. Both in his fiction and in his irregular domestic life, Collins flouted respectable conventions. Nervous attacks and overdoses of opium contributed to the imaginative intensity of his characteristically dark novels with their disturbing, eccentric characters and evocative settings.

Marie [Isabel Marie] Corelli [née Mills, later Mackay] (1855–1924)

A struggling solo pianist, Mary Mackay first adopted the pseudonym 'Corelli' when publishing *A Romance of Two Worlds* (1886), a novel of the reincarnation and the 'gospel of electricity' based, she claimed, on a psychic experience. It sold well and even attracted a favourable notice from Oscar Wilde. *Ardath, the Story of a Dead Self* (1889), an extravagant, chaotic sequel set in Babylon in 5000 BC, provoked hostile criticism, but was admired by an expanding audience that now included Gladstone and Queen Victoria. *Barabbas* (1893), a startling reworking of Christ's final days before crucifixion, sold fourteen editions in three years. **The Sorrows of Satan* (1895) was even more successful and pioneered the modern 'bestseller'. Although this proved the climax of her success, Corelli continued to write extravagant novels, of which the most popular were *The Mighty Atom* (1896), an attack on secular education, and *The Master Christian* (1900), an anti-Catholic account of the Second Coming. Written with scant regard for grammar, plotting or reason, exploiting the avid hunger for mystical, quasi-religious and pseudo-scientific fiction that was a feature of the last decades of the century, her work was phenomenally popular in England, and was translated into most European languages.

Charles [John Huffam] Dickens (1812–70)

Dickens' genius transformed the novel genre both in England and internationally. Establishing his brilliant career without the traditional advantages of class, money or higher education, he exemplified the new spirit behind the rise of nineteenth-century Britain, yet transcended his age, and remains a creative force to the present. His childhood was divided between the naval dockyard of Chatham in rural Kent, the happy 'birthplace of my fancy', and London. Here from the age of 10 he struggled to make his own way in the world against the background of his family's financial struggles and, briefly, imprisonment for debt. Early careers in a legal office, and in journalism ranging from street crime to Parliamentary debates, gave him multiple insights into the stresses of a rapidly changing society, while his enthusiasm for the stage rooted his future writing in the energies of popular culture.

Dickens came to public notice with *Sketches by 'Boz'* (1836) ('Boz' was the nickname of a favourite brother), miscellaneous sketches contributed to London journals from 1833 that contain his early experiments on the interface between reportage and fiction. *Pickwick Papers* (1836–7) began as text to accompany caricatures of cockney sportsmen. Developing into the boisterous adventures of the benevolent Pickwick and Sam Weller, his street-wise servant, and backed by Hablôt K. Browne's spirited etchings, the monthly numbers became the sensation of the day with sales of 40,000.

In 1836 Dickens married Catherine Hogarth amid intensifying pressures on his time. While *Pickwick* was still in progress, he wrote *Oliver Twist* (1837–8) for *Bentley's Miscellany*, which he was editing. The dark mood of the story was intensified by George Cruikshank's illustrations and introduced Dickens' vision of the contrasting social worlds of London. Writing the picaresque *Nicholas Nickleby* (1838–9) brought Dickens to the verge of exhaustion, but established him as England's most popular novelist. Published within the framework of *Master Humphrey's Clock* (1840–1), sales of *The Old Curiosity Shop* topped 100,000, but the failure of *Barnaby Rudge*, which succeeded it, drove Dickens to North America, drawn by its images of democratic freedom. *American Notes* (1842) records a more mixed impression. He was appalled by the country's vulgarity, its slave culture and its disregard for international copyright. His masterly analysis of self-interest, *Martin Chuzzlewit* (1843–4), was set partly in America, but although it contained the timeless characters of Mrs Gamp and Pecksniff, the novel proved relatively unpopular.

A Christmas Carol, also published in 1843, began a tradition of Christmas books continued in *The Chimes* (1844), *The Cricket on the Hearth* (1845), *The Battle for Life* (1846) and *The Haunted Man* (1848). These and the 'Christmas Stories' Dickens and others contributed to his periodicals from 1850 to 1868 helped establish Christmas as a time of family warmth, social benevolence and ghost stories for Victorian society. During 1844 to 1846 Dickens travelled in Europe and briefly edited *The Daily News* before returning to novel writing with *Dombey and Son* (1846–8), his first great problem-of-England novel, a work attacking the economic materialism behind Britain's meteoric rise to world dominance. It was his first novel planned from the beginning, and its number plans have survived to give valuable insight into the author's methods of composition. *David Copperfield* (1849–50) followed, whose gallery of vivid characters shows Dickens brilliantly humanizing the caricature method of his earlier work. Its sensitive evocation of childhood was to influence Proust and Graham Greene in the next century.

Dickens was by now deeply involved in social projects, supporting Angela Burdett Coutts' home for fallen and homeless women, and organizing the charitable Guild of Literature and Art. He reached out to a wider public with the twopenny weekly, *Household Words* (1850–9), succeeded by *All the Year Round* (1859–68), using these to publish *Hard Times* (1854) and *A Tale of Two Cities* (1859), and recruiting the work of other major novelists, including *Elizabeth Gaskell and *Wilkie Collins. During these years his vision of England darkened. *Bleak House* (1852–3) portrayed England floundering in a fog of legislation and deadening conventions. In *Little Dorrit* (1855–7), the enervated morality of life in a debtor's prison pervaded society, in which the one free spirit was Amy Dorrit who had been born in gaol and so was free from its illusions.

Dickens' depression was intensified by the break-up of his own domestic life. In 1857, acting in Wilkie Collins' *The Frozen Deep*, he began a passionate but carefully concealed relationship with the young actress Ellen Ternan, and in 1858 he separated publicly from his wife. He flung himself into a sensational series of public readings from his books, gaining both financial and emotional rewards from his packed, enthusiastic audiences. His fiction became more extrovert, with the mysteries of *A Tale of Two Cities* and *Great Expectations* (1860–1) leading the new vogue for *sensational novels.

Dickens' many styles of fiction converge in his last completed novel, *Our Mutual Friend* (1864–5). Boffin the literary dustman and the one-legged ballad singer Silas Wegg provide comedy in the spirit of *Pickwick*. The satire of a visionary London dominated by the river and the 'dust heaps' (tips of waste) recall his dark middle novels, while the sensation-style plot of double identity reflect the emancipated style of his recent fiction. *The Mystery of Edwin Drood* (1870), in which Cloisterham is based on Rochester, returns to Kent. But a consciousness of the expanding British Empire brings references to opium, dark-skinned twins from the east, and Egypt, into the enclosed world of Dickens' childhood. Dickens never wrote two successive novels in the same vein. Just where his last work was leading will never be known, for he died with only six monthly numbers written, taking Drood's mystery with him to the grave.

Benjamin Disraeli (1804–81)

Disraeli's vivid journalistic eye, combined with an ebullient imagination, allowed him to extend the scope of the 'silver fork', industrial and political novel genres. An intended legal career was abandoned when he found success with his flamboyant novel *Vivian Grey* (1826–7), written when he was barely 20, which charts a sensitive youth's career through high society. *The Young Duke* (1831), *Contari Fleming* (1832) and *Alroy* (1832) were in a similar genre. His florid, idealistic love story *Henrietta Temple*, indebted to *Bulwer Lytton, and *Venetia*, a fictionalized account of Byron's later years, were published in 1837.

In the same year Disraeli was elected Tory Member of Parliament for Maidstone. As leader of the Young England movement, he furthered his Utopian vision for England based on medieval chivalric ideals in a novel trilogy. In *Coningsby* (1844), a mysterious Jew, Sidonia, inspires the eponymous hero to unite England's aristocratic past and its industrial future: he marries an industrialist's daughter, enters Parliament, and finally inherits the ancestral wealth of his grandfather, Lord Monmouth. In *Sybil* (1845), the emblematic nun-like heroine comes together with the enlightened working-class Radical Walter Gerard to reconcile the ancestral and industrial worlds of the northern district of Marney. *Tancred* (1847) takes the hero to the Middle East to find a political vision inspired by Christianized Judaism, a theme that anticipates George Eliot's *Daniel Deronda* (1876). Towards the end of his life Disraeli wrote two popular but self-indulgent novels, *Lothair* (1870), a romanticized *Bildungsroman*, and the partly autobiographical *Endymion* (1880).

[Sir] Arthur Conan Doyle (1859–1930)

Conan Doyle cannot be credited with inventing the formula of the detective story, but in Sherlock Holmes, a character based on Joseph Bell, Doyle's medical lecturer in Edinburgh, he created the apotheosis of the genre (see above, p. 64). First attracting attention with *The Sign of the Four* (1890), the popularity of Sherlock Holmes made his lodgings, the fictional 221B Baker Street, one of the most famous addresses in London. Although for Sherlock Holmes the solution of a crime is more important than its morality, he subversively champions individuals against the incompetence and corruption of the social system. Holmes' appeal was enhanced by the presence of Dr Watson, the foil to his exotic and sometimes sinister personality, by the bizarre and violent nature of his cases, and by a taut narrative structure indebted to the short stories of Guy de Maupassant. Doyle himself became embarrassed by Holmes' popularity, and attempted to kill him off in 'The Final Problem' (1893). Doyle saw the *historical novel as a more worthy form of fiction, and the Brigadier Gerard series, set in Napoleonic Europe, replaced Holmes in *The Strand Magazine* from 1894 to 1903. Doyle's other historical fiction, with its sharp detail, masterful male characters and rattling good narrative, included *Micah Clarke* (1889), set around the Monmouth Rebellion of 1685, *The White Company* (1891), on a band of European mercenaries in the fourteenth century, and *The Great Shadow* (1892), which led up to the Battle of Waterloo.

George Eliot [née Mary Anne/Marian Evans] (1819–80)

'George Eliot', one of the finest scholars of her day, was to transform the mid-century novel with her knowledge of European literature and sciences, and with imaginative fiction written as 'a set of experiments in life' (*Letters*, 25 Jan. 1876). Yet she never lost her roots in an artisan childhood as the daughter of a well-to-do land agent in rural Warwickshire. While the most intellectually accomplished of novelists, all her work reflects her early love of Sir Walter Scott, Wordsworth and the Romantics, and she was valued most by her readers for insights into the working of the common heart.

On the death of her father she entered London literary life in 1852 as effective editor and major contributor to *The Westminster Review*, the leading radical quarterly that brought her into contact with the prominent intellects of the day. Always fascinated by religious issues and human motivation, Eliot questioned orthodox Christianity, translating Feuerbach's humanist reassessment of the historical Christ as *The Essence of Christianity* (1854), and Spinoza's *Ethics* (1856). From 1853 she scandalized contemporary society by living out of wedlock with the writer G. H.

Lewes, sharing his interests in literature, science, philosophy and theatre, including the sociology of Auguste Comte and the evolutionary behaviourism of Herbert Spencer. Out of this matrix of ideas she evolved her humanist belief in the power of sympathy, and in the role of art 'as a mode of amplifying experience and extending our contact with our fellow-men beyond the bounds of our personal lot' (*Essays*, p. 271; see above, p. 69).

In 1858, encouraged by Lewes, she published *Scenes of Clerical Life* under the pseudonym of 'George Eliot', a novella exploring with exceptional sensitivity three tragedies within unexceptional provincial lives. Its modest success encouraged her to write *Adam Bede (1859), a work whose popularity led to the author's true identity being revealed. *The Mill on the Floss* (1860) reflects conflicts in her own childhood family in the tensions between Maggie Tulliver and her idolized but censorious and less intelligent brother Tom. Mr Tulliver loses the family home, Dorlcote Mill, through bankruptcy, creating a feud with the opposing lawyer, Wakem. When Tom finds Maggie has been seeing Wakem's son, the intelligent, hunchbacked Philip, he cruelly forbids the relationship, and Maggie, repressing her desires, leaves to become a teacher. The last part of the novel, which culminates in the final reconciliation of Maggie and Tom before they are drowned together in the flooding river, is less successful, but the earlier account of Maggie's upbringing forms one of the most passionate evocations of childhood in English literature.

An uncharacteristic novella about the intolerable burden of clairvoyance, *The Lifted Veil* (1859), disappointed readers, but *Silas Marner* (1861), half rural idyll, half moral fable, charting a miser's redemption through love for an abandoned child, delighted critics as a return to the form of *Adam Bede*. Her intensively researched historical novel *Romola* (1862–3) met with more respect than affection, while her 'social problem' novel, *Felix Holt the Radical* (1866), lacked sympathy with her subject. However, *Middlemarch (1871–2) restored her to popularity. The parallel stories of the idealistic Dorothea Brooke and the young doctor Tertius Lydgate quickly established the novel as arguably the finest literary achievement of the century.

Having explored the roots of the Victorian era, Eliot's last major work considers its future possibilities. In *Daniel Deronda* (1876) Gwendolyn Harleth, coming from an impoverished middle-class family, marries the heartless aristocrat Grandcourt to escape the fate of becoming a governess, a story contrasted with the spiritual odyssey of the Jewish Daniel Deronda and his happy marriage to Mirah. Although it is now established as a major work, critics found the double plot unsatisfactory. Its writing left George Eliot exhausted, and in 1878 she was devastated by Lewes' death. Her last work, *The Impression of Theophrastus Such* (1879), was a series of ironic, largely autobiographical sketches. Shortly after marrying her much younger biographer, John Walter Cross, she died in 1880.

Elizabeth Cleghorn Gaskell [née Stevenson] (1810–65)

Elizabeth Gaskell first made her name with the industrial novel, *Mary Barton* (1848), and her fearless willingness to confront controversial issues has led to her being compartmentalized as a 'social problem' novelist. But this does her scant justice. She was a versatile author, deeply involved in a range of contemporary issues, finely sensitive to class and individuality, and, although occasionally she could lapse into the clichés of melodrama and the *sensation novel, tirelessly developed her skill as a writer. Her experience of both London and the north gave her an unusually broad perspective on English society. While as a 'provincial' novelist she lacked the social range of *Anthony Trollope, the intellectual depth of *George Eliot, or *Thomas Hardy's sense of landscape, her work is distinguished by unfailing intelligence and sympathetic insight into common humanity. As Kathleen Tillotson noted, in her *Novels of the Eighteen-forties* (1954), 'Not even George Eliot shows such reverence for average human nature'. Best known as a novelist, some of Gaskell's finest work lies in her short stories written for periodicals, which often draw on local lives and legends. A selection of these was republished in *Round the Sofa* (1859) and *My Lady Ludlow* (1861).

On her mother's death Gaskell lived with her Aunt Lumb in the country town of Knutsford in Cheshire, some 16 miles from industrial Manchester, where she received a sound grounding in science and classics. She had been brought up among Unitarians, a sect that shared the social concerns of the evangelical movement without its dogmatism. In 1832, after a period in London, she married the Reverend William Gaskell, sharing his life as a Unitarian minister in a working-class area of Manchester. The London middle-class bias in writing about the northern industrial unrest of the 'hungry forties' provoked her to write *Mary Barton*. The original focus was on John Barton, a worker driven by suffering and despair to murder the son of a factory owner, but in the interests of gaining a popular audience she added the romantic subplot of Barton's daughter, and concluded the novel in an act of reconciliation that owed more to melodrama than to social reality. Nevertheless, its vivid detail, dramatic immediacy and passionate empathy gave the work an authenticity lacking in other *social problem novels.

Its success led *Dickens to recruit her for his new weekly, *Household Words* (1850–9), which published two of her best-loved works, the sketches of the rural Cheshire she had known as a child, *Cranford* (1851–3), and *Ruth* (1853), a novel that bravely challenged middle-class attitudes to the unmarried mother. Manchester mill owners had protested that *Mary Barton* was prejudiced towards the workers, a bias she tried to correct in the more complex novel of industrial relations, *North and South* (1854–5). She was asked as a friend of the family to write *The Life of Charlotte Brontë* (1857), a work that remains one of the best of Victorian literary biographies.

Gaskell was now associating with the leading English and American writers of the day. She made the mandatory venture into historical fiction with *Sylvia's Lovers* (1863), a novel set in Whitby at the time of the Napoleonic Wars with its press gangs and clandestine smuggling. Sylvia is caught between two suitors, the passionate harpooner Charley Kinraid and her morally obsessive shop assistant cousin Philip, who in order to win her hand treacherously conceals the fact that Kinraid has been press-ganged. Gaskell's one wholly tragic fiction, it is relieved by her compassion for her characters. In *Cousin Phyllis* (1864), one of her finest works, Phyllis' lost love is again lightened by the sensitivity of its characterization and the idyllically evoked Lancashire countryside. *Wives and Daughters* (1864–6), her most ambitious novel, is set in Hollingford, a village community based on her childhood Knutsford. The relationship between the widowed Dr Gibson and his devoted but independent daughter Molly reflects her own fond memories of her father. Gaskell died suddenly, leaving the work unfinished but largely complete, in 1865.

George [Robert] Gissing (1857–1903)

While the determining act of Gissing's career was an impulsive and disastrous love match, much of his fiction was a bitter reaction against romantic ideals. The intellectually precocious son of a pharmaceutical chemist in Wakefield, Yorkshire, Gissing studied classics and modern languages at Owens College, Manchester. He appeared set for a brilliant university career when in 1876, aged 18, he fell desperately in love with Marianne Helen Harrison [Nell], an alcoholic young prostitute, and served imprisonment with hard labour for thieving to provide for her. After a year in the United States hiding from his disgrace, he returned to Wakefield, where marriage to Nell failed after four years. Nell's slum life inspired his grim first novel, *Workers in the Dawn* (1880). This caught the notice of Frederic Harrison. Harrison's positivist philosophy, together with the socialism of Eduard Betz, underpins Gissing's novel of working-class life, *The Unclassed* (1884).

Gissing's writing was now becoming recognized, but his social outlook remained bleak. In *Demos* (1886) he satirized contemporary socialist movements. *Thyrza* (1887), an uncharacteristically idealistic story of a pure working-class girl in love with the son of a factory owner, followed. *The Nether World* (1889) was his darkest account of slum life. After the lighter tone of the satirical *The Emancipated* (1890), set in Italy, came his mordant account of London literary life, *New Grub Street* (1891). At this time Gissing made another catastrophic marriage to a working-class girl, the mentally unstable Edith Alice Underwood.

He turned to contemporary controversies, addressing the public response to agnosticism in *Born in Exile* (1892), women's rights in *The Odd Women* (1893) and *In the Year of Jubilee* (1894), and the destabilizing effects of suburban life in *The Whirlpool* (1897). In 1897 he travelled to Italy and wrote the important literary reassessment, *Charles Dickens: A Critical Study*. From 1899 he lived happily with the French intellectual Gabrielle Fleury, the translator of *New Grub Street*, and died in France shortly after the publication of his remarkable autobiographical reflections, *Private Papers of Henry Ryecroft* (1903).

[Sir] H[enry] Rider Haggard (1856–1925)

Haggard was the leading writer in what Patrick Brantlinger has called the 'Colonial Gothic', a genre that emerged at the close of the century as a reflection of the unease surrounding imperial expansion. In 1875, aged 19, Haggard was sent to South Africa, and stayed there for most of the next sixteen years. He was enthralled by a life of travelling, hunting and being a colonial administrator at a time of turbulent conflicts between British, Boers and Zulus. When he returned to England with a wife and son at the start of the First Boer War in 1881, he escaped the boredom of his legal studies by writing about his experiences.

In 1885, challenged to write a story as good as Stevenson's *Treasure Island* (1883), he completed *King Solomon's Mines*, reputedly in six weeks. Its take on imperialism is ambivalent. If the white aristocrat Sir Henry Curtis represents the superiority of the Anglo-Saxon race, the magnificent black chief Umbopa reflects an idealized view of feudal African society, while the descriptions of bloody massacres give an elegiac note to Haggard's celebration of empire. The story combines adventure with the mythic elements of quest, initiation and a journey to an underworld of the dead, all given colour by Haggard's vivid recollections of Natal. Its immediate success was even exceeded by its successor, *She (1887)*, but two sequels, *Alan Quartermain* (1887) and *Ayesha* (1905), were relative failures. Although his popularity waned in his later years, Haggard remained prolific, and sustained by his gifts as an instinctive storyteller, wrote over fifty novels.

Thomas Hardy (1840–1928)

In more senses than one, Hardy took the *regional novel into new territory. Other novelists had created imaginary landscapes for their novels, but Hardy, more than any novelist since Sir Walter Scott, grounded his fictional world on a living sense of the earth, of folk tradition and history. The land itself becomes a central element in the narrative, and the vibrant individuality of his characters stand in precarious relationship to the physical presences of earth and sky. Hardy is a great original, a novelist whose work both culminates and reacts against the achievement of the Victorian novel. While he shared the contemporary interest in realism and solidly realized his scenes and characters, he was hostile to materialism and his fiction is closer to poetry than to realist prose. Flouting the conventions of the well-made plot, he created some of the most compelling narratives in English fiction.

Hardy was born the son of a stonemason and jobbing builder in the little Dorset hamlet of Higher Bockhampton, an environment virtually untouched by the railway and the outside world. A sickly child, he spent his early years close to his family and neighbours, taking in a culture rich with folklore, country traditions and music. Considered too frail for his father's physical occupation, he was apprenticed as an architect. In 1862 he went to London, where he came under the influence of Darwin's *Origin of Species*, and began writing poetry. But city smoke affected his health, and in 1867 he returned home as an architect.

Hardy abandoned his first, fiercely socialist novel, *The Poor Man and the Lady*, on the advice of *George Meredith, and *Desperate Remedies*, written in the style of the *'sensation novel', was published anonymously in 1871. But it was with *Under the Greenwood Tree* (1872) that Hardy found his true subject, the rural Dorset of his childhood. This short, unpretentious work remains one of Hardy's most perfect and unclouded fictions. In 1874 he married Emma Gifford, a solicitor's daughter, causing the strains of an unequal marriage partnership that were reflected in the plots of his novels. But Emma gave him invaluable support and stimulus as a writer. His novel *A Pair of Blue Eyes* (1873) was moderately successful, but it was *Far from the Madding Crowd* (1874) that first identified the territory of 'Wessex' and launched Hardy to fame. Tragic elements of misguided marriage, murder and death were set against an idyllic country setting, and the final marriage of the landowning Bathsheba Everdene to the faithful Gabriel Oak ended the novel on a warm, positive note. After a minor comedic novel, *The Hand of Ethelbert* (1876), *The Return of the Native* (1878) goes back to the southern Dorset heaths. Dominating the sombre novel is the tempestuous figure of Eustacia Vye, a complex heroine, part temptress, part victim, whose passions find tragic fulfilment in drowning with Wildeve in the raging weir within the brooding presence of Egdon

Heath. The returning 'native', the disillusioned and finally blinded Clym Yeobright, may stand for the alienated Hardy.

Domestic tensions and Hardy's worsening health adversely affected his historical novel, *The Trumpet Major* (1880), and *The Laodicean* (1881) and *Two on a Tower* (1882). But setting up a permanent home at Max Gate in Dorset brought new energy. There he wrote *The Mayor of Casterbridge* (1886), whose plot of unforgiving retribution is set appropriately within a town built within the foursquare plan of the Romans who laid down Britain's system of justice. *The Woodlanders* (1887), set among the winding byways of Hardy's mother's forested Dorset, troubled reviewers by its lack of moral direction, ending as it did with the tragic death of the worthy Giles Winterbourne and the reconciliation in marriage of the rootless Edred Fitzpiers, with Giles' great love, Grace Melbury.

Although he was now celebrated as an author, Hardy was increasingly out of sympathy with his age. In *Tess of the D'Urbervilles* (1891) he directly confronted late Victorian attitudes to the 'fallen woman', asserting that Tess, though not a virgin, was 'a pure woman'. *Jude the Obscure* (1895) caused outright scandal with the stonemason Jude, torn between his love for Arabella Donn, a sensual, extravert pig farmer's daughter, and for his highly strung and sexually inhibited cousin, Sue Brideshead. Protests caused by its overt treatment of sexual passion and its attacks on orthodox Christianity, popular education and the institution of marriage drove Hardy to abandon writing fiction for poetry.

Wessex Poems (1898) began a series of volumes of verse. *The Dynasts* (1904–8) was an ambitious verse drama partly based on the Napoleonic Wars. After Emma's death in 1912, Hardy married Florence Dugdale, who composed *The Life and Work of Thomas Hardy* (1828, 1830) largely from his memoirs.

G[eorge] P[ayne] R[ainsford] James (1801–60)

G. P. R. James was the most prolific of a group of authors, which included *Bulwer Lytton and *William Harrison Ainsworth, who followed the popularity of Sir Walter Scott's historical *Waverley* novels. Scott himself encouraged the 28-year-old James to publish his first work, *Richelieu*

(1829). Its immediate success confirmed James' decision to live by his pen. Following a regime of writing rapidly four hours a day, he produced approximately one novel every nine months for most of his remaining life. His popularity was founded on the breathless élan of his narratives. James gained the soubriquet 'the solitary horseman' from the dashing lone rider that introduced *Richelieu* and subsequent novels, but he ceased using this motif when this was pointed out to him. His stories were based on his passionate belief in the values of chivalry, an ethos in which he anticipated Victorian interest in Arthurian legend, and which he expounded in *The History of Chivalry* (2nd edn, 1830). But James also prided himself on the historical accuracy of his stories, which he backed by extensive quotations from his sources, covering a wide variety of periods and topics. However his novels, with their stereotyped characters and crude plotting, failed to survive the historical vogue that made them popular. Among the more readable today are *Richelieu*, *The Gypsy* (1835) and *The Fate* (1851).

As well as being a prolific author of histories and novels, James lived an active family, social and public life, lecturing and agitating for reform of the copyright laws. Cheap piracies of his work and legal complications brought financial difficulties that forced James and his family in 1850 to move, first to the United States, and then, with failing physical and mental health, to Venice, where he died as British consul.

Henry James (1843–1916)

Henry James is omitted from most studies of the Victorian novel because he was an American by birth and his work extends into the twentieth century. However, it is hard to justify his total exclusion. James settled in Britain in 1876, associated with many of the major English writers of the day, including *H. G. Wells and *Robert Louis Stevenson, and was a British citizen at the time of his death. If his attitudes appear those of an outsider, they were influenced by intellectual movements in continental Europe as much as by those in America – by Turgenev, Flaubert, Balzac, Zola and the Goncourt brothers as much as by Hawthorne, Poe and Melville. While his novels were never widely popular in England, his perceptive reviews, which appeared as early as 1865, and his seminal 1884 essay 'The Art of the Novel', made a central contribution to the development of English prose fiction.

James' novels fall into three phases, only two of which are Victorian. The first novels look at the world from an American perspective. *Roderick Hudson* (1876) and **Portrait of a Lady* (1881) used an expatriate American as a touchstone against which to set European culture; *Washington Square* (1880) and *The Bostonians* (1886) address the effects of changing social attitudes on individuals in America, while *The Princess Casamassima* (1886) explores clandestine socialist movements of the 1880s in London and Europe. The novels of his second phase, *The Tragic Muse* (1890), *What Maisie Knew* (1897) and *The Awkward Age* (1899), are set in England and their moral concerns transcend nationality, marking his more settled life in Rye, Sussex. Much of his best writings were short stories and novellas. *The Turn of the Screw* (1898) remains one of the finest tales of the *supernatural in English. Although James has become identified with the reaction against Victorian 'baggy monster' novels, and his concern with structure and psychological nuance looks forward to the practices of Modernism, in his concern with morality and the problems of realism he remains rooted in the nineteenth century (see pp. 25–6).

Douglas [William] Jerrold (1803–57)

Although little read today, in the 1840s Jerrold was classed with *Dickens and *Thackeray as a leading literary figure. Born into a Kent theatrical troupe, he wrote one of the most popular plays of the century, *Black-Ey'd Susan* (1829), and further anglicized domestic melodrama with *The Rent Day* (1832). He then turned to journalism, in 1841 becoming a staple contributor to *Punch*. Here he published a popular novella, *The Story of a Feather* (1844), in which an ostrich feather changes hands, revealing the contrasts between rich and poor, and the comic monologues for which he is best remembered today, *Mrs Caudle's Curtain Lectures* (1845). His ambitious satire on the worship of wealth, *A Man Made of Money* (1848), proved too ingenious for most readers, who preferred his savage social critique contrasting the careers of two protagonists, one rich and one poor, *The History of St Giles and St James* (1845–7). While his reputation rapidly collapsed after his early death, his work played an important role in the social controversies of the 1840s.

Geraldine E[ndsor] Jewsbury (1812–80)

Jewsbury, the daughter of a Manchester manufacturer, grew up a precocious child. She studied Italian and French, which led to the admiration for George Sand that was to shape her fiction, and found her Calvinist faith undermined by her reading of science and metaphysics. Painfully aware that provincial society undervalued the intellectual ability of middle-class women, she moved to London, where she found kindred spirits in Jane and Thomas Carlyle.

She poured her concerns with female emancipation into *Zoe. The History of Two Lives* (1845), a novel that scandalized readers with its frank depiction of sexual passion and its controversial religious views. This was followed by *The Half Sisters* (1848), which contrasts the restricted life of a woman who marries a businessman with the fulfilment of her sibling's career on the stage. *Maria Withers* (1851) draws on her knowledge of industrial life in Manchester. Her later novels, which included children's fiction, are of less interest. Apart from her outspoken fiction, Geraldine Jewsbury made an important contribution to the development of the novel as an active reader for publishers Hurst and Blackett, and for Bentley. She also reviewed an estimated 2,000 works, mostly novels, for *The Athenaeum*.

Charles Kingsley (1819–75)

Kingsley was the leading writer of *religious novels of the Broad Church 'muscular Christian' school. Rector of Eversley in Hampshire from 1848 to 1852, during the height of the Chartist agitation he became an ardent disciple of the Christian socialist F. D. Maurice. He pamphleteered against sweatshop labour under the pseudonym 'Parson Lot', and was temporarily banned by the Bishop of London for his radical views. His novel *Yeast* (1848) showed Tregarva, a radical Cornish gamekeeper, introducing the Cambridge graduate Lancelot Smith into the brutal sufferings of the rural poor. *Alton Locke* (1850), Kingsley's finest novel, takes an autobiographical form to record the career of a Chartist poet from childhood in the sweated labour of the London clothes industry. He becomes involved in physical force Chartism, and finds celebrity as a working-class poet. But Cambridge academia pressures him to reject his radicalism, while a Chartist leader attacks him for betraying the cause. Catching a fever after witnessing the Chartist debacle of 1848, he dies on a pilgrimage to seek new social vision in America.

Kingsley's historical novels were an often violent mixture of anti-Catholicism, imperialism and belief in male athleticism. In *Hypatia* (1853), a historical novel set in fifth-century Egypt, Philammon, a pagan ascetic turned Christian, meets the Neo-Platonist teacher Hypatia. But before she, too, can declare her conversion, corrupt monks brutally murder her as an infidel under a giant icon of Christ. Philammon enters a reformed monastery as abbot. *Westward Ho!* (1855) is a saga of bloody revenge against Catholic Spaniards in the reign of Elizabeth I. In such stories Kingsley's high-spirited, violent but engaging adventure narratives have worn better than his serious religious concerns.

In 1860 Kingsley became Regius Professor of Modern History at Cambridge. Fascinated by marine biology from boyhood, he embraced Darwin's evolutionary theories, which underlie his most enduringly popular work, *The Water-Babies (1863). Hereward the Wake* (1865) goes back to the years surrounding the Norman invasion of 1066. The boisterously physical Hereward, the embodiment of early British muscular prowess (see above, p. 39), cudgels his way across England, defeating a succession of opponents from a polar bear to heavily armed knights. The princess Torfrida finally marries him and tames his unruly nature, preparing the way for his British successors to combine his primitive energy with the virtues of civilization. But Kingsley's own health was never the strongest. In 1869 he travelled to the West Indies and the United States, but died during a visit to North America.

[Joseph] Rudyard Kipling (1830–76)

Although more important as a short story writer and poet than a novelist, Kipling earns his place here as arguably the finest British *colonial writer. He was born in India, a country that shaped his imagination and sensibility. He returned there after education in England as a journalist, a profession that brought him into contact with a rich variety of racial and social types, and gave him both an outlet and the inspiration for much of his finest writing. His writing set in England, including his 'decadent' novel of a blinded war artist, *The Light that Failed* (1891), and the school stories in *Stalky and Co.* (1899), reveals his profound alienation from Britain. But with the *Jungle Books* (1894–5), and supremely with his 'labour of love', *Kim* (1901), he brought new ways of seeing and thinking about the cultures of the 'Other' into fiction, and opened the way for the emergence of postcolonial studies.

[Joseph Thomas] Sheridan Le Fanu (1814–73)

One of the finest writers of the *supernatural, Le Fanu was the son of Irish Protestants, and his fiction draws on a rich fund of Irish folklore traditions. His experimental early tales, mainly contributed to *Dublin University Magazine*, were collected as *Ghost Stories and Tales of Mystery* (1851). The successive deaths of his wife and mother in 1858 and 1861 respectively isolated the temperamentally reclusive Le Fanu, and drove him to find solace in the Gothic recesses of his imagination. The ghostly murder mysteries *The House by the Churchyard* (1861–3) and *Wylder's Hand* (1863–4) followed. His best-known novel, *Uncle Silas* (1864), uses the sensibility of its vulnerable young heroine, threatened by her murderous Uncle Silas, who is after her inheritance, to create a terrifying sense of menace. Le Fanu's interests in Swedenborg and the occult underpinned his sensational and often violent fiction, culminating in *In a Glass Darkly* (1872). This collection of tales included 'Carmilla', a sexually ambivalent vampire story (both the narrator and the vampire are feminine) that provided a source for Bram Stoker's *Dracula* (1897), and 'Green Tea', an artfully constructed tale of occult possession. Blending the supernatural and mundane, and fine-tuned to psychological nuance, Le Fanu's 'Gothic' fiction explored issues of sexuality, gender and national identities that were closed to the contemporary 'realist' texts.

Edward Bulwer-Lytton [until 1843, Edward George Earle Lytton] (1803–73)

Edward Bulwer-Lytton was one of the most prolific, widely read and innovative writers of the Victorian era. An aristocrat by birth, from boyhood he was precociously intelligent, yet with the conflicting self-confidence and inner diffidence that continued into adulthood. Studious and never physically strong, educated at home under the eye of his smotheringly possessive mother, he nevertheless assumed a Byronic panache, and cut a dashing figure in Regency London. Then at the age of 24 Lytton's fortunes crashed when he married the Irish adventuress Rosina Wheeler against the wishes of his mother, who cut him off without a penny. The marriage was a disaster. Lytton was forced to write rapidly to survive, and the figure of the struggling outsider was to recur in his novels and plays. He found success with his second novel, *Pelham* (1828), the progress of a world-weary dandy from a life of vanity to the assumption of responsibility. The work caught the spirit of the waning Regency, and launched a vogue for novels of fashionable life. He followed this success with *Paul Clifford* (1830), the life of a high-spirited gentleman highwayman complete with criminal slang and racy songs, written partly as a protest against indiscriminate capital punishment. This began a fashion for 'Newgate novels', and both this and the murder mystery *Eugene Aram* (1832), which probed criminal impulses within middle-class respectability, provoked attacks as fiction that glamorized crime.

Failing health took Lytton to Italy, from whence he returned with an all-time bestseller, *The Last Days of Pompeii* (1834), and the politically inspired *Rienzi* (1835). These established the enduring genre of 'toga' fiction and drama. *Zanoni* (1842), a neo-Gothic novel involving the elixir of life, made Lytton a pioneer in fiction of the *supernatural, while *The Caxtons* (1849), an idiosyncratic, discursive family history, and its sequel, *My Novel* (1853), opened the way for the development of the mid-Victorian domestic novel. By 1850 Lytton was also a successful dramatist and poet, and a central figure of the literary scene. In this year he became a close friend of *Dickens, and with him co-founded the Guild of Literature and Art. The ending of Dickens' serialized *Great

Expectations (1860–1) was revised on Lytton's suggestion, and Dickens' masterwork was followed by Lytton's occult fiction, *A Strange Story* (1862), in *All the Year Round*. In 1871 Lytton's *The Coming Race* was an early forerunner of *science fiction. When he died two years later, Lytton's reputation faded as rapidly as it had risen. His mannered style, which delighted his original readers, quickly dated, and other writers developed the genres that he had innovated. Nevertheless, the Victorian novel owes much to Bulwer Lytton.

George Macdonald (1824–1905)

Macdonald's highly individual vision had its base in dual imaginative worlds, the folklore and superstition that surrounded his childhood in a Scottish farming community, and its dour Calvinism. His imagination drew him to German Romanticism, while a spirit of intellectual inquiry led him to take a university degree in science. His unorthodox views cut short a career in Congregational ministry. He settled in London, becoming Professor of English at Bedford College, London, from 1859. The Christian socialism of F. D. Maurice drew him to the Anglican Church, and he entered a career of miscellaneous journalism and editing.

Macdonald's fiction, which reflects his interest in mysticism, myths and folk legends, moves from dreamlike allegory to gritty everyday reality, and often combines the two dimensions, reflecting his rejection of conventional views of death. In *Phantastes* (1858), a 21-year-old boy travels through a hazardous dream world on a spiritual initiation into manhood. Other works are realistic in approach. *Robert Falconer* (1868) describes the Calvinist community of Aberdeen that Macdonald knew as a child, a repressive world from which Falconer has to emancipate himself by becoming a doctor among the London poor. It is here, in a melodramatic coup, that he discovers the father who abandoned him in childhood. *Sir Gibbie* (1879) vividly portrays the struggles of a Scottish street urchin.

His stories written for children are among his finest work. These include the visionary *At the Back of the North Wind* (1871), which takes the son of a struggling London cabbie into the world on the other side of death, and his fairy fantasy *The Princess and the Goblin* (1872). But Macdonald's imagination, like that of his friend Lewis Carroll, was timeless, and appealed to all ages. In the next centuries his fantasies were to become

a major influence on the work of C. S. Lewis, Charles Williams and
J. R. R. Tolkien.

Frederick Marryat (1792–1848)

Marryat came to novel writing after having served in the British navy with
distinction from the ages of 14 to 32, rising to become post-Captain CB
(Companion of the Order of the Bath). Leaving the navy, he sought a literary career. From 1832 to 1835 he edited *The Metropolitan Magazine*, to
which he contributed his own naval fiction. These drew on the rich
resources of his naval life. He became the most popular of a group of
naval writers that included Edward Howard, Captain Frederick Chamier
and Michael Scott. He wrote rapidly, drawing on stock plots, and his
novels typically record the picaresque adventures of an eponymous
foundling or lost heir in search of a father. But Marryat's informal style,
his bluff, often rough, humour and his ability to bring common characters to life on the page, gained him a large and devoted readership. *Peter
Simple* (1834) is his most accomplished sea novel, handling with assurance
the *Bildungsroman* of an innocent finding maturity in a life of action. *Jacob
Faithful*, also published that year, is interesting for its account of sailing
life on the Thames. *Snarleyyow; or the Dog Fiend* (1836–7) and *The Phantom
Ship* (1837) revealed a melodramatic interest in the *supernatural.

By the 1840s, the naval novel was becoming worked out, and Marryat
turned to writing for children, finding success with *Masterman Ready*
(1842), a family version of *Robinson Crusoe*, and *Children of the New Forest*
(1847), his most enduring work. Marryat's robust tales prepared the way
for the boy's adventure fiction written by G. A. Henty, Captain Mayne
Reid and R. M. Ballantyne later in the century.

Harriet Martineau (1802–76)

Harriet Martineau was educated largely at home, where, a precocious
intellect, she voraciously studied economics, philosophy and literature.
Faced with the failure of the family firm in 1829, and her chances of marriage reduced by her deafness, she rejected the occupations of needlework
and being a governess for writing. Her *Illustrations of Political Economy*

(1832–4), twenty-three homely parables illustrating Utilitarian political and economic theory published in cheap monthly parts directed to a popular readership, sold up to 10,000 copies. Although they confirmed middle-class conservative attitudes rather than proselytizing the poor, they prepared the way for the *'social problem' novel. *Poor Laws and Paupers Illustrated* (1833–4) followed.

Martineau's one full-length novel, *Deerbrook* (1839), describes the impact on a rural community when two orphaned sisters arrive and attract the attention of the village's young surgeon. While the complicated love story appears stiff to modern tastes, its portrayal of female passion was frank enough to influence the work of *Charlotte Brontë, and its account of the hierarchies, rivalries and gossip within a tightly knit community pioneered the novel of *provincial life that culminates in George Eliot's *Middlemarch* (1871–2). Martineau became an advocate of the healing power of mesmerism. Her *Dawn Island: A Tale* (1845) was notable for championing the Haitian revolutionary Toussaint L'Ouverture. Abandoning her early Unitarian faith, she became an early advocate of sociology, in 1853 translating and condensing Auguste Comte's *Cours de philosophie positive* (1830) into English. While a minor novelist herself, as an intellectual she played an important role in the world of ideas on which the Victorian novel thrived.

George Meredith (1828–1909)

Meredith's childhood was blighted by his mother's death when he was 5, and the bankruptcy of his father's naval outfitting business. After a brief period in a lawyer's office, he turned to the career of writing. His early life was unhappy. His marriage to Mary Ellen Nicholls went sour, a breakdown achingly explored in his sonnet sequence *Modern Love* (1862), and his wife eloped with the painter Henry Wallis. His bitter attitude towards family life is reflected in his first novel, *The Ordeal of Richard Feverel* (1859), in which the eponymous hero is damaged by his father's strict 'scientific' principles of education. Breaking away, he secretly marries a neighbouring farmer's niece and flees to London, where he suffers the heartbreak of marital failure. It was too sexually frank and stylistically innovative for Mudie's Circulating Library, which withdrew it. *Evan Harrington* (1860), which returns to Meredith's background in its plot of a tailor's son's aspirations to be a 'gentleman', met with a better reception. But Meredith was becoming independent of the need to write novels for a living. He contributed columns to newspapers, travelled abroad as a journalist, and from 1860 to 1894 was chief reader for the publishers Chapman and Hall, exercising considerable influence in selecting and editing the scripts of many leading novelists, including *George Gissing, Olive Schreiner and *Thomas Hardy.

By 1864 Meredith was established in London as a respected man of letters. He remarried, and was elected to the Garrick Club. *Emilia in England* (1864, reissued as *Sandra Belloni* in 1886) and its sequel *Vittoria* (1866) were set in England and Europe, reflecting his travels as a journalist. *Harry Richmond* (1871), one of his most popular novels, returned to the subject of the fraught relationship between father and son. In his idiosyncratic essay 'The Idea of Comedy' (1877), Meredith advocated the detached comic perspective embodied in the work of Cervantes, Fielding and Molière. He embodied these ideas in *Beauchamp's Career* (1875), an ironic view of a young naval officer's pursuit of high-minded ideals, and also in his masterpiece *The Egoist* (1879) and in *The Tragic Comedians* (1880). His last three works, *Diana of the Crossways* (1885), *One of Our Conquerors* (1891) and *The Amazing Marriage* (1895), reflect his growing involvement in the feminist cause. He became President of the Society of Authors in 1892.

Oscar Wilde wrote that Meredith 'was a child of realism who is not on speaking terms with his father'. His fiction represents a reaction against the values embodied in the mid-Victorian novel, and his dense epigrammatic style deliberately flouted the expectations of general readers, whom Meredith called 'porkers'. His fiction embodied Darwinian views of social behaviour evolving from animal passions to intellectual and moral refinement. His work was widely respected, but only the late *Diana of the Crossways*, a novel made popular by its connection with the spirited Caroline Norton who had died in 1877, enjoyed popular success. His novelistic reputation was revived in the twentieth century by the Bloomsbury coterie of Virginia Woolf and E. M. Forster.

George [Augustus] Moore (1852–1933)

Moore was the son of a landowning Roman Catholic father, G. H. Moore, MP, in County Mayo, a world he was to recreate from the servants' viewpoint in *Esther Waters* (1894). He was educated in England, but on the death of his father moved to Paris, where he led a Bohemian life, and met Manet and Degas. He came under the influence of Impressionism, the use of light to recreate the artist's experienced perception, and naturalism, whose aim was to show human character scientifically determined by environment, evolution and biology. These twin poles of artistry and realism were to direct his career. He returned to London in 1880 as a journalist, art critic and novelist.

Moore's first novel, *A Modern Lover* (1883), recreated the sordid social world of young artists in London, while *A Mummer's Wife* (1885) depicted dingy life in an acting troupe. Both scandalized the bourgeois reading public with their uncompromising portrayal of sexual passion and the squalor of lower-class life, and were excluded from circulating libraries. Later Moore turned to the aestheticism of Walter Pater and Huysmans, a major influence on *A Drama in Muslin* (1886). *Mike Fletcher* (1889), the story of the dissolute life and suicide of an indigent London poet, was a partially successful return to the style of Zola. But it was the perspective of his unsentimental, humane servant-girl that provided the key to 'realism' in his enduring masterpiece, *Esther Waters*. He continued to experiment with fictional form, relating literature to music in *Evelyn Innes* (1898). In 1901 he returned to Ireland where he became part of the *Irish revival, writing short stories collected in *The Untilled Field* (1903) and a symbolist novel, *The Lake* (1905).

Margaret Oliphant [née Wilson] (1828–97)

Margaret Oliphant was one of the most prolific and versatile writers of the mid-nineteenth century, writing over eighty novels besides collections of short stories, biographies, histories and reviews. She was brought up in lowland Scotland and in Birkenhead, where she gained the insights into the nonconformist society shown in her remarkably mature first novel, *Passages in the Life of Mrs Margaret Maitland* (1849), the work that made her name. Her historical novel of the 1775 rebellion, *Katie Stewart* (1853), began her long connection with the publishing firm of Blackwood's, and she contributed regularly to *Blackwood's Magazine*.

After the early death of her husband she provided for three children and his alcoholic brother with her pen, a story movingly told in her *Auto-biography* (1899). The popularity of her novel *Salem Chapel* (1862–3) in *Blackwood's Magazine* led to the 'Chronicles of Carlingford' (*The Rector and the Rector's Family* [1863], *The Perpetual Curate* [1864], *Miss Marjoribanks* [1866] and *Phoebe Junior* [1876]). Although the name of the series echoes *Anthony Trollope's *Barsetshire Chronicles*, the focus is wider, including both dissenting and Anglican communities, and there is only a loose connection between the tales. While *Salem Chapel* has remained the best known of the series, critics have preferred *Miss Marjoribanks*, in which the imperious Lucilla tries to impose her views and tastes on her father and the village, but finally turns down a fashionable marriage to a newly elected MP in favour of her devoted cousin Tom. Although Mrs Oliphant came to fame as a 'realistic' writer, her later popularity was based on her ghost stories and writing of the occult, including *A Beleaguered City* (1880) (see above, pp. 57–8) and *A Little Pilgrim of the Unseen* (1882).

Written rapidly to support her extended family, Mrs Oliphant's fiction nevertheless remained consistently engaging, and its sympathetic characterization and social observation occasionally led to her work being attributed to *George Eliot. Her *Annals of a Publishing House* (1897) was a pioneering study of publishing history, and her widely ranging writing did much to confirm women's status in the profession of letters.

Ouida [Marie Louise de la Ramée] (1839–1908)

Ouida's exotic romances were more typical of the end of the century than the 1860s in which they first appeared. As a child, she invented a French secret service identity for her frequently absent father. She was barely 22 when her first novel, *Granville de Vigne* (1861–3), was serialized in *The New Monthly Magazine*. It was later republished as *Held in Bondage* (1863), 'bondage' referring to marriage, recently modified by the 1857 divorce law reform. It recounts the adventures of two athletic public school friends in England, India and the Crimea, entangled with glamorous scheming women and a complex of bigamous, or apparently bigamous, relations. More muscular Byronic heroes and extravagant plotting motivate *Strathmore* (1865), in which the eponymous hero is tricked by his paramour into killing his closest friend in a duel, but makes amends by marrying his dead friend's daughter. The novel's morality was questionable, but the narrative verve was not. Ouida built on her popularity with the equally racy *Chandos* (1866), in which the hedonistic but honourable aristocrat is the intended victim of his steward, John Trevenna, who, unknown to Chandos, is his envious bastard half-brother. Ouida's greatest popular success was *Under Two Flags* (1867). She published over forty novels and short-story collections, including a vigorous satire on English high life, *The Massarines* (1897). Her ebullient style and preposterous plots won her a huge readership, but, careless with her copyrights and resistant to charity, she died in poverty.

Charles Reade (1814–84)

Charles Reade, sometimes classed as a *sensation writer for his melodramatic plots and subjects, distanced himself from 'this slang term', preferring to be regarded as a *social problem novelist. He grew up obsessive and idealistic, a loner who never married and never settled comfortably into his society. With a background in academia and in law, he led a rootless life between Oxford and Paris before finding success collaborating with Tom Taylor in *Masks and Faces* (1852), a comedy set in eighteenth-century theatre land which formed the basis for his first novel, *Peg Woffington* (1853). But Reade was drawn to contemporary social issues. His melodrama of the Australian diggings, *Gold* (1853), enjoyed a successful run at Drury Lane, and he combined this material with an exposé of the penal system in England and Australia, *It's Never Too Late to Mend* (1856), adapting the novel back onto the stage in 1865. *Hard Cash* (1868), the best of Reade's exposé novels, gruesomely portrayed the cruelties of the private lunatic asylum system, a topic he revisited in *A Terrible Temptation* (1871). His 'newspaper novels' continued to dramatize the topics of the day. *Put Yourself in His Place* (1870) denounced trades unions' closed shops, and *Foul Play* (1868), the scuttling of ships for insurance. Reade himself considered *Griffith Gaunt; or Jealousy* (1866), a novel campaigning against public hypocrisy in sexual matters, as his finest work, but it scandalized too many of his readers to prove popular.

Reade's career declined in the 1870s, although *The Wandering Heir* (1872), based on the Tichborne case, sold a million copies in magazine form, and *Drink* (1879), his melodrama of Zola's *L'Assommoir* (1877), achieved worldwide popularity. At the height of his success he was one of the most widely read writers of his day, with a massive following in the United States and in Australia. Contemporaries ranked him with authors as diverse as *George Eliot and Victor Hugo. But his work, which diverted fiction and drama towards gritty social concerns, has worn badly, too often remaining an undigested mix of documentation and melodrama. His most enduring achievement was *The Cloister and the Hearth* (1861), a massively researched *historical novel in which the father of the scholar Erasmus travels across a vast panorama of fifteenth-century Europe at the dawn of the Reformation.

G[eorge] W[illiam] M[acarthur] Reynolds (1814–79)

Reynolds was 'the most popular writer of our time', according to his obituary in *The Bookseller*, with more readers than *Dickens. He had been intended for a military career, but on his father's death his legacy enabled Reynolds to pursue a journalistic life in Paris, strengthening his radical views and helping him acquire the affection for French literature that motivates his study *The Modern Writers of France* (1838). There he married Susannah Frances Pearson, herself a minor novelist. But the first of the many financial disasters that dogged his career struck. He returned to England, and in 1836 was declared bankrupt. His novel *The Youthful Impostor* (later reissued as *The Parricide*) had appeared in 1835, and the success of Dickens' *Pickwick Papers* (1836–7) prompted his own *Pickwick Abroad; or the Tour in France* (1837–8). He insisted that this was not plagiarism but a 'continuation', and it indeed conducted Dickens' characters through new and sometimes unsavoury situations, attracting some respectful reviews – and Dickens' lasting hatred.

It was not, however, *Pickwick* but Eugene Sue's *Mystères de Paris* (1842–3) that set Reynolds on the road to success. Sue's work provided a model for Reynolds' cruder *The Mysteries of London* (1844–6), which was published, in weekly penny numbers with sensational woodcuts, by George Vickers, a publisher specializing in pornographic and radical works. When Reynolds quarrelled with Vickers, he engaged John Dicks to publish the continuation as *The Mysteries of the Court of London* (1848–56). This huge compilation of tales and exposés was loosely held together by Reynolds' vision of a society divided sharply between an oppressive aristocracy and the criminalized poor, the actual middle classes being generally absent from the narrative. In spite of its ostensibly radical stance, Reynolds' perspective remained bourgeois rather than working class, and the heroic virtues are found not in socialist reformers but in his spirited and emotionally emancipated young heroines' resistance to predatory aristocrats.

His industry was prodigious. Possibly assisted by 'ghost' writers, he composed over twenty lengthy novels. These included the Gothic and oriental tales *Wagner the Werewolf* (1846–7) and *The Coral Island* (1848–9); the *social problem novels *The Seamstress* (1850) and *Mary Price* (1851–4); and *historical fiction *The Rye House Plot* (1853–4) and *Mary Stuart* (1859). He launched *The London Journal* (1845–1912), which he brought to a circulation of 50,000, before leaving it to start his own magazine, *Reynolds' Miscellany* (1846–69), besides editing *Reynolds' Weekly Newspaper* (1850–1924).

Reynolds remains an invisible presence behind the middle-class urban novel. He and *Thackeray shared a common literary apprenticeship in Paris, and *The Mysteries of London* influenced the view of London in *Vanity Fair* (1847–8). Dickens reviled Reynolds, and he ventured into popular publishing with *Household Words* partly to counter the effect of *Reynolds' Miscellany*; nevertheless, reviewers saw elements of Reynolds' *Mysteries* in *Bleak House* (1852–3). *Mary Elizabeth Braddon modelled her early serial, *The Black Band* (1861–2), on the work of Reynolds, and his fiction influenced the serpentine plots and strong ambivalent heroines of the *sensation novel. But his fiction, which caught the taste of the mid-Victorian popular reader, remains today largely locked in the age for which it was written.

James Malcolm Rymer (1803?–84)

Rymer is included as an example of the sensational novelists, like J. F. Smith and *G. W. M. Reynolds, who wrote fiction for the massive but largely lost body of literature published at a penny an issue for the masses in the mid-Victorian period. Rymer came to England from Scotland and set up in London as a civil engineer, mechanical inventor and engraver in about 1838. In 1837 Edward Lloyd launched the first of his immensely popular penny-issue plagiarisms of *Dickens, Thomas Peckett Prest's *The Penny Pickwick* (1837–8), finding a huge market of readers, many of whom had been weaned by political and educational publications and were looking for more entertaining matter. Rymer became the major writer for Lloyd in the early 1840s, producing a series of sensational penny-issue novels that have now become prized collectors' items. They include *Ada the Betrayed* (1843), *The Black Monk* (1844) and, most famously, two works that were to become bywords in middle- as well as working-class cultures, *Sweeney Todd* (1846) and *Varney the Vampyre, or the Feast of Blood* (1847–8), a probable source for Bram Stoker's *Dracula*. Rymer has been credited with over 120 titles. He also edited a number of periodicals, including *Lloyd's Weekly Miscellany* (1845). A clever and versatile writer in the literary genre that was to resurface into respectability in the *'sensation' novel, he used a series of pseudonyms such as 'M. J. Errym' to hide his identity from the middle-class society in which he lived, and died in West London a relatively wealthy man.

Robert Louis [Lewis Balfour] Stevenson (1850–94)

Stevenson was born in Edinburgh, a sickly child dependent on his Calvinist nurse, 'Cummie', whose tales of damnation haunted his dreams, and his mother, who gave him his enduring fascination with Highland history and legend. At Edinburgh University Stevenson's religious conflicts with his Presbyterian father intensified. He lived a secret Bohemian life, read widely and experimented with creative writing. An insatiable explorer, his first publications were travel books and essays, including *Travels with a Donkey* (1879). He fell in love with an older American divorcée and author, Fanny Osbourne. In spite of poverty and ill health, he pursued her to America and married her in 1880. But he had begun to show the symptoms of tuberculosis, and the couple began a life that was to be a constant search for a convalescent climate.

The map of a Scottish island he once visited as a youth inspired the archetypal tale of boyhood initiation, *Treasure Island*, published in book form in 1883. This was an instant success as a boy's adventure story. But Stevenson was never interested simply in excitement, and the darker forces within the self haunt all his work. His terrifying *The Strange Case of Dr Jekyll and Mr Hyde (1886), which reflected his own double life as an Edinburgh student, also struck a popular chord in an era questioning the moral certainties of the mid-Victorian period and became an instant classic. Kidnapped (1886) was set in the aftermath of the 1751 Scottish rebellion and was based on an actual murder. The chase plot drove together two contrasting personalities, the pragmatic David Balfour, pursued by murderous kidnappers intent on his inheritance, and the romantic Alan Breck Stewart, a Jacobite rebel escaping the forces of the crown. The work related character to historical and geographical setting with an authenticity not achieved since the work of Scott. Catriona (1893), its sequel, was relatively unsuccessful, but the period was used again for his adult novel, The Master of Ballantrae (1889), a psychologically gripping tale of rivalry between two brothers who take different sides in the Jacobite uprising. Stevenson's last years were spent in Samoa, where his publications included his slight but popular historical yarn for boys, The Black Arrow (1888), and his grim study of father–son conflict, the unfinished The Weir of Hermiston (1896).

R[obert] S[mith] Surtees (1805–64)

Surtees, a comic novelist of the hunting life, began writing sporting journalism while in London in 1830. The next year, inheriting his father's estate near Newcastle-upon-Tyne, Co. Durham, he became a public figure and never publicly acknowledged authorship of his roistering fiction. His best-known creation, Jorrocks, a vulgar parvenu City grocer who wears a 'vig' and aspires to social respectability as a member of the Surrey hunt, gallops his way through Jorrocks' Jaunts and Jollities (1838), Handley Cross (1843) and Hillingdon Hall (1845). But his popularity with Victorians readers began with Mr Sponge's Sporting Tour (1853) about a shifty Londoner who 'sponges' his way up into rural hunt society. This was illustrated by John Leech, who was to provide lively coloured etchings for five of Surtees' novels, and did much to ensure Surtees' continuing popularity. Hawbuck Grange (1847) was a loosely connected collection of hunting sketches, while Ask Mamma (1858) and Plain or Ringlets? (1860) venture into the domestic side of provincial life. In *Mr. Facey Romford's Hounds* (1865) Surtees returned to the cockney confidence trickster imposing himself on provincial society.

Much of Surtees' fiction was first serialized in sporting magazines, and although it was republished in three-volume form, it stands outside the central ambience of the Victorian novel. The characters are thin and stereotypical, the men loud and vulgar, the women lacking in decorum. The narratives have little plot, and often betray their periodical origins. Yet Surtees' slapdash method gives his best work a delightful brio. He has a cartoonist's eye for human idiosyncrasy, and a fine ear for cockney speech. More Regency than Victorian in spirit, his novels reflect in comic form Londoners' nostalgia for the disappearing country ways, and embody Surtees' own considerable knowledge of the hunting life.

William Makepeace Thackeray (1811–63)

Born in India the son of a senior civil servant, he received a gentleman's education there and in England, but left Cambridge without a degree. He began careers in law, art and journalism, but, unable to settle in any of them, lived a Bohemian life in Paris, squandered his inheritance, and married a penniless Irish girl who was later certified incurably insane. He was forced to write for a living. Having experienced both wealth and adversity, Thackeray became an ambivalent observer of polite society. He wrote ironic, conversational pieces for a range of periodicals, and found a sympathetic outlet in the lively, newly formed *Fraser's Magazine*, which in 1841 published *The Luck of Barry Lyndon*, a bitter picaresque novel set in the Seven Years' War.

But in 1840 he had found the perfect channel for his talents in the newly founded *Punch*, for which he wrote a successful series republished as *The Book of Snobs* (1848). This anatomy of social pretensions fed directly into the novel *Vanity Fair, published in monthly numbers from 1847 to 1848, with Thackeray's own illustrations. While it never approached the popularity of *Dickens' novels, by the fourth number sales verged on 10,000 a month, and the work brought Thackeray critical acclaim and social respectability. The partly autobiographical *Pendennis (1848–50), which includes vivid insights into the London journalistic scene, again appeared in parts illustrated by Thackeray. *Henry Esmond* (1852), which adapted the prestigious form of the *historical novel, drew a panorama of Europe at the time of the Jacobite rebellion and the Spanish War of Succession. *The Newcomes*, a leisurely panorama of contemporary middle-class family life, followed in 1853–5. *The Virginians* (1859), the American sequel to *Henry Esmond*, was less successful. But journalism was absorbing more and more of Thackeray's energies. As editor of *The Cornhill Magazine* (1860–1957), he launched the first and best of a new wave of illustrated, high-quality magazines, published monthly at a shilling. *Cornhill* published his last completed novel, *The Adventures of Philip* (1861–2), besides the work of *Anthony Trollope, *Wilkie Collins, *Elizabeth Gaskell, *Thomas Hardy and *George Eliot.

Thackeray's deepest interests lay in the era of Hogarth and Fielding, which he believed had freer manners, a franker morality and a finer taste, and to which he paid tribute in his lectures, *The English Humorists of the Eighteenth Century* (1852) and *The Four Georges* (1855). Like Dickens, he came to novel writing through journalism. But where Dickens transformed what he observed in his imagination, Thackeray sought to present social life as he observed it, in its unvarnished reality, creating a touchstone of social realism for novelists like Trollope, and critics like Lewes and David Masson.

Anthony Trollope (1815–82)

Trollope was, after *Dickens, the most popular 'serious' novelist of the mid-Victorian period. He was also one of the most prolific, writing some forty-seven novels, many short stories, four travel books, a mass of essays and journalistic pieces, besides an admiring study of Thackeray (1879). Underlying his extraordinary discipline as a writer lay the experience of an early life blighted by the financial failures of his father which finally exiled his family to Belgium. But after these dark years, in 1847 Trollope emerged from poverty, illness and depression with a new sense of purpose, began surveying for the Post Office in Ireland, married happily, and published his first novel.

His best-known work, which only represents under a quarter of his total output, falls into three groups. The experience of a summer evening wandering among the surrounds of Salisbury Cathedral led to his writing *The Warden* (1855). This provided the basis from which Trollope was to write the loosely linked *Barsetshire Chronicles*: **Barchester Towers* (1857), *Doctor Thorne* (1858), *Framley Parsonage* (1861) and *The Small House at Allington* (1864). The final volume, *The Last Chronicle of Barset* (1867), a work partly set in London, is generally considered the finest. The 'Palliser' novels, named after its central character, the liberal politician Plantagenet Palliser, followed, including *Can You Forgive Her?* (1864), *Phineas Finn* (1869), *The Eustace Diamonds* (1873), *The Prime Minister* (1876) and *The Duke's Children* (1880). His novels showed a considerable range of subject. *Castle Richmond* (1860) is a tale of the Irish famine; *Orley Farm* (1862), published in shilling numbers with illustrations by Millais, was a tale of criminal intrigue in which a mother forges a will to benefit her son. His vision of England, like that of Dickens, darkened as the century progressed. *He Knew He Was Right* (1868) is a novel of dark obsession, and **The Way We Live Now* (1874–5) is a comprehensive condemnation of British life and culture. Readers who valued Trollope for the gentle humour of his Barchester series disliked it, and the circulation of his novels fell.

Trollope was mainly interested in the eccentricities of human nature and the moral complexity of social interaction. He paid relatively little attention to the outward appearance of his characters, and his plots, in which he professed little interest, were often conventional and peremptory. But he aimed to portray lives with which his readers could identify. With deceptive simplicity he wrote in his *Autobiography* (1883) that a novel 'should give a picture of common life enlivened with humour and sweetened with pathos. To make that picture worthy of attention, the canvas should be crowded with real portraits not of individuals known to the world, but of created personages impregnated with traits that are known' (ch. 7). In his imagination he knew his characters as 'speaking, moving, living creatures', and believed the novelist's task was to make them as real to his readers.

Academic opinion has been divided as to Trollope's literary status. His extraordinarily disciplined writing habits, which produced ten pages a day before going to work at the Post Office, reinforced the picture drawn in his own *Autobiography* of writing firstly for money, and his popularity with the general reading public has tended to alienate academics concerned with the 'art' of writing. In the 1950s, however, Trollope emerged as a central figure in the rediscovery of the Victorian period, and subsequent scholarship has demonstrated the depth of his understated artistry as a novelist.

Mrs T[homas] Humphry Ward [née Mary Augusta Arnold] (1851–1920)

The future Mrs Ward grew up in atmosphere of controversy. Her father, Thomas Arnold, the son of the headmaster of Rugby, lost his post as a teacher when he briefly converted to Roman Catholicism, and when he turned back to Anglicanism, allowing him to take up a post in Oxford, the family found the university torn by religious debate. All this stimulated Mary's precocious academic interest. Although there were as yet no women's colleges at Oxford, she took the opportunity of university life to educate herself into an authority on Spanish history and literature, worked for women's access to university education, and married an Oxford don. In 1881, moving to the wider intellectual sphere of London, she became an eminent journalist and literary hostess, and met *Henry James, who encouraged her writing.

Translating Amiel's *Journal intime* (1885), a work that hovered between faith and doubt, led her to write an apprentice novel, *Miss Bretherton* (1887). Her second, *Robert Elsmere* (1888), made a huge impression, and, with the help of a long review from Gladstone in *Nineteenth Century*, became one of the best-selling novels of the century. Elsmere, a sensitive young clergyman, wrestles with religious doubts planted by the contemporary philosophical, intellectual and historical debates he encountered studying at Oxford, a scene that directly draws on Mrs Ward's own experience. He abandoned creed for practical action, setting up 'the New Brotherhood of Christ', a commune working for the poor in East London. It succeeds, but he dies prematurely of tuberculosis and overwork, leaving his wife (who has remained an Anglican) to continue his work. A less successful sequel, *David Grieve*, followed in 1892. *Helbeck of Bannisdale* (1896) recalls her own father's crisis in its sensitive portrayal of the austere Roman Catholic Helbeck and Laura, who comes to share his love but, influenced by scepticism and Protestant faith, cannot accept his doctrine. She finally drowns herself, while he becomes a Jesuit.

Profits from her writing enabled her, like her characters Elsmere and Grieve, to establish a London 'settlement' for the working classes. She campaigned for evening crèches for working-class women, but she opposed woman's suffrage. Focused on the cross-currents of contemporary religious belief, her novels lacked the wider human vision required to survive her period.

H[erbert] G[eorge] Wells (1866–1946)

Wells' literary career was to be distinguished in several genres of fiction, but it is as a late Victorian that he is significant as the precursor of modern *science fiction. He himself noted that while 'hitherto, except in exploration fantasies, the fantastic element was brought in by magic . . . I made it as near actual theory as possible'. He combined scientific speculation with everyday experience and, like Swift in *Gulliver's Travels* (1726), a work that he admired, used fantastic situations to comment on contemporary society.

Wells wrote five minor masterpieces in as many years. *The Time Machine* (1895) took the concept of time's 'fourth dimension' to question Victorian concepts of human progress in the light of evolution and contemporary scientific theory. It was followed by *The Island of Dr Moreau* (1896), which shows evolution, accelerated through vivisection, creating not Utopia but a 'vision of the aimless torture in creation'. *The Invisible Man* (1897) is a wry comment on the isolating effect of scientific discovery, while in *The War of the Worlds* (1898) ruthless and virtually invulnerable space invaders expose the fragility of late nineteenth-century civilization. *When the Sleeper Wakes* (1899) describes the dreamer waking two hundred years in the future to find himself in a totalitarian capitalist state, a work that prefigures countless dystopias of the next century.

[William Hale White] Mark Rutherford (1831–1913)

White grew up in Bedford, the cradle of East Midlands dissent, and his novels offer a unique and objective record of the life, values and sensibility of a segment of Victorian society that usually lies outside the scope of Victorian literature, except in satire. White himself was intended for the Congregational ministry, but was expelled from his training college for questioning biblical fundamentalism. He found spiritual healing in the nature poetry of Wordsworth, and, settled in London, became a civil servant, journalist and a respected man of letters. But while deploring its decadence in the later century, he never lost his allegiance to the non-conformist culture of his youth, and his writing reflects its concern with scrupulous truth.

He came to fiction late, at the age of 50, doubly distanced behind a fictional identity, Mark Rutherford, and a pseudonymous 'editor', Reuben Shapcott. *The Autobiography of Mark Rutherford* (1881) is a thinly veiled confessional account of his early life and spiritual struggles. Its sequel, *Mark Rutherford's Deliverance* (1885), finds Rutherford working as a Parliamentary journalist, opening an (unsuccessful) religious mission in Drury Lane, and marrying Ellen, a girl from his provincial past. A grim life is ended by Rutherford's heart failure. His best novel, *The Revolution in Tanner's Lane* (1887), mordantly contrasts the integrity of nonconformist radicalism in Bedford in the political agitation of 1814–17 with its decline into shallow hypocrisy in the 1840s. It is distinguished by its empathetic and detailed account of the inner life of the working class, its reading, attitudes and circumstances, in two contrasting eras. Two domestic novels, *Miriam's Schooling* (1891) and *Catharine Furze* (1893), fill out his picture of East Midland village life. *Clara Hopwood* (1896), in which Clara's sister refuses to marry the unloved father of her child, reveals White's sympathy with feminist issues, and drew accusations of immorality.

Ellen Wood [Mrs Henry Wood, née Ellen Price] (1814–87)

Ellen Wood brought uncompromising moral purpose to bear on the form of the *sensation novel. Her first novel, *Danesbury House* (1860), which won a prize in a temperance competition, was a grim monitory tale of disasters wreaked by alcohol on a manufacturing family in a northern town, and her most famous, *East Lynne* (1861), dramatizes the appalling consequences of a woman's momentary impulsive lapse. The popularity of the latter work has distorted her literary reputation. In all, she published some twenty-seven novels, not including children's books and short stories, most of which have a quieter domestic focus. These illustrate her conviction that adversity brings moral strength, and typically are dynastic accounts of middle-class families. Two of her most popular are set in the same cathedral town. In *The Channings* (1862), a devoted family triumph over financial adversity and an unjust legal prosecution for being suspected of stealing a twenty-pound note. *Mrs Haliburton's Troubles* (1862) describes how a widow brings up her children in the face of being cheated out of her inheritance by the lawyer head of the affluent Dare family. Behind the criminal intrigue and emotional deathbed scenes that spice her fiction, Wood was an accurate and informed observer of critical issues facing middle-class family life, for men as well as for women.

Charlotte Mary Yonge (1823–1901)

Charlotte M. Yonge, the leading novelist of the Tractarian High Church movement, wrote nearly two hundred books, a quarter of which were fiction. She was strictly educated by her magistrate father in Otterbourne, near Winchester, reading the classics, sciences and modern languages, but no fiction other than the novels of Sir Walter Scott. Teaching in the village Sunday school from the age of 7, she relieved her childhood loneliness by telling stories. In 1835 John Keble, the doyen of the Oxford Movement, became a neighbour and friend, supervising her work and encouraging her to keep it free from overt moralizing.

Her first popular success, *The Heir of Redclyffe* (1853), ran through five editions in the first year of publication. *The Daisy Chain* (1856) was even more popular. This imagined the extended family life she never knew, having herself only one younger brother. Dr May, 'extremely skilful and clever, with a boyish character . . . ardent, sensitive and heedless', eschews a brilliant career in London to give time to his large family. But his wife is killed in a coach crash, leaving eleven children. The 'daisy' of the title is the youngest, Margaret, crippled in the crash, whose care provides a focus for the family. The eldest, Ethel, dedicates her life to building a church in the local village, although this consigns her to a single life. While there is little plot, the characters are clear-cut and sympathetically observed, creating a warm domestic chronicle with great appeal to its family-centred readership.

Declaring that 'history never failed to have great power over my imagination', she was a prolific writer of *historical novels and short stories. Among the most popular were *The Lances of Lynwood* (1855), in which Christian chivalry overcomes Norman barbarity, and *A Dove in the Eagle's Nest* (1866), a fifteenth-century tale of Germany, in which the 'dove' Cristina Sorel, seized by Baron Eberhard to nurse his sick daughter, civilizes the pagan household and secretly marries the baron's son. From 1851 Yonge edited and contributed to *The Monthly Packet* (1851–94,) a High Church periodical for younger readers, and the parental *Mothers in Council* (1890–1900), besides writing some enlightened and incisive literary essays.

Her strengths and weaknesses as a novelist come from her isolation from the intellectual turmoil of the period, removed from which she remained securely rooted in her High Anglican faith. Her friendships were strong but largely local: she only once ventured out of England. When she died in 1901 she was buried in Otterbourne churchyard, appropriately at the foot of a memorial cross to Keble.

Key Texts

Major Presences

John Bunyan, *The Pilgrim's Progress from this World to the Next* (Part I, 1678; Part II, 1684)

Bunyan's *Pilgrim's Progress* was widely read by all classes in the Victorian period, particularly in the earlier decades, and had a significant impact on the development of the novel particularly in the first half of the century (see above, pp. 31–2). It is in two parts, presented as a dream. The first and most important records the pilgrimage of Christian, who discovers he is living in the City of Destruction and sets off on a perilous journey in search of salvation. Each episode creates the vivid emblem of the stages of a Christian's life: the Wicket Gate leading to the Pilgrim's narrow path; the Slough of Despond; Giant Despair and Doubting Castle; the Valley of the Shadow of Death where Christian has to fight with Apollyon; Vanity Fair; the Delectable Mountains; and crossing the river of death to the Celestial City. The more leisurely Part II tells how Christian's wife Christiana, her children and fellow-Pilgrims follow Christian to salvation.

Bunyan's narrative drew its vigour from his own courageous life of struggle against religious persecution for his faith. His vision united the allegorical interpretation of the biblical Old and New Testaments found in the medieval miracle plays and William Langland's *Piers Ploughman* (1550) with the imaginative dimension of folklore. The purity and strength of the English vernacular, recently formalized in the 1611 Authorized Version of the Bible, sustained him through eight years in a Bedford jail and turned a semi-literate tinker into one of the supreme prose masters of the English language. Enhanced by George Cruikshank's striking illustrations, *Pilgrim's Progress* became embedded in the Victorian popular imagination.

Sir Walter Scott, *Waverley; or, 'Tis Sixty years Since* (1814)

It is difficult to select a single text from the *Waverley* novels with which to illustrate Scott's contribution to the Victorian novel. Most modern readers see *The Heart of Midlothian* (1818) as his masterpiece. Its heroine, Jeanie Dean, is Scott's most fully realized character, and the plot embodies his most complex examination of the compromises confronting the folk tradition in the face of modernity. But *Waverley* illustrates all of Scott's major qualities. It was his first novel, a sensational success that sold out three editions in its first year of publication, and critics compared each successive volume of the *Waverley* novels against it. Scott, who never put his name to his fiction, signed himself 'the author of *Waverley*'.

In its first chapter, Scott sets out his intention to write within strict bounds of realism and historical accuracy. 'By fixing, then, the date of my story sixty years before the present 1st November 1805, I would have my readers understand, that they will meet in the following pages neither a romance of chivalry, nor a tale of modern manners.' The story is set in the time of the 1745 Jacobite rebellion. Waverley becomes the 'ordinary' hero caught between conflicting phases of history and culture. After a desultory education in England in the charge of his uncle, Sir Edward Digby, a man of Jacobite leanings, he takes up a commission in the army. Travelling to Scotland he becomes embroiled in both sides of the conflict, a division of loyalties embodied in his competing affections for the domestic, gentle Rose Bradwardine and the passionate, Romantic Flora McIvor. A lucky chance enables him to redeem himself through an act of bravery, and escape execution for treason by the forces of the crown. He marries Rose, their marriage representing a compromise between Romantic idealism and the political realism of the new social order. Besides its immense impact on the development of the *historical novel, *Waverley* pioneered the English *Bildungsroman* (see above, pp. 36–8, 44).

Mary Shelley, *Frankenstein; or, the Modern Prometheus* (three volumes, 1818; significantly revised into one volume, 1831)

Mary Shelley's *Frankenstein* and Robert Louis Stevenson's *The Strange Case of Dr Jekyll and Mr Hyde* (1886) were the two great new myths created in the nineteenth century, and both originated in nightmares. Mary's original dream, of a sleeper awakening to see the Monster he had created staring in through the bed curtains, accreted to itself the various literary and philosophic debates of the Shelleys' circle, and was influenced by Erasmus Darwin and Sir Humphrey Davy's argument about the origins of life. Reviewing the novel in *Blackwood's Edinburgh Magazine*, Walter Scott praised it for its powerful exploration of 'the workings of the human mind'. In the revised 1831 edition, Mary Shelley edited out earlier scientific references, and Frankenstein's free will becomes more compromised by his flawed character and unleashed forces beyond his control.

Mary Shelley's image of the Monster focused the age's fears and uncertainties. In public debates and visual cartoons it embodied in turn slave emancipation, the Irish Fenians and Russian imperialism. Misnaming the Monster Frankenstein, *Elizabeth Gaskell used the story to plead for the industrial masses in *Mary Barton* (1848): 'Why have we made them what they are; a powerful monster, yet without the inner means for peace and happiness?' (ch. 15). It provided the organizing theme for Dickens' *Great Expectations* (1860–1). Its presence has been traced in fiction from Ahab's pursuit of the White Whale in Melville's *Moby Dick* (1851) to Kurtz confronting 'the horror' in Conrad's *Heart of Darkness* (1902). It became a foundation text for an emerging sub-genre of *'scientific romance'.

Literary critics of many persuasions, from Marxists to feminists, from followers of Freud to disciples of Nietzsche, have used Mary Shelley's fable. George Levine, in *The Endurance of Frankenstein* (1981), provocatively argued that Mary Shelley's work was central to the nineteenth-century novel, for the Monster gave visible form to the repressed psychic and emotional energies concealed within 'realist' imaginative creations.

Pierce Egan, Sr, *Life in London; or the Day and Night Scenes of Jerry Hawthorne Esq. and his elegant Friend Corinthian Tom accompanied by Bob Logic, the Oxonian in their Rambles and Sprees through the Metropolis*. With coloured plates by George and Isaac Robert Cruikshank (1820–1)

Pierce Egan, Sr's *Life in London* was a loosely linked series of urban sketches, recording the travels of a countryman, Jerry Hawthorne, and his streetwise friend Corinthian Tom through the sights of London, written in a tradition going back to Ned Ward's *London Spy* of 1698–1700. Its success was so great that when it first appeared, the monthly parts, each with the Cruikshanks' coloured etchings, required a second edition before the first run had ended. The Preface to *The Finish of Tom, Jerry and Logic* (1828) listed over a hundred plagiarisms, dramatizations and derivative publications. Dramatizations of *Life in London* dominated the London stage throughout the 1820s, with the stage designers 'realizing' the plates as stage settings, creating a theatrical iconography of London city life that was to survive into the twentieth century.

The organizing perspective of the serial, that 'THE EXTREMES, in every point of view, are daily to be met with in the Metropolis', shaped the urban novel. *Dickens followed Egan's part-issue method of publication for *Pickwick Papers* (1836–7), and Egan's use of a man about town, Tom, and an innocent observer, Jerry, may be one model for Dickens' Sam Weller and Pickwick. But Egan's biggest contribution to the urban novel was his enthusiasm for London, an interest that overrode concerns with class or morality. He proclaimed, 'there is not a *street* in London but what may be compared to a large or small volume of intelligence, abounding with anecdotes, incident and peculiarities', opening up the urban world for the writer and artist of Victorian England. The book's 'flash' slang, sensationally exploited by *William Harrison Ainsworth in *Rookwood* (1834), introduced vernacular idioms into contemporary plays and novels. A French translation of *Life in London* may have prompted Eugene Sue to write the *Mystères de Paris* (1842–3), which itself inspired *G. W. M. Reynolds' English bestseller, *The Mysteries of London* (1844–6). By mid-century, the work itself was becoming forgotten.

Thomas Carlyle, *Sartor Resartus* (serialized in *Fraser's Magazine* 1833–4; first volume edition, 1838)

Claiming to have been edited out of sacks of papers left by Professor Diogenes Teufelsdröckh (Devil's-dung), Carlyle's narrative was presented as 'indeed an "extensive Volume," of boundless, almost formless contents, a very Sea of Thought, neither calm nor clear, if you will; yet wherein the toughest pearl-diver may dive to his utmost depth'. With its puns, speculations, flights of fancy and recurrent images of light and dark, heat and cold, it embodied Carlyle's sense of a fragmented age. The first part examines the riddle of 'reality' (do appearances clothe reality, or are they reality itself?); the second progresses through 'the Everlasting Nay', the 'Centre of Indifference to the Everlasting Yea'; the third envisages the world 'reclothed' in idealistic vision. While it cannot be classed as a novel, Carlyle's idiosyncratic work was an important influence on the Victorian *Bildungsroman* (see above, p. 45).

Main Texts

Charles Dickens, *Oliver Twist; or the Parish Boy's Progress* (1837–8)

The first major Victorian novel, *Oliver Twist* began as a serial in *Bentley's Miscellany*, which Dickens was editing, in January 1837, and published in three volumes in 1838. With its brooding illustrations by Cruikshank, the novel startled its readers with its exposé of child exploitation and the criminal underworld. No one since Hogarth had shown the dark underbelly of respectable London so vividly. But its impact came from the way this world was seen through the eyes of Oliver, a vulnerable child. Although it is Dickens' most accessible story, its theme is ambiguous. In the 1838 Preface Dickens wrote: 'I wished to show, in little Oliver, the principle of Good surviving through every adverse circumstance, and triumphing at last.' Oliver feels loneliness, hunger and fear, but more usually serves as the novelist's point of view, his recurrent moments of waking out of sleep providing fresh visions of the worlds through which he moves. Simplified, Oliver attains mythical status, and his plea in the workhouse, 'Please sir, I want some more', has become the universal voice of deprived childhood. Opposing his innocence, Fagin becomes demonic.

Yet the book's moral and social perspectives are ambivalent. Few remember that Oliver is finally revealed as Edward Leaford, the victim of a plot to deprive him of his inheritance. The respectable world for which Oliver is destined is also that of the callous 'gentleman in the white waist-

Plate 3 George Cruikshank, 'THE FIENDS FRYING PAN or Annual Festival of Tom Foolery & Vice . . . In the AGE OF INTELLECT!!' (1832), from Cruikshank, *Scraps and Sketches* (1828–32), no. 23.

Cruikshank demonstrates the demonic vision of London's 'Vanity Fair' he imports into his *Oliver Twist* illustrations (see 'Oliver introduced to the Respectable Old Gentleman', overleaf).

coat', the workhouse system that starves him, offers him to a chimney sweep, and where Fang the magistrate condemns him as a thief without waiting for evidence. In contrast, Fagin's kitchen provides food and warmth, and his pupils enjoy moments of animal high spirits. Characterizations shift within the story itself: a violent murder turns Sikes from a two-dimensional melodramatic villain into the haunted soul Dickens obsessively impersonated in his public readings. Nancy, a common prostitute, becomes an icon of self-sacrificing womanhood. Dickens attempted to resolve the novel's ambiguities by repeated revisions to the text, suppressing details of Nancy's occupation and minimizing Fagin's demonic and Jewish associations. But neither the rural subplot of the

George Cruikshank

Oliver introduced to the respectable Old Gentleman.

Plate 4 George Cruikshank, 'Oliver introduced to the Respectable Old Gentleman', from Charles Dickens, *Oliver Twist* (1837–8), ch. 8.

The scene with its hellish atmosphere has echoes of Cruikshank's earlier etching, 'THE FIENDS FRYING PAN' (see previous page). Fagin is now the demonic figure holding a frying pan over the glowing fire, while his fork points to a broadsheet of three hanging criminals, intimating the future fate of his pupils. The ominous bottle beside it adds the social dimension of alcoholism Cruikshank was to develop in his later sequence, *The Bottle* (1847).

Maylie family, nor that of Oliver's Gothic half-brother Monks, could be convincingly integrated into the story.

For all its inconsistencies, *Oliver Twist* placed social concerns at the heart of the emergent Victorian novel. It created a visual panorama of London that led Eisenstein to claim it as the precursor of modern cinematic technique, and its larger than life characters, hallucinatory atmosphere and melodramatic situations have extended its life into a long succession of stage, film and television versions.

G. W. M. Reynolds, *The Mysteries of London* (1844–6)

With its continuation *The Mysteries of the Court of London* (1844–56), *The Mysteries of London* is the longest and probably most popular single Victorian work of fiction. It contained four and a half million words and was claimed to have sold, including translations, over a million copies. Its subject and staccato style were indebted to Eugene Sue, whose serial *Les Mystères de Paris* had run in the *Journal des débats* from 1842 to 1843. But where Sue created bizarre fantasy, Reynolds wrote in the genres of melodrama and sensational journalism. Central plots loosely unified each series: in the first series the lives of two parting brothers, who have agreed to meet in twelve years to compare careers. The noble Richard Markham follows a path of virtue, surviving villainous plots and persecutions, while the depraved Eugene seduces and schemes his way under a succession of aliases. His valet finally stabs him to death, while Richard ends an Italian duke with a lovely wife. But the main interests of the story lay in the sensational lives of a succession of low-life characters, and in the journalistic exposés of such social scandals as grave-robbing, exploited needlewomen and child labour in the mines.

Reynolds' wordy style and the length of his novels deter modern readers. Yet they had an influence on the urban fiction of better writers. The urban 'mysteries' cult of the 1840s reflected the alienation of city life for the mass population, and Reynolds' attacks on aristocratic privilege, bankers, clergy and economic exploitation formed a bridge between the old radicalism of Cobbett and Paine and the new socialism of Marx and Engels.

Geraldine Endsor Jewsbury, *Zoe. The History of Two Lives* (1845)

Jewsbury's historical novel, set in eighteenth-century Europe, centres on the passionate, vivacious Zoe, the illegitimate daughter of an English army officer and a young Greek woman he rescues from pirates in the Aegean, given a classical education by her uncle, a clergyman. In order to escape spinsterhood Zoe marries Mr Gifford, a rich older widower. But she subsequently falls in love with Everard, a Catholic priest wrestling with his faith. His unconsummated passion for Zoe drives him from the priesthood in despair. On the death of her husband, a love letter from Everard calls Zoe to his sickbed, but he dies before she arrives. The novel, with its frank portrayal of sexual passion (Everard dramatically declares his desires after rescuing Zoe from a fire) and its combined themes of religious doubt and the emotional needs of women, caused a critical sensation. Zoe's choice of marriage to the elderly Gifford has been seen as an original for Dorothea and Casaubon in George Eliot's *Middlemarch (1871–2), but Gifford is sympathetically portrayed, and of a very different character.

Charlotte Brontë, *Jane Eyre. An Autobiography* (1847)

The novel is characterized by an unusual intensity, constantly moving from Jane Eyre's progress in life to the inner pilgrimage of her spiritual life, with both meeting in her final union with Rochester. The narrative, which is discussed elsewhere in this study (see pp. 52–4), was immensely popular from its first appearance, and was one of the novels all Victorians would have known from childhood. Uniting the actual domestic life and trials of a governess with the Byronic figure of Rochester and the mysteries of Thornfield Hall, the novel was the first work of fiction to use Gothic conventions to give imaginative expression to the emotional needs of a 'real' woman. *Jane Eyre* was a seminal work in the development of what Ellen Moers in *Literary Women* (1972) called the 'Feminine Gothic', which created a basis for the *'sensation novel' of the 1860s. Critics have seen the mad wife concealed in the attic as the embodiment of the repressed identity of women in the middle-class household. Her Caribbean identity has also been taken to represent the rejection of the racial 'Other' within the imperial system (see pp. 195–6): Jean Rhys, herself born in the West Indies, wrote *Wide Sargasso Sea* (1960) to tell the story from Bertha's point of view. However, in the Brontës' imaginative world the Caribbean had appeared as a setting for violent passions in their childhood narratives of Gondal and Angria, in which Branwell had been closely involved. Now Branwell was drinking himself to death behind the closed doors of the isolated Haworth parsonage. His swollen face and *delirium tremens* may also have contributed to the horrifying image of Rochester's deserted wife.

Emily Brontë, *Wuthering Heights* (1847)

The plot of Emily Brontë's violent, powerful novel is complex but precisely drawn. It falls into three sections working out the theme of thwarted passion, revenge and final reconciliation in two generations of a family. Mr Earnshaw brings Heathcliff, a mysterious waif, into his family. Heathcliff enters a wild, intense childhood romance with the daughter, Cathy, but he is bullied and humiliated by her brother, Hindley. Heathcliff and Cathy visit Thrushcroft Grange in the valley below, home to the wealthy Linton family and a pastoral contrast to Wuthering Heights. The son, Edgar Linton, befriends Cathy. After the death of his father, Hindley Earnshaw returns with a wife to take over the farm, further maltreating Heathcliff: Hindley's wife dies after bearing a son, Hareton. Cathy agrees to marry Edgar Linton, prompting Heathcliff to leave in despair, without hearing Cathy declare her perpetual love for him.

The second section involves Heathcliff's revenge. He returns mysteriously educated and wealthy, ruins Hindley through gambling and drink, and mistreats, before finally marrying, Edgar's sister Isabella. Cathy, sick with brain fever, meets Heathcliff alone, and the passionate scene precipitates her death. She has just given birth to a daughter, also called Cathy. Isabella escapes from Wuthering Heights and bears Heathcliff a son, Linton. Hindley dies, leaving Heathcliff owner of the Heights and guardian to young Hareton.

The last phase concerns the third generation, and reconciliation. Heathcliff forces his son Linton to marry the younger Cathy. But by now his enemies are dead, and his demonic passions burnt out. Lockwood, visiting the Heights, in a terrifying scene encounters the ghost of the first Cathy crying to enter, and Heathcliff later is found dead by the open window. Local legends tell of the lovers wandering the heath. The second Cathy, widowed, tames and marries Hareton.

The novel subtly uses different views and perspectives. It opens out like a nest of Chinese boxes, with the passionate voices of the main characters mediated through the narrative of their matter-of-fact family nurse and servant, Nelly Dean, which in turn is relayed through the journal of a repressed, emotionally brittle outsider, Lockwood, who at its climax himself enters into the story. None of these, however, is a totally reliable witness. The novel is realistic in setting, and visionary in theme; it begins with a precise recorded date, '1801', and ends with intimations of timeless spirits. It revolves around universals – human passions, rock, heath, rain, wind and the revolving seasons. Yet it is a family saga, precisely plotted in time and place over forty-six years. With its roots in Emily's love of poetry and drama rather than in prose precedents, it remains resistant to conventional critical approaches and is, wrote Dorothy van Ghent in *The English Novel* (1953), 'of all English novels, the most treacherous for the analytical understanding to approach' (p. 153).

W. M. Thackeray, *Vanity Fair. A Novel without a Hero* (1847–8)

Charlotte Brontë, dedicating **Jane Eyre* (1847) to Thackeray, declared that 'no commentator on his writing has yet found the comparison that suits him, or the terms which rightly characterise his talent'. With its subtitle, *Vanity Fair* proclaimed its departure from the normal novel form. Although the story revolves around five main actors, none can be termed heroic. It also lacks a conventional plot. There are no hidden wills, mysteries of parentage, development of character or progress from rags to riches. Marriage, the standard culmination of the Victorian novel, comes early in the marriage of Amelia to George Osborne, and Thackeray notes the absurdity of thinking that in life 'wife and husband had nothing to do but link each other's arms together, and wander gently downhill towards old age in happy and perfect fruition' (ch. 26). Good is not rewarded, and pleasures are usually alloyed with disappointment; dark moments are relieved by comedy, and heartlessness by generous impulse, and the tone is wry observation rather than cynical rejection.

The novel chronicles the English middle classes evolving from the Regency towards the Victorian era in the years 1813–30. The Crawley family represent a decaying landed aristocracy; the Sedleys in their comfortable Bloomsbury a new class that make their money from stock-broking, their obese Anglo-Indian son Jos a hangover from the wealthy Raj. The Osbornes typify the rising wealthy merchant class. The society lacks moral direction. If the novel has no hero, it has a striking anti-heroine, Becky Sharp, the green-eyed orphan daughter of a derelict artist and a French opera girl. Her wits honed by the hard graft of poverty, she is armed with spirit, unscrupulous ambition and, although not pretty, she has abundant sexuality. Her devices can backfire and Thackeray never hides Becky's unattractive qualities. But the 'good' Amelia is also compromised: she only marries George because she does not want to lose him, and her self-absorbed widowhood stands in sharp contrast to Becky's life-asserting resilience.

Where Dickens or George Eliot would have woven the social panorama into a narrative structure, in Thackeray's story characters appear and disappear with the inconsequence of actual experience. They also remain largely independent of Thackeray's authorial voice. He rarely penetrates their consciousness, and if we do overhear their thoughts, as in Becky's famous reflection, 'I think I could be a good woman on two thousand a year', the words 'I think' remind us that it is only another piece of uncertain evidence of life's ultimately unknowable diversity.

W. M. Thackeray, *The History of Pendennis. His Fortunes and Misfortunes, his Friends and his Greatest Enemy* (1848–50)

On first appearance Thackeray's partly autobiographical *Bildungsroman* sold between 8,000 and 10,000 monthly numbers, more than **Vanity Fair* (1847–8), and the work held a central place in the affections of

Thackeray's readers. The success of *Vanity Fair* had freed Thackeray from financial constraints and established him as a major author. Where the earlier work gives an outsider's view of society, *Pendennis* is written from within. Thackeray designed a cover for the part issues showing a young man being tugged by wife and children on one side, and a fish-tailed siren and horned satyr on the other, indicating the book's moral concerns. Arthur Pendennis, who first appears aged 16, is the basically honourable son of a deceased prosperous chemist, but is impulsive, self-centred and spoiled by his adoring mother. He survives the temptations offered by a coarse stage actress, a flirtatious porter's daughter, Fanny Bolton, and the attractive, manipulative Blanche Amory, before, in a melodramatic climax, choosing Laura Bell, his patient, adopted half-sister who has loved him from boyhood.

Like *David Copperfield* (1849–50), Thackeray's novel traces the moral education of a young man's heart. Far more than *Copperfield*, however, *Pendennis* records England changing as it moves towards the Victorian period. As the book opens in the 1820s, Arthur's conservative uncle, Major Pendennis, serves as guide and preserver to him and his mother. But later we see his moral corruption, and Arthur glimpses the major and his ageing cronies through the window of their St James' club like 'a chamber of horrors' (ch. 36). Arthur, by birth one of the rising middle classes, must find a new definition for the term 'gentleman'. Thackeray also assesses the changing role of the author. After a largely wasted 'Oxbridge' education, Arthur works his way into a literary London dominated by ephemeral serials and fashionable novels. Like Dickens, Jerrold and Thackeray himself, it is his only immersion in the realities of London life that brings him respectability as a novelist. Even Major Pendennis is forced to admit 'the times are changed now – there's a run upon literature – clever fellows get into the best houses in town, begad' (ch. 36) – clever fellows like Thackeray himself.

Charles Dickens, *Bleak House* (1852–3)

Bleak House, the first of the dark symbolic works of Dickens' maturity, was an experiment in fiction uniting a multiplicity of characters and subplots within the dual perspectives of two narrators, the omniscient authorial voice in the present, and first-person recollections of a participant in the action, Esther Summerson. The opening scene depicts the fog irradiating out from its centre in the Court of Chancery, as if London and England around it were relapsing into prehistoric slime, an image that later in the book elides into that of vaporous clouds infected with cholera. The novel is, for Dickens, an unusually direct satire on the times. The floundering Russell government is reflected in the antics of Buffy, Coodle, Doodle and Foodle; the fragmentation of the Church in the evangelical bombast of Mr Chadband, the High Church foppery of Mrs Pardiggle and the moral myopia of the missionary activist, Mrs Jellyby. London is littered with relics of the past (see above, p. 42). The animal names Dickens gives the members of the legal profession suggest a predatory jungle – Vholes, Weevle, Guppy and the indefinably monstrous Tulkinghorn. Abutting the 'blind' wall of Chancery, the stifling rituals of the court of justice are parodied in the paper and waste repository of Krook, who, despite collecting legal documents, cannot read.

The story pulsates between immediate action and prevailing mood and atmosphere. Esther Summerson, the novel's first-person narrator, is its moral touchstone: like Oliver Twist, she is the 'Principle of Good' surviving all. The novel's subplots are held together within a precisely mapped area of legal London, and by a web of chance meetings and relationships within it. Probing the story's mysteries is Inspector Bucket, the English novel's first detective. Esther finds her mother, Lady Dedlock, a figure also emotionally crippled by society, and marries the doctor Alan Woodcourt, a practical healer living in a diseased society. The name of her guardian, Jarndyce, which suggests 'jaundiced', and the title 'Bleak House' given to Esther's two homes, hint at the reserve necessary for survival in the false optimism of mid-Victorian England. *Bleak House* was a novel ahead of its time. Although it attracted initial sales of 34,000 monthly parts, reviews were mixed. Modern criticism, however, has claimed it as Dickens' greatest work, the subject of intensive study for its form, symbolic complexity and contemporary relevance.

Charlotte Brontë, *Villette* (1853)

'So curious a novel as *Villette* seldom comes before us,' wrote *The Athenaeum* reviewer of Charlotte Brontë's last novel, and this extraordinary work has intrigued readers ever since. What plot there is – the love affair between the teacher Lucy Snowe and the waspish school proprietor M. Paul Emanuel, and a Gothic subplot of a spectral nun – appear to lead nowhere. The first-person narrator remains ambiguous. Lucy Snowe tells her story in old age, a white cap on her white hair, and Lucy's surname, Charlotte Brontë told her publisher, signified her cold detachment. But M. Paul, like most readers, finds Lucy fiery (ch. 27). Both reticent and enterprising, a congenital depressive with an intense passion for life, she remains an enigma. 'Lucy, I wonder if anyone will ever comprehend you altogether?' asks Paulina (ch. 37).

Charlotte Brontë's narrative gives no answers, but draws the reader into Lucy's own passionate quest to find meaning in a life of tragic frustration. 'Villette' translates as 'little town', and Charlotte Brontë used her memories of Brussels to create an alien community, neither village nor city, in which Lucy must find her independent way. Watching and being observed is a constant motif. Madame Beck investigates Lucy's belongings, thinking her asleep, but Lucy is awake, watching Madame Beck. Lucy's search for identity is projected onto scenes and objects. Costumed for a part in M. Paul's play, Lucy tries on another identity; her reaction to pictures in the museum externalizes her revulsion at sensuality; the acting of Vashti reveals her ambivalence towards physical passion. Lucy and M. Paul duel against each other, patience against choler, cool against fiery, Protestant against Catholic. In doing so they become mirror images: as M. Paul insists, 'there is an affinity between us. Do you see it, mademoiselle, when you look in the glass?' (ch. 31).

The dream-like intensity of the narrative dissolves the borders between vision and reality that alternate throughout Charlotte Brontë's earlier *Jane Eyre* (1847). At the climax of the novel, Lucy's drug-enhanced vision illuminates the nocturnal Villette as a bright carnival, creating the obverse to the night-side depression of her waking day. Tempest and shipwreck move beyond metaphor to become the very experience of spiritual crisis, and in the final pages actual storms appear to seal the fate of M. Paul. But Charlotte Brontë does not break the tension by resolving the ending. Brontë believed that the disciplined spirit does not depend on the accidents of fortune for a meaningful closure. Lucy declares that 'I see no reason why I should be of the few favoured. I believe that this life is not all; neither the beginning nor the end.' That Charlotte Brontë brings the reader to share Lucy's intimation of immortality is one achievement of this unique novel.

Elizabeth Gaskell, *North and South* (1854–5)

In her second industrial novel Gaskell aimed to show a greater under-standing of the mill owners' position than she had shown in the earlier *Mary Barton* (1848). Milton is still recognizably Manchester, but the novel moves away from the documentary approach of the earlier book. A reli-gious crisis leads Margaret Hale's father, an Anglican clergyman, to leave the idyllic southern village of Helstone to find teaching in the North Midland industrial city of Milton. There Margaret makes friends with a mill hand, Nicholas Higgins, and his daughter, Mary, who is dying with factory-congested lungs. She is also drawn to the mill owner John Thorn-ton, who, with his forbidding mother, represents the hard aggressive spirit of the Industrial Revolution, but whose cultural potential is shown in his interest in learning the Greek classics. When a labour dispute ends in a lockout, Margaret heroically saves Thornton from the rioters. Later Mar-garet returns to Helstone, but is now no longer satisfied with its rural decadence. She receives an unexpected legacy, and after saving Thornton from bankruptcy they marry. Thornton and his workers resolve to settle disputes by discussion.

Milton, the central location, is set against the Hales' rural home in southern Helstone (based on Hollingbourne in Hampshire), while behind them stand London, the commercial and legal centre, and Oxford, source of the classical culture that Mr Hale uses to mediate between north and south. The contrasting regions are distinguished by Mrs Gaskell's eye for local detail and her interest in dialect speech. But they are also seen through the changing consciousness of Margaret as she gains a more mature understanding of their realities. The narrative has some weak-nesses of plotting, and even Victorian readers complained of the large number of deaths in the narrative. But Gaskell's understated art, and her sympathetic understanding of character and place, give the work endur-ing interest.

Anthony Trollope, *Barchester Towers* (1857)

Barchester Towers, the second novel in Trollope's *Barchester Chronicles*, was the first to establish his popularity with the general reading public. Quintessential Trollope, it exhibits his comic spirit at its most generous. Although the darker *Last Chronicle of Barset* (1866–7) is a profounder work, it remains the most accessible and most carefully crafted of his *provincial novels. The story is a sequel to *The Warden* (1855), in which Septimus Harding resigned his post as warden to the town's almshouses (see above, pp. 55–7). 'Towers' suggests a fortified bastion, and the Barchester ecclesiastical community comes under siege when the new Liberal government imposes Dr Proudie as bishop instead of the local candidate, the Broad Church Archdeacon Grantly. Proudie is dominated by his aggressive, vulgar, evangelical wife, whose character Trollope never softens by giving her a Christian name. A fierce opponent of anything pleasurable, particularly on the Sabbath, Mrs Proudie (Prude) became a byword for censorious repression in mid-Victorian society. The new bishop's loathsome chaplain is Obadiah Slope, literally oleaginous with his clammy hands and greased hair, whose evangelical piety is a cover for social and marital ambitions. Another intruder is the daughter of Dr Stanhope, the Signora Madeline Vesey Neroni, who only appears in public, seductively dressed, on a sofa, kept within the bounds of the novel's propriety only by her crippled legs. She is more than a match for Mrs Proudie, but because she lacks any moral responsibility the moral touchstone for the book is the Reverend Francis Arabin, the energetic and eloquent High Churchman whom Archdeacon Grantly calls in to counter the faction of Proudie and Slope.

A *fête champêtre* organized by Wilfred Thorne, squire of Ullathorne, and his sister, who represent the old feudal order, provides a set piece that brings together the different elements in the community. Slope has his ears boxed by Harding's daughter, Eleanor Bold, and, with his ambitions of becoming dean thwarted, leaves Barchester in disgrace. Harding refuses the deanship in the interest of Arabin, who marries Eleanor. Even the disputed position of warden to Hiram's Hospital is settled when Mr Quiverful, a penurious curate with fourteen children to feed, is given the sinecure, making it the one Barchester novel to have an optimistic ending.

George Eliot, *Adam Bede* (1859)

Adam Bede is set in the 'Eden-like peace and loveliness' of Hayslope in Loamshire. Adam, a sturdy, honest carpenter, blindly loves Hetty Sorrel, who works as a dairymaid on the farm of her aunt and uncle Poyser. But the pretty, self-centred Hetty prefers the dashing regimental captain Arthur Donnithorne, and, unknown to Adam, she allows Arthur to seduce her. Adam violently persuades Arthur to end the relationship, but Hetty finds she is pregnant, and, failing to find Arthur, kills her baby. Discovered, she is sentenced to hang. Dinah Morris, a Methodist preacher, spends a night with Hetty, bringing her to confession and inner peace. On the scaffold Arthur saves Hetty, bringing a reprieve, but she is deported and dies in exile. Adam marries the saintly Dinah, while the desolated Arthur goes abroad seeking atonement.

The novel draws on George Eliot's warm childhood memories of Warwickshire. Adam is based on her worthy estate manager father. Her aunt Elizabeth Evans, a Methodist preacher, in 1802 consoled a condemned murderer, as did Dinah. The novel contains Eliot's declaration of interest in the dense detail she admired in Dutch painting, and the writing creates the glowing world, at once sensuous and unsentimental, of a community based on physical labour, closeness to nature and simple faith. This contrasts with the grim neighbourhood of Stonyshire and the mining town of Snowfield. Much recent criticism has focused on Hetty Sorrel, whose potential as a character appears to be abandoned by George Eliot once she has fallen into temptation. Raising questions of narrative structure, realism and moral point of view, the novel, which launched Eliot's career, has been the subject of critical debate since its original publication.

Wilkie Collins, *The Woman in White* (serialized in *All the Year Round*, 1859–60; three-volume edition, 1860)

Coming at the beginning of the **'sensation novel'* vogue, *The Woman in White*, with the clever plotting of the story and its use of multiple viewpoints, was widely influential. As Henry James noted, 'To Mr Collins belongs the credit of having introduced into fiction those most mysterious of mysteries which are at our own doors. This innovation gave a new impetus to the literature of horrors.' Collins used the 'realistic' format of law court evidence, contrasting witnesses, journals, letters and even a doctor's report. Yet the novel is Gothic in its use of atmospheric settings – Limmeridge Hall in Cumberland has echoes of Charlotte Brontë's Thornfield Hall, Blackwater Park of Anne Radcliffe's castles, while the menacing villain Count Fosco has been compared to Radcliffe's evil monk, Schedoni, in *The Italian* (1797).

No summary can do justice to the complexity of the plot, or to Collins' skill in unravelling it. At the centre is the dastardly Sir Percival Glyde, contriving with the sinister Count Fosco to deprive the beautiful Laura Fairlie of her fortune, first by marriage, and then by engineering her apparent death. Laura's feisty half-sister, Marian Halcombe, and Walter Hartright, who is in love with Laura, defeat their plots. Parallels and contrasts intensify the story's mysteries. Laura looks like her half-sister Anne Catherick, while she is the physical and psychological opposite to the masculine Marian, who is in turn opposed to the Machiavellian Count Fosco.

Collins wrote that the vulnerability of identity in the face of evil was basic to the story: 'The destruction of [Laura's] identity represents the first division of the story; the recovery of her identity marks a second division' ('How I Write My Books', *The Globe*, 26 Nov. 1887). Her story is mediated through contrasting sensibilities, including those of the terrified Anne Catherick, the neurasthenic Mr Fairley and the pragmatic Marian Halcombe. The story reflects current concerns. The nature of insanity, and the relationship between physical health, nervous disorders and the strains of 'modern' life, were being discussed in the issues of *All the Year Round* in which *The Woman in White* appeared. Although the novel ends with the happy marriage of Walter to Laura, and the death of Fosco, Collins' tale disturbs rather than assures.

Charles Dickens, *Great Expectations* (1860–1)

Magwitch's terrifying apparition in the lonely churchyard introduces a brilliant succession of scenes redolent of Dickens' own childhood memories of Kent, and perfectly modulated to reveal the developing consciousness of the impressionable Pip. The characters and situations are drawn with masterly economy, and the story moves at a pace Dickens never bettered. The intricate plot, which aligns the work with the *sensation novel, is constructed like a set of Chinese boxes, reduplicating the theme of Frankenstein's creation of his Monster. Compeyson creates the time-warped Monster Miss Havisham by leaving her at the marriage altar, Miss Havisham shapes Estella to break men's hearts, Estella breaks Pip's. Compeyson makes Magwitch a criminal outcast; Magwitch makes Pip into a 'gentleman' as a surrogate self. Even Pip's London servant, his new identity formed by fashionable livery, is described as created to be Pip's 'avenging phantom' (ch. 27).

The linked stories serve to examine the nature of innocence and responsibility. Dickens' earlier work idealized childhood. But in Pip, childish 'innocence' is corrupted by egotism, leading him to despise Joe and lose the hand of Biddy. Orlick serves as Pip's dark alter ego, carrying out the violent actions that Pip is too 'respectable' to contemplate, notably the attack on Pip's bullying sister. The story reflects Dickens' inward turmoil at the time of the break-up of his marriage, and his attraction to the young actress Ellen Ternan, whose name is echoed in 'Estella'. Published shortly after Samuel Smiles' celebration of personal achievement, *Self-Help* (1859), had become a bestseller, the novel identifies true moral values as lying in the self-effacing honesty of Joe and Biddy, and in the unostentatious hard work of Herbert Pocket, with whom Pip goes into partnership. Dickens originally intended Pip to lose Estella; but on the urging of Bulwer Lytton he substituted a more optimistic, though still ambiguous, ending: looking into the future, Pip foresees 'no shadow of another parting from her'.

Mrs Henry [Ellen] Wood, *East Lynne* (1861)

Ellen Wood's best-selling novel revolves around the high-spirited Lady Isobel Vane's marriage to the high-principled lawyer Archibald Carlyle. Falsely suspecting her husband's unfaithfulness, an uncontrolled impulse leads her to elope with a raffish acquaintance of her early years. Carlyle divorces her, and later remarries. Deserted by her seducer, her face disfigured in a train crash, Isobel returns disguised by green spectacles to East Lynne, where as a governess she nurses her own child. The boy dies in her arms. Isobel confesses all, and Carlyle pardons her before she too dies. The novel sold over 400,000 copies in Bentley's edition alone, and the stage version, which invented the famous line 'Dead! Dead! And never called me mother', became a staple of touring repertory companies.

But the novel is more than sensationalism. Ellen Wood was morally aware and socially observant. As Lyn Pykett has pointed out in *The Improper Feminine* (1992), Carlyle as a successful lawyer embodies the middle-class ideal of success through conscientious work. In marrying Lady Isobel, the daughter of the profligate Lord Mountsevern, he hopes to set up its ideal, the respectable home, to bring order, grace and comfort to a commercial life. Lady Isobel, with her moral weakness, fails him, eloping with an aristocratic wastrel; in Barbara Hare, Carlyle's second wife, a model of domestic virtue replaces her. Lady Isobel is compared to other women's identities in the book, and she herself progresses through a series of roles from dependent wife, fallen woman to again (if suffering and unacknowledged) mother. The central tension in the novel, one felt strongly by its many readers, comes from the fact that Wood's uncompromising condemnation of Isobel's moral lapse coexists with powerful sympathy for her sufferings.

Mary Elizabeth Braddon, *Lady Audley's Secret* (1861–2)

Together with Wilkie Collins' *The Woman in White* (1860), to which it was indebted, *Lady Audley's Secret* was a foundation text for the *'sensation novel'. It was constantly reprinted, and, like *East Lynne* (1861), became a stock subject for stage melodrama. Stage versions simplified her character into that of a villainess, but in the novel Lady Audley is ambivalent. The story, like that of *Jane Eyre* (1847), is of a vulnerable governess attracted to an older, wealthy man. But Lady Audley has none of Jane's innocence. When she marries the elderly Sir Audley, she takes elaborate steps to conceal her earlier existence as the wife of an army dragoon who deserted her for the Australian goldfields, and whom she believes is dead. Although writing at great speed, Braddon unpacks the layers of mystery surrounding the identity of her main character with considerable skill. Lady Audley's disintegration as a woman is paired with the developing masculinity of Sir Audley's barrister nephew, Robert, who begins as a desultory observer and becomes a committed sleuth. In what was to become the stock business of the sensation novel, the story juxtaposes crime, deception and bigamy with 'respectable' domestic life. 'No species of crime has ever been committed in the worst Rookeries about Seven Dials that has not also been done in the face of . . . rustic calm' (ch. 7), and the benign exterior of Audley Hall hides a Gothic tunnel which leads to the secrets of Lady Audley's boudoir. In Lucy Graham, Braddon subverted the models of the middle-class domestic novel (see above, pp. 78–9), and was careful not to identify the nature of Lucy's 'madness', leaving the reader uncertain whether this is the result of hereditary insanity or her rebellion against the restricted lives open to women in Victorian society.

Charles Kingsley, *The Water-Babies. A Fairy Tale for a Land Baby* (1863)

Tom, a chimney sweep terrorized by Grimes his master, falls down a chimney at Harthover House and finds himself in the bedroom of the squire's daughter, Ellie. Horrified to realize he is dirty, he leaps into a stream, but, in a parable of baptism, finds himself not drowned but reborn. Tom sets off on underwater adventures in which he meets Ellie, sees Grimes punished (he has to sweep out Mount Aetna), and undergoes his moral education. One of the most extraordinary fantasies of the nineteenth century, Kingsley's fable combines, in a surrealist dream, personifications from Bunyan, Blake's vision of innocence and experience, satire, religious debates, Darwinian theories of evolution, and such social issues as child employment and the provision of clean water. While no one could imitate it, *The Water-Babies* encouraged the movement into worlds of fantasy that characterized the novel in the later decades of the century.

Lewis Carroll [Charles Lutwidge Dodgson], *Alice's Adventures in Wonderland* (1865), *Through the Looking Glass; and What Alice Found There* (1871)

In the *Alice* books, the journeys underground and through the looking glass become tropes by which Carroll interrogates the issues that were also preoccupying the 'realist' novel, from the meaning of history and biography to scientific discovery and Darwinian theories of evolution. The books' genius lies in the completeness with which Carroll abrogates the point of view of a 30-year-old male academic for the gaze of a pre-pubescent girl. Alice challenges the conventional images of the child, curious but independent, neither the unregenerate child of noncon-formist faith nor the Romantic figure of innocence. The dream frame-work of *Alice's Adventures in Wonderland* has been compared to that of Bunyan's **Pilgrim's Progress* (1678, 1684), with the Cheshire Cat an evanes-cent evangelist. But Alice has no sense of sin, there is no preordained direction, and moral progress is exchanged for the chance manoeuvres of games. The climax of the first book comes when Alice, by asserting her identity, turns the court that is judging her into its original form, playing cards; in the second book, progress becomes a game of chess. Carroll was fortunate in having one of the era's finest illustrators, Tenniel, to visually interpret his imagination. The *Alice* books live on in Tenniel's pictures as vividly as in Carroll's text.

Ouida [Marie Louise de la Ramée], *Under Two Flags* (1867)

In this, the most popular of Ouida's novels, the 'two flags' are of Britain and France. The Hon. Bertie Cecil, an insouciant, fearless Life Guards-man and heir to the estates of Royallieu, is plotted against by an envious younger brother and betrayed by Princess Corona, whom he loves and saves from ignominy. A paragon of self-sacrificing virtue, rather than expose the princess he allows himself to be presumed dead, and takes a second life as Louis Victor, a common soldier in the French Foreign Legion serving in Algeria. Cigarette, a dark-skinned, gamine camp follower, herself a heroic if uncommissioned warrior, falls in love with him. Bertie defends the honour of Princess Corona against a superior officer, and is condemned to death for insubordination. The splendid Cigarette, although aware she is surrendering him to her rival, reveals Bertie's aristocratic identity. She saves him on the point of his execution by throwing herself in front of the firing squad, and dies in his arms. Bertie is reconciled to his repentant brother, assumes his noble title, and marries Corona. Told in a breathless style, full of action set against backdrops of high society and stirring military exploits, with heightened melodramatic characters and extravagant moral gestures, Ouida's fiction pioneered a new dimension of romance in the novel in ways that look forward to early cinema, where the book became a successful film.

R[ichard] D[oddridge] Blackmore, *Lorna Doone, A Romance of Exmoor* (1869)

Blackmore wrote *Lorna Doone*, the most popular *regional romance of the century, out of childhood memories of northwest Devon, recollections enhanced by his precocious interest in local folklore, history and the natural world. The story, which is set in the seventeenth century, is told through the consciousness of John Ridd, a forthright yeoman who comes to maturity through the book. Ridd farms Plover's Barrow, a pastoral world threatened by the outlawed Doone clan in their hidden moorland glen. There Ridd courts the radiant Lorna, stolen as a child and reared as a Doone. He rescues her from marriage to their villainous chief, the giant Carver Doone, and discovering her noble birth, believes her to be beyond his reach. He becomes involved in the Monmouth Rebellion and narrowly escapes execution as a rebel, but a chance to serve the king brings him release and a knighthood. At Ridd's marriage to Lorna, Carver shoots and wounds her, but after a furious chase, he is caught by Ridd and dies in a bog. The couple's story ends happily.

Victorian readers admired its powerful evocation of place. The high-born Lorna's associations with fertile nature were seen to give her mythical status, while her marriage to John Ridd celebrated the triumph of Saxon yeomanry over political tyranny. The hard-won simplicity of the action-filled narrative, which made it so popular with its first readers, has detracted from its literary status today, and although it has never been out of print, it is now read largely as a children's book.

George Eliot, *Middlemarch. A Study of Provincial Life* (six parts, 1871–2; one-volume edition, 1874)

Based on long and painstaking research, the novel recreates the society, culture and ideas of an isolated Midland community in the 1830s, a period at the cusp of wide changes creating the Victorian period. It brought together two independently begun but related stories: Dorothea Brooke searches for spiritual fulfilment as a St Theresa without a cause; the young doctor Lydgate wishes to bring scientific benefits to the community benighted in medical ignorance. Within the limiting confines of the Middlemarch community, both fail by weaknesses caused by their strengths. Dorothea's generous enthusiasm blinds her to the petty selfishness of the pedantic Casaubon; Lydgate's high-minded aspirations leave him unconscious of the 'spots of commonness' in his character that make him vulnerable to the predatory social climber Rosamond Vincy. Other characters reflect different aspects of ambition. Bulstrode, anxious to establish his respectability as the town banker, stoops to allow the death of Raffles, a companion from his murky financial past, to protect his own reputation. The young Fred Vincy is saved from the temptations of an idle life when his sweetheart, Mary Garth, refuses to help change his uncle Featherstone's will in his favour.

George Eliot uses the image of a microscope to describe the book's observation of individual characters modified by minute interactions, weakening moral resolve and stifling action. But the book's vision also shows how suffering can bring self-knowledge, and sympathy move individuals towards compassion and insight in the 'roar on the other side of silence'. Henry James said of the novel that it was 'a treasure-house of details, but it is an indifferent whole'. But its multiplicity is organic. Characters gradually develop through the story. Dorothea's ways of thinking, feeling and even her speech patterns change as she matures. The novel centres on the theme of selflessness versus the many subtleties of self-love, a unity reinforced by recurring images of the web, the mirror, water and the labyrinth. Within this the authorial voice constantly shifts to create new perspectives. Its multiple ways of seeing and feeling demonstrate both the historical process and history's failure to provide a final explanation of human existence. The novel continued to germinate in George Eliot's imagination even while the part-number publication was under way, and the reader, drawn into this process, also participates in an open-ended exploration.

Anthony Trollope, *The Way We Live Now* (1874–5)

The Way We Live Now is Trollope's most sustained critique of his age, a wide-ranging attack on Victorian class, finance, politics and culture. The story is broadly contemporary with the time of its writing, 1872. The heads of two feudal families face the problem of adapting to a changing age. Roger Carbury, squire of Carbury Manor, Suffolk, is the moral conscience of the novel. He feels responsible for his aunt, Lady Matilda Carbury, a widow of unfounded literary pretensions, and her handsome wastrel son Sir Felix. Adolphus Longstaffe, Roger's neighbour, faces financial ruin from his wife's extravagance and her matrimonial ambitions for their daughters. Roger Carbury loves his virtuous cousin Hetty, but Hetty is attracted to his younger friend, Paul Montague. Montague travels to America, where he becomes engaged to the fearsome Mrs Winifred Hurtle, and is involved in railway speculation and the shady intrigues of the financial confidence trickster Augustus Melmotte. The inevitable financial crash brings retribution. Melmotte commits suicide, Felix is packed off to the continent, and Lady Carbury marries an honourable journalist. Roger Carbury blesses the marriage of Paul and Hetty, with the prospect that their child will inherit Carbury Manor.

Written in the last decade of Trollope's life, the novel reflects contemporary scandals surrounding the 'railway king' George Hudson, whose empire crashed in 1849, and the fraudulent financier and Member of Parliament John Sadlier, who committed suicide in 1856. Its broad scope invites comparison with Dickens' late panoramic social novels. But where Dickens uses complex plotting and symbolic images, Trollope's novel gives the impression of haphazard actuality as it focuses on a representative swathe of English society over some nine months. Within this there is considerable variety of tone. Solid characters like Roger Carbury and Hetty are contrasted with the meretricious Lady Carbury and the inept Sir Felix. At the centre of the novel is Melmotte, a vulgar bully, yet ultimately bleakly empty, not so much a villain as a catalyst bringing disaster on a directionless, predatory society. While its pessimism and wide-ranging plot alienated its first readers, it is now recognized as arguably Trollope's finest achievement.

George Meredith, *The Egoist* (1879)

Meredith's wry study of male pride and women's rights to independence is set largely in Patterne Hall, the ancestral home of the proud, pampered and self-centred Sir Willoughby Patterne. Coming into his inheritance, he wishes to choose a wife as a decorative accessory to his social position. But his fiancée, Constantia Durham, sees through his egotism, and instead elopes with a captain in the hussars. Returning after three years travelling abroad, Patterne becomes engaged to Clara Middleton, and when she also becomes unhappy about the match, covers himself against a second humiliating refusal by secretly proposing to Laetitia Dale, a reserved, sensitive woman whose love he has previously ignored. To his dismay Laetitia rejects him, and Clara, learning of his duplicity, also breaks off her engagement. Finally, Laetitia accepts Willoughby, but lays out the condition that she herself will adopt a disillusioned 'spirit of egoism'.

The most tightly organized of Meredith's novels, *The Egoist* was conceived as comedy observing the dramatic unities. Willoughby's surname suggests an ironic comparison with the traditional story of the Willow Pattern plate, in which the daughter of a rich widower escapes from the wealthy suitor proposed by her father, and marries her true but impoverished lover. The novel itself is a formal 'pattern' through which, Virginia Woolf wrote, 'Sir Willoughby, our original male in giant form, is turned slowly round before a steady fire of scrutiny and criticism which allows no twitch on the victim's part to escape it'. But Meredith's artistic detachment both choreographs the action and weakens its relevance to actual human experience.

Henry James, *Portrait of a Lady* (1881)

The novel is the masterpiece of Henry James' middle phase. Isabel Archer, an orphan, leaves New York for England to stay with her aunt, married to a retired banker. Through the offices of her cousin Ralph, a tubercular invalid, she inherits a fortune on her uncle's death. A vital independent spirit, she rejects proposals from her neighbour, Lord Warburton, and a rich American, Caspar Goodwood. While visiting Florence in Italy she is introduced by Madame Merle to Gilbert Osmond, a widower with a daughter Pansy, and his cultured self-possession persuades her to marry him. She soon discovers he is cold, shallow and self-centred, with designs on her fortune, and later learns that the sinister Madame Merle is Pansy's mother. Against Osmond's command she returns to England to be at Ralph's deathbed, and when she meets Goodwood, longs desperately to accept the support of his offered love. But this would be for her an act of surrender, and she returns to Osmond and Pansy in Italy to face the consequences of her choice.

James entitled his work a 'Portrait'. As an American coming from outside Europe, Isabel is the constant centre of the book as James composes successive pictures of her passing with her open consciousness through brilliantly nuanced frameworks of other places and cultures: Gardencourt, the tranquil but decaying English country house; Paris; and behind it the splendours and decadence of older Europe, where Osmond's villa waits among the flowering orchards like a mask with 'heavy lids, but no eyes' (ch. 22). An innocent abroad, her instinctive sympathy for others leaves her defenceless against the coldly calculating Madame Merle and mercenary ambition of the heartless Osmond. But as James' images of darkness underline her intensifying isolation, Isobel's integrity and independence shine out the brighter, leaving her paradoxically triumphant over those who have unscrupulously used her.

[Olive Schreiner] Ralph Iron, *The Story of an African Farm* (1883)

The novel was immediately successful on publication for besides its controversial exploration of feminism and a newly sensitive masculinity, it focused central religious and philosophical debates of the later Victorian period. In form, it is episodic and sometimes elliptical, leaving sections of the narrative blank, and denying the reader the solace of any moral conclusions. The story takes place mainly on a farm in the High Karoo, and a sense of place unifies the narrative. The monstrous Boer-woman Tant' Sannie, rigidly Calvinist and crudely sensual, presides over a household that includes her stepdaughter Em, whose father left her heir to the farm on his death, and Em's orphaned cousin Lyndall. In the first section the brutal interloper Napoleon Blenkins cruelly ousts the gentle resident German overseer Otto. Blenkins takes his place, and savagely maltreats Waldo, Otto's mystically inclined son, whose search for meaning in life parallels Lyndall's search for identity as a woman. However, when Sannie discovers Blenkins making love to her visiting niece, she furiously banishes him.

In the second half of the novel, Lyndall returns from school, deeply read in the issues of woman's emancipation. She refuses to marry Gregory Rose, who exemplifies a new male sensitivity, fearing that marriage will end their freedom, and leaves with an unidentified stranger. Gregory pursues her, finds her in a hotel dying after having given birth to a short-lived child, and tends her disguised as a female nurse. To fulfil her wish, he returns to the farm and marries Em. Waldo dies alone, his consciousness merging with the glowing African landscape. Tant' Sannie gleefully embarks on a third marriage. Only the bad appear to prosper, but the spiritual aspirations of Lyndall, Waldo and Gregory raise the hope that human consciousness will evolve to higher things. Critics have questioned the book's feminist perspective. But Schreiner's work was pioneering, looking forward to the *'new woman' novels of the 1890s, and the novella retains the freshness and moral urgency of a deeply felt minor classic.

Robert Louis Stevenson, *The Strange Case of Dr Jekyll and Mr Hyde* (1886)

Originating in a nightmare, as did the other two seminal myths of the century, Mary Shelley's *Frankenstein* (1818; revised 1831) and Bram Stoker's *Dracula* (1897), the story has psychic roots that reach deep into the personality of its author. As Jenni Calder has remarked, although set in London, the novel has the smoky atmosphere of Edinburgh, where Stevenson lived a double life as member of the respectable middle class and a visitor to the underworld of the Old City's murky wynds and dark courtyards. Calvinism, with its inexorable moral judgement on the sinner, left an indelible imprint on his imagination, and *Jekyll and Hyde* looks back to an earlier Scottish tale reflecting the same obsession with good and evil in a single personality, James Hogg's *Confessions of a Justified Sinner* (1824). But the plot also focuses fears raised by evolutionary theory: if humans have evolved from the savagery of apes, can the cultured Jekyll return to become the 'ape-like' Hyde?

The story unfolds with brilliant economy. It begins with a chapter on a door, a motif that becomes increasingly significant as we realize the barrier not only between Jekyll's public and private life, but also between two modes of existence. Third-person narrative turns to the immediacy of first-person witness with heightening tension. The climax is all the more terrifying for what it leaves unsaid. Hyde's physical appearance remains shadowy, the nature of his crimes, apart from their murderous violence, unspecified. Jekyll's terror is that 'that insurgent horror was knit to him closer than a wife, closer than an eye; lay caged in his flesh, where he heard it mutter and felt it struggle to be born'. Stevenson's myth revealed the truths that were becoming charted by the investigations of Charcot and Freud. Jekyll did not need to create his Monster: the Monster was within him.

Sir Henry Rider Haggard, *She* (1887)

Massively popular on publication, the novel is a key example of what Patrick Brantlinger has termed the late-century 'Imperial Gothic', and it has drawn the interest of postcolonial and feminist critics alike as a pivotal work in the emergence of the modern. It unites Haggard's fascination for Africa with his interests in the occult, anthropology and mythology. Ludwig Holly, a Cambridge fellow, is entrusted with Leo Vincey, the son of a dying student, on a journey into central Africa to avenge Leo's ancestor, Killikrates, murdered in ancient times by a fatally beautiful but immortal white Queen Ayesha ('She-who-must-be Obeyed'). After perilous adventures they meet in the ancient city of Kôr, where Leo is recognized as the reincarnation of Killikrates. However, when Ayesha takes the enamoured Leo into the fire of eternal life, preparatory to their return to England, she becomes a stunted ape-like figure two thousand years old in the flames, and apparently dies. Holly and the now emaciated Leo escape back to England.

Told with a mixture of tongue-in-cheek pseudo-scholarship and stirring action, the story revolves around a series of contradictions. Leo, Ayesha's lover, is foppish and ineffectual; the story's hero Holly is physically ugly. The Amhaggar, a matriarchal tribe of amiable cannibals who entertain the explorers, invert European gender roles. The protagonists travel to the centre of black Africa, and find a queen who is white. The story reveals Haggard's ambivalence towards imperialism, and the novel with its inner contradictions has been seen as a pioneer work of Modernist fiction.

George Gissing, *New Grub Street* (1891)

New Grub Street, an attack on the writing of three-volume novels itself published in three volumes, explores the isolation of the independent serious writer in a market increasingly dominated by economics and literary fashion. As an aspiring writer, Reardon also struggles with ill health and depression. When his failure to earn a living by writing fiction reduces him to working for poverty wages as a clerk and living in wretched lodgings, his wife Amy leaves him with their son, Reardon's obstinate refusal to be an object of her pity preventing any reconciliation.

Amy is contrasted with Marian, trapped by her responsibility to her father Edmund Yule, a selfish, irascible man of letters of an earlier school, whose later blindness condemns her to a life of journalistic drudgery in his support. Reardon's tragedy is set against the calculating rise of Jasper Milvain, who ruthlessly exploits the publishing situation, and when Marian is reduced to poverty, rejects her. Instead, after Reardon's death, Milvain marries Reardon's wife Amy, who has ironically become a wealthy widow. Among the memorable minor figures is Reardon's friend Biffen, who writes the ultimate 'realist' novel, a work so true to life that it is unreadably dull. Yet Gissing's novel is both realistic and readable, and debates literary issues in terms of vividly animated characters and a compelling plot.

Thomas Hardy, *Tess of the D'Urbervilles: A Pure Woman Faithfully Presented by Thomas Hardy* (1891)

The character of Tess dominates Hardy's penultimate novel, both as a sensuous girl rooted in traditional country life and as a self-conscious child of modern education: as Hardy comments, when she and her mother stand together, 'the Jacobean and the Victorian ages were juxtaposed' (ch. 3). Out of balance with her time and situation, Tess's goodness becomes a liability, driving her to fatal self-blame and a futile anxiety to do right. She drifts half awake between the worlds of instinctive impulse and self-conscious, judgemental morality. The decisive moments of her tragedy take place when she is in a dreaming state – the accidental killing of the family horse that throws her into the path of the upstart Alec D'Urberville; her rape; her disastrous confession to Angel Clare, and her final capture at Stonehenge. Her feminine body makes her both a temptress and a victim. Her one moment of positive action, her stabbing of Alec, frees her from her past, but also locks her into the nemesis of the present.

Much of the novel's power comes from Hardy's use of poetic prose to shift between contrasting imaginative worlds, in which the luminous evocation of natural landscape merges with intimations of timeless myth. Seen within a moonlit haze, the drunken peasants inhabit a primitive, amoral environment; with their few possessions loaded on a lurching cart, they become wandering children of Israel. Tess is raped in a cyclical history of victimization and sacrifice in the Druidic woods, and her changing fortunes are embodied in landscapes of lush fertility or frozen sterility. Angel Clare brings a fatal knowledge of good and evil into the Eden of the Vale of Dairies, while her malevolent D'Urberville ancestors, painted into the ancestral walls of their manor, glare down on Tess's fatal confession to Angel. The satanic Alec D'Urberville reappears as preacher in his pursuit of Tess, and his murder leads her to her fate on the stones of Stonehenge.

The book's complex elements do not always cohere. Hardy's reductive final comment that 'the President of the Immortals . . . had ended his sport with Tess' (ch. 52) conflicts with our positive sense of Tess's vibrant humanity. In a final detail, the reformed Angel is to marry Tess's sister Liza Lou, suggesting that after Tess's tragedy society can move forward; but this is unprepared for and unconvincing. Nevertheless, the ending cannot diminish the imaginative power that irradiates Hardy's masterpiece.

George Moore, *Esther Waters* (1894)

Moore's finest novel began with the idea of a scullery maid, seduced and struggling to bring up an illegitimate child, within the world of racing stables he knew intimately from his own County Mayo childhood. It developed into the story of the 17-year-old Esther, who enters service in the Barham household to escape the violence of her drunken stepfather, is seduced by William Latch, a footman, is dismissed, and flees to London to bear her child. She survives the dangers facing an unprotected single mother in the city with great courage, and turns down a respectable suitor in order to marry Latch and so make her son legitimate. Latch becomes a hardworking publican and bookmaker in Soho, but dies ruined by alcohol and the betting laws. The novel ends on a note of hope, with Esther becoming reunited with her son, for whose independence she has given all.

The work earns its 'key' status as one of the very few English novels to benefit from the example of French realism. Moore's total identification with the resilient, unselfconscious Esther enabled him to create an authentic account of working-class life, free from moralizing and deeply humane.

Marie Corelli, *The Sorrows of Satan* (1895)

Marie Corelli's hugely popular novel marked a reaction against the changes of the *fin de siècle*. Geoffrey Tempest, who tells the story, is an impoverished opportunist and agnostic author whose lack of religious or artistic convictions makes him an ideal subject of attention for the mysterious aristocrat Lucio Rimânez. Rimânez is the incarnation of Satan who is roaming an England sunk in egotism and moral corruption, hoping to find a soul with the virtue to resist temptation. He gives Tempest untold wealth, literary success and the beautiful society belle Lady Sibyl. They marry, but she has been morally corrupted by modern literature, in particular the poetry of Swinburne and *'new woman' novels. She is seduced by Rimânez and finally commits suicide in despair. Sibyl is contrasted with the sweet, generous literary genius Mavis Clare (Corelli's highly idealized self-portrait), who writes in the classical spirit of Shakespeare and Homer. She is also tempted by Satan, but serenely resists. She sows the seeds of redemption in Tempest's consciousness. Tempest is taken on an extraordinary visionary voyage, where he too finally escapes the toils of Rimânez and gratefully returns to honest poverty. Rimânez is finally seen arm in arm with a cabinet minister entering the House of Commons.

Helped by being the first popular novel to be published at sixpence on the demise of the 'three-decker' format, the work had huge sales and went through thirty-seven editions in three years. It has claims to be the most popular work of the century, and the pioneer of the modern 'bestseller'. For all its absurdities, the tale is energized by Corelli's extraordinary imagination, and her uncritical belief in her ideas and literary talent.

H. G. Wells, *The Time Machine* (1895)

The first and most brilliant of Wells' novellas exploring contemporary scientific theories takes the 'Time Traveller' through the 'fourth dimension' of time to reach the year 802,701. He is at first delighted by the flowery landscape and idyllic lives of the pleasure-loving Eloi and is befriended by one of them, the child-like Weena. The Thames runs clean, and the Kensington Science Museum stands as a deserted green porcelain palace amid parkland. But he finds that when progress ended the stimulus of the struggle for existence, humanity divided into the effete vegetarian Eloi and the flaccid, sinister Morlocks, who live in a ruined industrial under-world and eat the flesh of Eloi they kill by night. His only weapon against the Morlocks proves to be the one human invention surviving intact in the abandoned museum, a safety match. A new Prometheus, he brings fire back to earth to free his time machine from their grasp and return to the present. In a final coda, he moves ahead three million years to see the final ending of the earth in the planetary system.

Wells was the precursor of modern *science fiction in his combination of down-to-earth realism and conjecture, and in his use of fantasy to examine contemporary issues. The hedonistic Eloi offer a mordant comment on the *fin-de-siècle* aesthetic movement, and the blind under-ground world of the Morlocks reflects the contemporary view of the working-class masses, with their anarchic threat. The Time Traveller shares an identity with both the Eloi and the Morlocks, for he is both cul-tured and a meat-eater. The novel centrally questions the optimistic view of social progress of the earlier nineteenth century, and has an unchanged relevance for the twenty-first.

Arthur Morrison, *A Child of the Jago* (1896)

The most famous account of East End slum life in its time, Morrison's violent novella was based on life in 'Old Nichol', an actual if atypical East End slum area. It narrates the bleak, brief life of the young Dicky Perrot, stealing to survive, beaten by his violent father, harassed by warring gangs, and preyed on by the odious Mr Weech, a fence who gives him a pittance for his thefts. Father Sturt (based on Father Arthur Osborne Jay) attempts to save him, but Dicky is killed in a gang fight, lying as he dies to protect his killers. The most powerful presence of the book, however, remains the claustrophobic 'Jago'.

The book earned Morrison comparisons with Balzac, Zola and Hart Crane, and he was hailed as a leading British realist writer. But his personal detachment drains his characters of any real humanity, and the narrative survives best as a sequence of filmic scenes that still have the power to startle and shock.

Bram [Abraham] Stoker, *Dracula* (1897)

The novel moves outwards from Count Dracula's castle in the Carpathian Mountains, where Dracula has trapped the young solicitor Jonathan Harker to negotiate his acquisition of Carfax, a decaying building in Essex. When Harker escapes back to England, Dracula follows, landing at Whitby on a doomed ship bringing earth-filled coffins for his intended colony of vampires. In the complex plot, the Dutch doctor and polymath Abraham Van Helsing forms a 'League of Light' against the 'Un-dead' invasion. The plot involves two contrasting women. The conventional heroine, the beautiful but passive Lucy, has no defence against Dracula, and once bitten, her vampire life has to be ended by a stake driven through her heart by her fiancée. Mina is, however, a 'new woman' full of ingenuity and enterprise. Although she has been bitten by Dracula, a sacred wafer converts Dracula's curse into a redemptive cross, and her psychic communication with the count enables her to lead his pursuers across Europe. They catch up with him shortly before the setting of the sun enables him to take his vampire form. Stabbed through the heart, he crumbles to dust.

Bram Stoker wrote *Dracula* while he was business manager of Henry Irving's Lyceum Theatre in London, and the novel's Gothic settings, visual effects and confrontations draw on Stoker's knowledge of the stage. The two-dimensional characters are the cut-outs of melodrama, and the mesmeric actor Irving contributed to the character of Dracula. Like **Frankenstein* (1818, rev. 1831), *Dracula* created a modern myth that could embody the fears of its era. But where Mary Shelley's tale was haunted by the loneliness of mountain peaks and polar ice, *Dracula* is crowded with peoples, past histories and new inventions; if the pre-Victorian myth intimates the abyss of isolation, *Dracula*'s nightmare is of sexual intimacy and possession by another. Stoker's novel reflects *fin-de-siècle* fears of female sexuality. Moretti sees the story as a parable of capitalism, cited by Marx as 'dead labour which, vampire-like, lives only by sucking living labour'. It also reflects a sense of England's vulnerability in a world she no longer dominated. Dracula is a demonic force that has lain concealed in 'deep caverns and fissures' of middle Europe from the Dark Ages, waiting its time to colonize England, and he is only defeated because he is in a lower state of evolution, with the imperfectly formed mind of the criminal that can only look back, not improvise.

Samuel Butler, *The Way of All Flesh* (1902)

Although published a year after Queen Victoria's death, Samuel Butler's scarifying account of Victorian life had been written between 1873 and 1884, and held back in order not to offend its living originals. It is the family saga of three generations of the Pontifex family. Theobald, the pompous, weak-willed son of a printer of evangelical persuasion, is bullied into the profession of the Anglican priesthood in the family's pursuit of social respectability. There he quickly falls prey to the matrimonial designs of the scheming Christina Alaby. The marriage is a painful failure, and the couple turn their pent-up frustrations towards the severe upbringing of their only son, Ernest, born, like Butler, in 1835. His upbringing cripples him emotionally and morally, and as a young man, fumbling a respectable girl he mistakenly thinks is a prostitute, he ends up in gaol. But prison proves his salvation. Disgraced, he is able to break away from the constricting web of Victorian respectability, and evolves into a reclusive but happy philosopher and writer. Combining Butler's hatred of mid-Victorian middle-class hypocrisy with his own expert interests in scientific evolution, *The Way of All Flesh* provides a powerful culmination to the Darwinian novel.

Topics

Children's Novels

The great era of the novel coincided with the golden age of children's books, although it is not always easy to identify books with an intended age group. Family reading brought together all ages, and younger readers would have identified with the experiences of Oliver Twist, the young Jane Eyre, David Copperfield or Maggie Tulliver. Equally, parents would have been intrigued by Thomas Hughes' Tom Brown, *Charles Kingsley's Tom among the water-babies, or Lewis Carroll's Alice. Most writers for adults, including *Dickens, Kingsley, *Thackeray, *George Macdonald, *Charlotte Yonge, *Robert Louis Stevenson and Oscar Wilde, wrote for younger readers at some point in their careers, and sometimes used children's literature to explore worlds of the imagination inaccessible to the 'realist' novel. Nevertheless it is possible to identify a developing genre of juvenile fiction.

The Victorians inherited the fearsome evangelical legacy of moral instruction for the young. The woes of Byron's Don Juan began with a mother who was

> a walking calculation,
> Miss Edgeworth's novels stepping from their covers,
> Or Mrs Trimmer's books on education. (*Don Juan*, Canto 1, v. 16)

In Thomas Day's *Sandford and Merton* (1783–9), Tommy Merton, 'who unfortunately had been spoiled by too much indulgence' on his father's Jamaican estate, is painfully taught his unselfish duty to others by the exemplary behaviour of the virtuous farmer's boy, Harry Merton. Still more forbidding was *The History of the Fairchild Family* (1818) by Mrs

Sherwood (née Mary Martha Butt), whose children learned the transience of life by contemplating a corpse ('You never saw a corpse?' 'No papa, but we have a great curiosity to see one'), and the consequences of quarrelling are taught by a visit to view an executed fratricide rotting on the gibbet. *Sandford and Merton* went through over eighty editions during the nineteenth century, its popularity at mid-century being challenged by *Eric, or Little by Little* (1858) by Frederick W. Farrar, Dean of Canterbury Cathedral. Minor sins of smoking and cheating in class lead Eric down a precipitous slope through drink and criminal associates to exile and early death, killing his mother with shame.

But the realist spirit of the age was softening the moral edge of writing for children. Mrs Catherine Sinclair's *Holiday House* (1839) brought naturalistic characters and a sense of fun into children's reading. A bestseller of the mid-century was Elizabeth Wetherell's *The Wide, Wide World* (1850). The religious sentimentality of the story, in which the girl Ellen is sent to the country while her mother goes abroad to die and suffers under the harsh regime of her Aunt Fortune, is tempered by a sense of an actual adolescent facing adversity. Charlotte Yonge, a Tractarian writer sensitive to the dangers of overt moralizing, wrote *The Daisy Chain, or Aspirations* (1856) for all ages, and its rambling chronicle of children close knit by the death of their mother and the devotion of their father made it favourite family reading, preparing the way for such classics for girls as Louisa May Alcott's *Little Women* (1868).

The Romantic movement had directly challenged evangelical beliefs in original sin, and brought a new interest in the child's imaginative world. Fantasy was no longer identified with the nursery but with a higher reality the adult world had lost. The interest in fairy stories was boosted by English translations of *Grimm's Fairy Tales* (1823–6). In the 1840s readers could turn from the gloomy realities of *social problem novels to Mary Howitt's translation of the tales of the Danish author Hans Christian Andersen (1846). George Cruikshank's illustrations to Grimm startled the young Ruskin with the delicacy of their etching and opened a visualized fairyland for Victorian artists and writers, one Ruskin himself was to explore in *The King of the Golden River* (1855). Charles Kingsley's *The Water-Babies* (1863) used the dream world of Tom the chimney sweep to explore metaphysical issues and opened the way for such fantasies as Lewis Carroll's *Alice's Adventures in Wonderland* (1865) and George Macdonald's *At the Back of the North Wind* (1871).

The growing prosperity of the middle classes allowed parents to give children pocket money for periodicals and cheap books, creating a literary market for purely recreational reading for younger readers. This brought an increasingly clear distinction between boys' and girls' reading, and targeted particular age groups. Captain *Frederick Marryat's adult naval novels fostered a genre of stirring tales for boys, often based on the writer's personal experiences, and his own books for children included the enduring classic *The Children of the New Forest* (1847). R. M. Ballantyne wrote *The Young Fur Trappers* (1856) while a youthful agent for the Hudson's Bay Company, launching a career which produced such stirring bestsellers as *The Coral Island* (1858). Captain Mayne Reid, W. H. G. Kingston and G. A. Henty exploited the interest in overseas adventure that was drawing emigrants in their thousands to the outposts of empire. Much of this writing was published in a rapidly growing number of boys' magazines.

In 1866 Edwin J. Brett launched *Boys of England: A Young Gentleman's Journal of Sport, Travel, Fun and Instruction* offering sensational fare for the lower-middle-class boy readership created by an expanding public education. Aided by melodramatic woodcuts and advertising stunts, in the 1870s Brett's periodical was selling an estimated 250,000 a week, and had spawned a host of rivals with titles such as *Boys of the Empire*. The middle-class press countered with a raft of 'respectable' but often violent journals, ranging from Kingston's patriotic *Union Jack* (1880–3) to the Religious Tract Society's *The Boy's Own Paper* (1879–1967). Works read mainly by girls, such as the Quaker Anna Sewell's sympathetic equine autobiography *Black Beauty* (1877), make a startling contrast to the high-spirited slaughter of wildlife featured in boys' fiction, and *The Girl's Own Paper* (1880–1965), while morally bracing, provided milder reading than its male-orientated companion.

But the borders between adult and children's reading were constantly shifting. By the end of the century, the *historical novels of Walter Scott had become largely children's reading, while, as George Orwell was to note, young men avidly read boys' weeklies. In the 1880s two rival adventure books written for boys, Stevenson's *Treasure Island* (1883) and *Sir Rider Haggard's *King Solomon's Mines* (1885), became adult bestsellers. The 'adult' and 'juvenile' branches of literature continued to influence and live off each other.

Colonial Novels

The expanding British Empire affected Victorian life in many ways, from garden plants to words, clothes, food, beliefs and reading matter. Yet the novel, which recorded so much of English culture, provides a curiously opaque window on the nations that Britain was subjugating. These worlds entered fiction in the naval novels of Frederick Chamier, Edward Howard, Michael Scott and the prolific *Frederick Marryat, who wrote of a world overseas they had known during the Napoleonic Wars. While these works only incidentally engaged with colonial life, they shaped racial stereotypes and increased a taste for fiction set in exotic locations. Marryat's family-owned property in the West Indies, and plantation life, intruded into his reply to Johann Wyss' *The Swiss Family Robinson* (1814), *Masterman Ready* (1842), in which the Seagrove family colonize a desert island, fighting off native savages with the help of their faithful black servant Juno. This novel looked forward to boys' adventure yarns of the later century with their Anglo-Saxon boy Crusoes subduing the inferior races of the world.

In contrast to new world adventures, India in fiction was associated with devious natives and with the corrupt administration and lax colonial lifestyle of an East India Company that went back to Elizabethan times. The Indian-born *Thackeray portrayed Anglo-Indians as living on the degenerate outer edge of British culture. From the 1830s, while James Stuart Mill and Thomas Babington Macaulay were working to reform Indian society, Philip Meadows Taylor's *Confessions of a Thug* (1839) explored the murderous extremes of Hindu superstition. The Indian Mutiny of 1857–8 obliterated any illusions of tolerant coexistence, and some fifty novels, including Henry Kingsley's *Stretton* (1866), made melodrama out of the brutal deaths of white women and children, and the heroism of British soldiers. Notable exceptions were Meadows Taylor's masterly *Seeta* (1872) and Flora Annie Steel's later novel exploring the complexity of the issues, *On the Face of the Waters* (1886). In 1888 *Rudyard Kipling's first collection of short stories, *Plain Tales from the Hills*, brought a new engagement with the complexity of Indian life and the effects of imperialism, taking colonial literature into a new era.

Africa, shielded by an inaccessible seaboard and the dangers of malaria, had remained a relatively unknown continent. Mungo Park's pioneering *Travels* (1799) and David Livingstone's *Missionary Travels* (1857) created benign images of the African peoples. But this was changed by aggressive missionary and trading confrontation, colonial expansion with its wars of 'pacification', and in particular Darwinian beliefs in Anglo-Saxon racial and cultural superiority. Pseudo-scientific works like Robert Knox's *The Races of Men* (1850) did not directly advocate genocide, but saw the extinction of lesser breeds as inevitable. Africa became the 'heart of darkness', the world of cannibals, superstition and slavery of R. M. Ballantyne's *Black Ivory* (1873). Yet as Patrick Brantlinger and others have argued, fascination with savage Africa also reflected doubts concerning the civilization of *fin-de-siècle* Britain. The most popular African adventure of the late century, Sir Rider Haggard's *She* (1887), describes a perilous adventure into the heart of Africa to find a *white* queen, and has been seen as an influence on Joseph Conrad's definitive anti-colonial fable, *The Heart of Darkness* (1902).

If African natives were savages, and Indians deceitful Orientals, antipodean aborigines were seen as subhuman brutes to be ruthlessly exterminated. With a few exceptions such as Jacky in *Charles Reade's It's Never Too Late to Mend* (1856), they are absent from fiction. Australia and New Zealand occupied an ambivalent place in the Victorian consciousness. In *Bulwer Lytton's *The Caxtons* (1849), *Dickens' *David Copperfield* (1849–50) and Henry Kingsley's *Geoffry Hamlyn* (1859), Australia is a land of opportunity where those who have failed in England can find a new life. But the novel that established the status of Australian literature, Marcus Clarke's *For the Term of His Natural Life* (1874), gives a scarifying vision of cruelty and despair within the isolation of deportation, and the most popular Australian romance, *Robbery Under Arms* (1888) by Rolf Boldrewood (T. A. Brown), recounts the criminal exploits of a bushranger.

Colonial worlds in fiction embodied the complex and often contradictory impulses behind the Victorian period itself, its courage, idealism and scientific curiosity, its cultural myopia and brutal belief in Anglo-Saxon racial superiority. Just how far the general public supported or were even aware of British imperialism is a controversial matter. But colonial fiction both extended British curiosity about the wider world and created a range of symbolic spaces through which the Victorians could look inwards, embodying both their utopian hopes and the fears of the repressed energies within their own society that were being given form, among other places, in Stevenson's Mr Hyde, the stunted alter ego, aboriginal in more senses than one, of Dr Jekyll (see above, p. 181).

Historical Novels

The historical novel enjoyed great prestige in the Victorian period. All the major novelists tried their hand at the form, and both they and their readers often saw historical fiction as their most important work. The novels of Scott reinforced the belief of historians like Macaulay and J. R. Green that the nation was evolving towards a higher form of democracy, a process grounded in the common life of the Saxon peoples, although in the later century this liberal view of history was increasingly challenged by Darwinian views of social evolution. While Scott remained a central influence on the historical novel, few of his successors had his ability to make the historical context emerge out of the story, and their work tends to smack of the library rather than of the past worlds they try to recreate. The most prolific and erudite historical novelist of the century was *G. P. R. James. Among the most intelligent, *Bulwer Lytton used the form to reflect contemporary debate. His highway romance *Paul Clifford* (1830) campaigned against indiscriminate capital punishment; *Harold: The Last of the Saxon Kings* (1848) reflected the political uncertainties of the 1840s. *W. H. Ainsworth drew on interest in topography and archaeology in *Jack Sheppard* (1839), *The Tower of London* (1840), *Old St Paul's* (1841) and *Windsor Castle* (1843), but Cruikshank's brooding illustrations have lasted better than Ainsworth's over-plotted melodrama.

*Dickens, in spite of two attempts at historical novels, was temperamentally a journalist of the present hostile to the past (see above, pp. 40–3). *Thackeray was drawn to the eighteenth century, but scepticism limited his overall vision of the period, and *Henry Esmond* (1852), his accomplished novel of the Jacobite rebellion and the Wars of Spanish Succession, remains a vivid panorama that is unified only within Esmond's disillusioned consciousness. The historical novel involved the recreation of other locations as much as earlier times, as in *Elizabeth Gaskell's one historical novel, *Sylvia's Lovers* (1863), set in the isolated northern port of Monkshaven, a locale based on Whitby, at the turn of the century (see above, p. 118).

The historical novel overlapped with the *religious novel, and also related to contemporary controversies. John Henry Newman's account of a third-century North African martyr, *Callista* (1856), is both a Catholic tract for the times and a moving and intelligent exploration of the first impact of Christianity on a pagan community. The title of *Charles Reade's highly regarded *The Cloister and the Hearth* (1861) refers to the choice between domestic and religious vocations facing Gerrard Elias-soen, the illegitimate son of the theologian Erasmus, as he wanders across Holland, Italy, Germany and France, his trials and frustrations forming a prolegomenon to the European Reformation and providing a backdrop to Victorian religious controversy. Similarly, *George Eliot's one histori-cal work, *Romola* (1862–3), looks back to the Renaissance and forward to her own hopes for religious and female emancipation. It is set in fifteenth-century Florence, where the ascetic prior Savonarola challenges the venal conservatism of the papacy and the ruling Medici. Romola, the daughter of a blind scholar, lives through the era's turmoil, enduring marriage to a treacherous Greek to survive into the age of new humanist freedom. Burdened with its weight of meticulous research, *Romola*, however, remains George Eliot's least accessible major work.

The historical novel continued into the last decades of the century, in works such as *Thomas Hardy's *The Trumpet Major* (1880), which nostal-gically recalled Dorset at the time of the Napoleonic Wars, and the his-torical sagas of *Sir Arthur Conan Doyle. But as Darwinian determinism ousted earlier interest in history, the earlier popularity of historical fiction lessened. The uncertainties of the *fin de siècle* were creating a shift in the public interest – instead of looking backwards with the history novel, the reading public turned to stories of the future, and to *science fiction.

Illustrated Novels

It is not a coincidence that the great age of the novel was the golden age of English book illustration. Both reflected continuous developments in the processes of book production and the rapid expansion of the reading public, with pictures making books attractive to an increasingly diverse audience. Bewick's development of wood-engraving (cutting the design across the grain of boxwood) in the late eighteenth century provided a cheap, effective way of inserting pictures into the text, and played a central role in the dramatic growth of popular literature in the 1830s and 1840s. Illustrations had a major effect on the popularity of certain novels: they were crucial to the work of some writers, such as *Robert Surtees, and even *Dickens had his popularity extended by the illustrations of Cruikshank and Hablôt K. Browne.

The genius of George Cruikshank dominates book illustration in the first decades of the century, with work that drew on folklore, myth and satire. His versatile etchings illustrated Bunyan's *Pilgrim's Progress (1678, 1684), the fairy stories of the Brothers Grimm and Pierce Egan's *Life in London (1820–1) before helping launch the careers of Dickens and *W. H. Ainsworth. Meanwhile, William Hogarth's narrative art, which had fed into the rise of the novel, was developed in Browne's definitive illustrations for Dickens' Pickwick Papers (1836–7). For over twenty years, most of Dickens' fiction was to be identified with Browne's illustrations. Browne's distinctive characters and comic or melodramatic tableaux perfectly matched Dickens' fluent pen, and Browne extended the story's moral by adding symbolic detail – a clock, a peacock's feather, a significant picture on the wall – in the manner of Hogarth. By the 1860s the bond between fiction and pictorial illustrations changed as novelists explored psychological issues that lacked an appropriate visual language. By *Bleak House* (1852–3) Browne's illustrations were becoming less significant to the story, and he was experimenting with dark half-tone plates to convey atmosphere and mood. Dickens was a major influence on Victorian illustrated fiction. Dickens' practice of publishing his novels in monthly parts, each with two illustrations recapitulating earlier instalments and advancing the progress of the story, was followed, among others, by *Thackeray.

By the 1860s conventions of book illustrations with roots in the conventions of caricature, melodrama and folk art were being replaced by the more realistic style of Pre-Raphaelite art. This period saw the emergence of a new generation of book illustrators who returned to wood blocks, but drew characters from life and detailed landscapes from observation. They were dominated by art school artists and Academicians, including Millais, the Dalziel brothers, Arthur Hughes and Frederick Walker, and furnished illustrations for novels in prestigious new journals such as *Cornhill*. George Du Maurier was particularly active in this field, working for a range of magazines and illustrating the work of many leading novelists of the period, including *Wilkie Collins, *Thomas Hardy, *George Meredith, *Margaret Oliphant and Thackeray, and his own novel, *Trilby* (1894). Book illustrations were still related to the novels' text. *Anthony Trollope claimed that Millais' illustrations for his own work clarified his imagination: 'I have carried some of those characters from book to book, and have my own early ideas impressed indelibly on my memory, by the excellence of [Millais'] impressions.' But illustrations were now an art form in their own right, standing independent from the text.

New conventions also took shape, moving beyond realism. *Children's literature proved a particularly rich field, with Walter Crane, Randolph Caldecott and Kate Greenaway studying eighteenth-century art conventions to find new ways of exploring the worlds of a child's imagination. By the 1890s, art nouveau and the avant-garde were inspiring book illustration, and the break with the earlier 'realist' novel form became complete.

Florence & Edith on the Staircase

Plate 5 Hablôt K. Browne, 'Florence and Edith on the Staircase', from Charles Dickens, *Dombey and Son* (1846–8).

Edith (to the left) recoils in horror from Florence's familial claims on her, crying 'Don't call me [mother]', smothering her domestic instincts with the gesture Henry Siddons prescribed for the actress portraying Medea contemplating infanticide (see p. 94). The scene is both theatrical and symbolic. Edith descends the stairs of fortune that Florence is ascending, while pseudo-classical statues signifying Florence's relations with Dombey, and pictures reflecting the angelic presence of the dead Paul, surround the stairwell.

Irish Novels

The tragedy of Ireland haunts English consciousness throughout the nineteenth century. Deprived of an independent government by the Act of Union in 1800, Irish Catholics were disenfranchised in England until 1829. Then the death of the radical leader Daniel O'Connell in 1847, and the appalling effects of the potato famine from 1845 to 1848, which decimated the peasantry, drove many to emigrate and gutted a Gaelic culture rooted in the people. Nevertheless, until mid-century, with its Dublin intellectual base, Ireland did make a significant contribution to the Victorian literary scene. The Young Ireland movement of the 1840s attempted to recover Gaelic into the Anglo-Irish tradition. James Clarence Mangan (1803–49), Samuel Ferguson (1810–86) and Standish James O'Grady (1846–1929) wrote mainly in verse, but their vision influenced the broad conception of Irish life and culture.

The brothers John and Michael Banim pioneered the authentic representation of Irish life with their *Tales of the O'Hara Family* (2 series, 1825–31), John Banim's last novel, *Father Connell*, being published in 1842. But the first Dublin-based writer to live by the pen was William Carleton (1794–1849), who was steeped in the Gaelic tradition. His *Traits and Stories of the Irish Peasantry* (1830–3), with their unsentimental evocation of traditional life, made his name. The horrors of the famine were reflected in his mordant satire on absentee Protestant landlords and their agents, *Valentine M'Clutchy* (1845). But *The Black Prophet* (1847) and *The Emigrants of Ahadarra* (1848) adopted a more realistic style to describe the misery of the famine and its aftermath. However, Carleton wrote for an English as much as for an Irish audience, and the draw of London lessened his involvement with his home island.

Irish literature became associated with comedy. Dublin-born Samuel Lover (1797–1868) made his name in London with a tale of the Irish peasantry in the 1798 revolt, *Rory O'More* (1837), which featured also as a ballad and a popular play. He became associated with *Dickens through *Bentley's Miscellany*, the periodical that published his best-known novel, a high-spirited picaresque tale based on the bungling clumsiness of the eponymous manservant *Handy Andy* (1837–9). Comedy also spiced the work of the most popular Irish novelist of the century, Charles Lever (1806–72). *The Confession of Harry Lorrequer* (1839), tales of military high jinks in the 1790s, and *Charles O'Malley* (1841), set in the next century, were built around the roguish charm of their heroes, catching the taste of the reading public in the early 1840s and creating the stock figure of the wily Irishman. Lever was appointed editor of *The Dublin University Magazine* in 1842, an influential periodical in Britain in which he pioneered the publication of long fiction in magazines. In 1845 he left Ireland for continental Europe. In his later work his comic genius is overshadowed by the tragedy of the Irish famine, and his fortunes declined.

With Carleton and Lever gone, the popularity of the Irish novel faded, and Ireland, crippled by the effects of the famine and political turmoil, found itself caught between creating an Irish-based literature it could not itself support, and a London-based tradition out of touch with its cultural roots. The most popular Irish writing came not in the form of the novel but in the massively popular melodramas of Dion Boucicault (*c.*1820–90). The publication of W. B. Yeats' *The Wanderings of Oisin* in 1889 marked a new beginning. But its fruits would come in the next century, and most Irish expatriates did not feel themselves attached to their island. Even *George Moore was not a nationalist at the time of writing his Irish novel, *A Drama in Muslin* (1886).

Yet the contribution of Irish writers made a distinctive impact on the London-based British culture. Bernard Shaw and Oscar Wilde were dominating intellectual figures. *Sheridan Le Fanu's tales of the uncanny developed an Irish Gothic tradition that went back to Maturin's *Melmoth the Wanderer* (1820), and looks forward to that most popular of all nineteenth-century Gothic tales, *Dracula* (1897), written by the Irish stage manager Bram Stoker.

'New Woman' Novels

The phrase 'new woman' was coined in 1894 by Sarah Grand [Frances Elizabeth McFall] (1854–1943) to represent a new phase in female emancipation. Applied to the novel, however, the term referred to a body of fiction whose sensational form drew new attention to women's issues rather than to a specific social or political movement. It was initiated by Grand's *Heavenly Twins* (1893), which used three connected stories concerned with women's sexual frustration, cross-dressing and, most scandalously, venereal disease to attack double standards in the treatment of women. Also controversial, the sketches in *Keynotes* (1893) by George Egerton [Mary Chavelita Melville Bright, née Dunne] (1859–1945) set out to portray the crises facing women at crucial moments of their lives.

The provocatively titled *The Woman Who Did* (1895), by Grant Allen (1848–99), tells of a university-educated heroine, Herminia Barton, who, in her quest for liberation, lives happily with an artist out of wedlock and bears his daughter. After his death, public prejudice drives her to defeat and eventual suicide, while her daughter returns to respectability. Also raising a scandal, *A Superfluous Woman* (1894) by E[mma] F[rances] Brooke (1844–1926) told of a heroine who marries a syphilitic roué and gives birth to a hideously deformed child. Other 'new woman' novelists included Mona Caird (née Alison) (1858–1932), Ménie Muriel Dowie (1867–1945) and Iota (Kathleen Mannington Caffyn) (1852/3–1926). Lyn Pykett has noted in *The Improper Feminine* (1992) that 'the general effect of the new woman novel . . . is to suggest the "impossibility" of women's situation' (p. 148). Whatever course they adopt, women will end up defeated. While the 'new woman' novels were a cry of frustration, not a programme for emancipation, the short-lived genre sensationally drew attention to issues repressed during the mid-Victorian period.

Publishing Formats

The growth of the nineteenth-century novel is inseparable from technical innovation and commercial enterprise. It began, paradoxically, with books too expensive for most readers to buy and much of the massive growth in reading came through the extension of various forms of library, found in locations from working men's clubs and institutes to shops and coffee houses. In the aftermath of the Napoleonic Wars, book production costs rose, and governments taxed paper and cheap periodicals for fear of subversive literature. An over-ambitious attempt to bring down the price of books ended when Sir Walter Scott and the publishing houses of Ballantine and Constable went bankrupt in 1826, leaving debts of a quarter of a million pounds. The collapse cast a warning shadow over publishing for half a century.

Onto the scene came the unscrupulous, universally disliked but persuasive bookseller Henry Colburn. Colburn exploited Regency taste by publishing 'silver fork' novels about high society, introducing fiction by the young *Benjamin Disraeli, *Bulwer Lytton, Mrs Gore and *G. P. R. James and shamelessly puffing his wares in advertisements and journals. He priced his novels high at 30s 6d for fashionable circulating libraries, including his own, and published them in three volumes ('three-deckers') to treble the returns on borrowing. His practice was copied by Richard Bentley, his one-time partner and later his hated rival, and Colburn's successors, Hurst and Blackett.

Three-deckers became a central format for new Victorian fiction, used at some point by most major novelists, including *Anthony Trollope, *George Eliot, *Mary Elizabeth Braddon and *George Gissing, until it finally ended in 1894. Even *Dickens felt he had arrived as a serious novelist only when he could handle *Oliver Twist (1837–8) in 'separate and individual volumes'. This format was only for new fiction and even here there were cheaper alternatives. In 1831 Colburn himself had introduced 'standard novels' – one-volume reprints at 6s. But a three-decker was often the necessary springboard for a novel's publication. The three-volume novel's main advantage was commercial, for its high price could make a print run of 700, or even 500, viable. Writers universally disliked a format that demanded a specific length and three sections, but it paid. Reardon in Gissing's *New Grub Street (1891), a novel itself published as a three-decker, notes ruefully: 'An author of moderate repute may live on a yearly three-volume novel . . . who gets from one to two hundred pounds for it. But he would have to produce four one-volume novels to obtain the same income; and I doubt whether he could get so many published within twelve months' (vol. 2, ch. 15).

Although few could buy a three-decker, by mid-century most town-dwellers could borrow them cheaply from a library. The first circulating library open to the public had been established in London about 1742, an institution quickly copied in Edinburgh and throughout Britain. A hundred years later Charles Edward Mudie brought the spirit of tough Victorian enterprise to the business, slashing the annual single-volume subscription from four or five guineas to one, with more volumes borrowed priced pro rata. He also stamped Victorian decency on the institution. Libraries had been identified with romantic fiction: 'Madam,' Sir Anthony Absolute warns Mrs Malaprop in Sheridan's The Rivals (1775), 'a circulating library in a town is an evergreen tree of diabolical knowledge! And . . . they who are so fond of handling the leaves, will long for the fruit at last' (Act 1, sc. 2). But with half of his stock fiction, Mudie personally vetted his 'fruit' for decency and good taste. Mudie's sometimes absurdly cautious censorship was resented by authors, but it gave the novel a respectability with a middle class traditionally hostile to fiction, and confirmed the custom of family reading. Such was Mudie's success that in 1860 he opened enlarged New Oxford Street premises in a ceremony attended by the major literary figures of the day. By the same year he had branches or agencies throughout England, with boxes servicing overseas colonies. When his major competitor, W. H. Smith, struck gold by setting up a network of libraries and newsagents in railway stations, he exercised an equally draconian control over the moral respectability of his wares.

One alternative to the three-decker emerged when the success of Dickens' *Pickwick Papers* (1836–7), originally planned as text to a series of comic sketches in the style of Pierce Egan, Sr's *Life in London* (1820–1), established the publication of novels in monthly shilling parts. Dickens stayed with the part-issue format for all but two of his major novels. It was more flexible than the three-volume novel, suited his dramatic style, whose plots kept the reader anxious for the next instalment, and above all enabled him to build up an intimate relationship between writer and reader. The illustrations which accompanied each issue and reminded readers of characters and setting echoed Dickens' visual imagination, particularly in his work up to *Bleak House* (1852–3). Although the form attracted interest, it was expensive to produce and distribute, and only suited those whose reputation ensured large sales of their work. Of the major authors, only *Thackeray, Lever and *Ainsworth used it to any effect, and only Dickens remained with it.

In 1844 when the touchy Dickens quarrelled with Chapman and Hall over payments for *A Christmas Carol*, he turned to Bradbury and Evans, publishers of the journal *Household Words* (1850–9), which offered new quality fiction for twopence per issue, including his *Hard Times* (1854) and Elizabeth Gaskell's *North and South* (1854–5). The firm provided the new technical efficiency demanded by the ever-increasing size of the publishing market, and included Thackeray among their authors. Meanwhile, Chapman and Hall went on to be leading publishers of the *'social problem' novel and of the fiction of Trollope, although their fortunes declined in the 1860s. Dominating the quality publishers in mid-century was the Edinburgh firm of Blackwood and Sons, which established a London office under the energetic John Blackwood in 1840 and won the loyalty of a group of writers that included Bulwer Lytton, *Margaret Oliphant and George Eliot.

By the 1860s there was an increasing division between the 'serious' novel published by firms such as Blackwood's, and more entertaining fiction. Monthly parts, and to some extent the three-volume format, were superseded by shilling monthly magazines led by *The Cornhill Magazine* (1860–1975), edited by Thackeray. This offered not one but two serials running concurrently, together with high-class illustrations, poetry and other material, all for one shilling. It put a premium on stimulating interest, and the need for cliffhangers to raise circulation was an important element in the rise of the *sensation novel. Soon these magazines were challenged by periodicals priced at sixpence or below. A new generation of writers, including Mary Elizabeth Braddon and *Robert Louis Stevenson, had been apprenticed to writing for penny 'pulp' serials, and brought a new immediacy and pace to the writing of fiction. Novels were also being serialized in regional newspapers. The practice had started in the 1840s in imitation of the French *feuilleton*, but received a massive boost in the 1870s with the rise of Tillotson's 'Fiction Bureau', which operated from Lancashire but syndicated fiction in newspapers throughout the provinces and even abroad, and whose authors included Braddon.

Over this period, Victorian readers had access to an ever-growing range of cheap reprinted, out of copyright or American novels. From the 1820s publishers such as John Limbird had published reprints for twopence, but this popular press operated below middle-class notice. For the 'respectable' public, R. J. Cadell had successfully published a cheap collected edition of Scott's novels as early as 1829, and through the century publishers issued inexpensive editions of work by authors such as Bulwer Lytton, G. P. R. James and W. H. Ainsworth. Chapman and Hall's cheap edition of Dickens, published in parts, provided a novel for about 3s 6d. In Germany, the firm of Tauchnitz was formed in Leipzig to publish cheap one-volume paperback editions of current English fiction, and although much of its sales were confined to Europe, Tauchnitz became a major publisher of cheap reprints throughout the century. Exceptionally, Tauchnitz paid English authors a standard fifty-pound fee, and consulted them over the text, making some of his editions of bibliographical importance. This encouraged cheaper prices in England. From 1846 Sims and McIntyre's Parlour Library made a wide range of titles available at 2s 6d a volume. Cheap editions apparently did little to diminish sales of more expensive versions. *Oliver Twist* went into three-volume form while still being serialized in *Bentley's Miscellany*, and in Dickens' lifetime, in various formats, sold in seven differently priced editions.

Reading was no longer confined to the home. Routledge's Railway Library in 1848 preceded the 'yellowback' novels from the 1850s and provided convenient small octavo-volume editions for travellers. Through the century, books increasingly became the common part of everyday life in the way they are today. By the time the three-volume novel format ended in 1894, and the price of a new novel was set at six shillings, only the lack of paperbacks distinguished book production from that of the present.

Regional Novels

The Victorian novel was in many ways a London phenomenon. London dominated the book trade, helped by the centralizing impact of the railways. If writers like the *Brontë sisters, *Elizabeth Gaskell and *Margaret Oliphant were born and sometimes lived outside the metropolis, they were still dependent on London for its publishers and mass market often visiting it, and their provincial perspectives were framed by a metropolitan viewpoint. Even the alien world of *Wuthering Heights (1847) is seen through the wondering gaze of Lockwood, an outsider from the city.

Scotland had lost much of the literary eminence it had enjoyed in the time of Sir Walter Scott. Thomas Carlyle, Scotland's most powerful voice, settled in Chelsea in London in 1834. At the end of the century Scottish fiction saw a minor renaissance with the sentimental 'kailyard' (cabbage patch) novels of S. R. Crockett, J. M. Barrie and Ian Maclaren [John Wilson]; while *Irish literature, which after the novels of the Banim brothers had become associated with the comic picaresque, gained a new presence in the work of Bernard Shaw, Oscar Wilde and *George Moore.

The gentler pace of Elizabeth Gaskell's *Cranford* (1851–3) and *Sylvia's Lovers* (1863), and the chronicles of *Trollope's Barsetshire and Margaret Oliphant's Carlingford, provided a foil to the pace and style of characteristic urban fiction. *George Eliot turned to provincial life to explore human nature in a state of simplicity relative to the realities of many of her readers. But as England became overwhelmingly urban, railways blurred regional differences and rural poverty depopulated the countryside, the distinction between London and the provinces became less significant. When *Thomas Hardy created his imaginary provincial world of Wessex, he portrayed it as an isolated island increasingly eroded by change and loss.

Religious Novels

The evidence of actual religious adherence in the Victorian era is contradictory. Church leaders wrung their hands in 1851 when a census revealed that only 7 million out of 18 million adults in England and Wales attended places of worship. 'It is not that the Church of God has lost the great towns,' wrote the Anglican clergyman Winnington-Ingram in 1896, 'it has never had them.' At the same time, the Victorian age was visibly a period of intense religious activity. In mid-century there were over 1,200 places of worship recorded within inner London alone, serving the worshippers of over thirty religious denominations.

The same contradiction appears in literature. In *The Religion of the Heart* (1979), Elizabeth Jay notes that in the 1820s religious works made up 22.2 per cent of all books published: by mid-century this had increased to 33.5 per cent (p. 7). John Sutherland estimated that clergymen and their daughters made up the largest single category of 'serious' novelists (Sutherland, p. 529). When Leo J. Henkin categorized 'Problems and Digressions' in the novels reviewed in *The Athenaeum* between 1860 and 1900 (see above, p. 3), over a quarter of his categories concerned religious matters, while another related to topics such as 'Spiritualism' and 'Theosophy'. Even non-believers like *George Eliot and *Thomas Hardy explore issues of faith, and as theological certainties were challenged by social science and the implications of evolution, scientific belief itself assumed a quasi-religious authority. And yet the main development of the novel was secular and materialist.

Nevertheless, a significant number of Victorian novels were directly involved with matters of faith. The Oxford Movement's interest in the historical past, and the controversies it aroused, provoked a flurry of novels drawing on both Gothic and biographical genres. An extreme example is William Sewell's *Hawkstone* (1845), in which the introduction of a Roman Catholic establishment is associated with other radical forces intent on destroying the community. The noble conservative Villiers opposes an alliance between Pearce, a local Irish subversive, and the incoming Father O'Leary. At the end Villiers recovers his son, who has been brainwashed by the Catholics, while the villain is found trapped underground in an old abbey, eaten alive by rats. A more temperate work is *Margaret Percival* (1847), by his sister Elizabeth Missing Sewell. It recounts Margaret's long debates with an Italian family and a Father Andrea whether to accept the Romish faith. Finally she returns to the sureties of the Church of England. John Henry Newman's novel of spiritual pilgrimage to Rome, *Loss and Gain* (1848), was also a patient exploration of theological issues, provoking J. A. Froude's powerful novel of doubt and despair, *The Nemesis of Faith* (1849).

By mid-century, religious fiction had fallen into three broad groups. Low Church or evangelical writers were generally suspicious of fiction, and the little they wrote was severely didactic or directed towards conversion, as in the work of Charlotte Elizabeth Tonna ('Charlotte Elizabeth'), although her early industrial tale, *Helen Fleetwood* (1838–40), shows an ability to engage with wider social issues. While the *Brontë sisters attacked the repressive aspect of evangelicalism, their work owes much to its intense, apocalyptic introspection. Its main impact was in the first half of the century. A liberal side of the nonconformist tradition can be seen in a novel such as *Ruth* (1853), by the Unitarian *Elizabeth Gaskell, which attracted scandal with its sympathetic account of an unmarried mother rescued by a dissenting minister.

Broad Church novelists, influenced by Carlyle and by Christian socialism, turned to social and nationalistic issues, advocating the healthy engagement of 'muscular Christianity' against the devious wiles of intellectual persuasion. Thomas Hughes' *Tom Brown's Schooldays* (1857) applied these ideals to public school life. As noted above, *Charles Kingsley applied them to industrial society in *Alton Locke* (1850), and championed Protestant courage against barbaric Catholicism in *Hypatia* (1853) and *Westward Ho!* (1855). The High Church writers answered by showing the saintly qualities of pre-Reformation Roman Catholicism, as did Newman's tale of heroic Catholic martyrdom in third-century Carthage, *Callista* (1856). The most popular High Church novelist was *Charlotte

Yonge, although she carefully avoided overt proselytizing in her work. In historical novels such as *A Dove in the Eagle's Nest* (1866), she dramatized chivalric Christian qualities, values which were quietly transposed into such domestic stories as *The Daisy Chain* (1856).

As the century progressed, pressures on traditional belief intensified rather than lessened the vogue for religious fiction. In 1888 *Mrs Humphry Ward's account of faith tested to destruction, *Robert Elsmere*, became arguably the most popular serious novel of the century. Hardy's *Jude the Obscure* (1895) marked the advance of fatalistic agnosticism. But religious interests were also being diverted into fiction of the occult and *supernatural, which ranged from *George Macdonald's spiritual allegories to *Marie Corelli's wild psychic fantasies. An aesthetic approach to faith made J. H. Shorthouse's historical novel of returning from Catholicism to the Anglican faith, *John Inglesant*, the unexpected bestseller of 1880. Walter Pater's *Marius the Epicurean* (1885), set in second-century Rome, approached religious conversion in terms of exquisite sensibility.

While a large sub-genre of the Victorian novel was devoted to Christian topics, it is hard to read far in this fiction without encountering religious issues. Religion features both as private faith and as social institution in Victorian fiction in the novels of *Anthony Trollope and *Margaret Oliphant. George Macdonald's fiction explores the life of Scottish Calvinist communities; W. H. White's novels describe the life of Midland dissent; while the Jewish community surfaces in the novels of *Disraeli and Israel Zangwill, and in George Eliot's *Daniel Deronda* (1876). A largely hostile gallery of various clergy and ministers emerges in the novels of *Dickens and *Thackeray. However, a work such as George Eliot's *Scenes of Clerical Life* (1858) illustrates the sensitivity with which a non-believer can approach matters of religious conscience.

Science, Utopias and Dystopias

While the term 'science fiction' only became used in 1926, the genre had its roots in the nineteenth century. Mary Shelley's *Frankenstein* (1818, revised 1831), an important progenitor of the genre, was itself signally vague about science, but as the century progressed, scientific discoveries became increasingly a subject for debate and were discussed in popular journals. It was often a major feature of boys' magazines, and when Jules Verne's *A Journey to the Centre of the Earth* first appeared in England, it was in *The Boy's Journal* for 1864. *Bulwer Lytton's pioneering 'scientific romance' *The Coming Race* (1871) updated Johnson's *Rasselas* with an American explorer discovering a technological utopia hidden deep underground. Its advances included human flight, both aircraft and detachable wings, extra-sensory perception, and an inexhaustible source of energy called 'Vril' (a term taken up by the beef extract, 'Bovril'). But he is threatened by its totalitarian regime, in which women are the superior sex. When Zee, a princess, falls in love with him, he faces extermination lest he contaminate the race's gene pool. However, the winged Zee nobly snatches him back to upper earth, where he waits for the superior race to invade and destroy humankind.

Novels of Britain's invasion by hostile powers reflected public anxiety as the country's global power came under threat. Also published in 1871, Colonel J. T. Chesney's graphic *The Battle of Dorking* is set in a ravaged England fifty years after its defeat by German forces have reduced the country to a subject state. In M. P. Shiel's *The Yellow Danger* (1898), a Chinese potentate's passion for an English girl precipitates a world war; although she is saved by a Saxon hero in a mighty sea battle, there is no escape from the subsequent global disaster of a cholera epidemic. The following year *H. G. Wells' novel *The War of the Worlds* graphically described the decimation of England's population by the (literally) blood-thirsty Martians, before the invaders are themselves defeated by their one vulnerability, to human disease.

The Martian massacres, Wells notes, parallel the virtual extermination of Tasmanian aborigines by white settlers. Samuel Butler in *Erewhon* ('Nowhere') (1872), set in New Zealand, creates a mirror image of Victorian society. Religion is based on money and their god is Ydgrun (Mrs Grundy); students attend Universities of Unreason; and sickness is treated as crime, crime as sickness. Less successful is *Anthony Trollope's satire on treatment of the elderly, *The Fixed Period* (1882), set on an island republic off Australia where euthanasia is mandatory at age 68.

Moving from dystopia to utopia, the American Edward Bellamy's *Looking Backward* (1888), which envisaged Utopia under a nationalized economy, evoked William Morris' *News from Nowhere* (1891). In this work the narrator William Guest wakes to find himself in a twentieth-century, post-revolutionary Britain, the Thames teeming with salmon, and London a centre of art and learning. In a romantic voyage upriver, the dreamer experiences England returned to a pre-industrial beauty and prosperity. The story's lyrical warm charm outdates its optimistic socialism. But it was H. G. Wells with *The Time Machine* (1895), *The Island of Dr Moreau* (1896) and *The Invisible Man* (1897) who brought together the various elements of nineteenth-century 'scientific romance', uniting scientific concepts, social issues and human interest into one graphic narrative.

Sensation Novels

The term 'sensation novel' became widely used in the 1860s to refer to fiction written to surprise and shock. The term can be traced back to *The Colleen Bawn* of Dion Boucicault, a melodrama that was packing middle-class audiences into the Adelphi Theatre in 1860. While Boucicault kept the spectacle, mystery, action and intensified emotions basic to melo-drama, he subverted its moral opposition of good against evil, presenting his flawed 'hero' Hardress as dominated by his mother and shadowed by a crippled alter ego, and dividing the figure of the heroine into two women of contrasting appearance and character, the physically ebullient redhead Anne Chute, and the dark-haired Eily, Hardress' good but timid secret wife, a pure-spirited peasant. The climactic 'sensation scene', the apparent drowning of Eily in a huge sea cave, is not used to show the final working out of justice as in traditional melodrama, but comes in the middle, to startle and create mystery.

Many of these features passed into the sensation novel as first identified with Wilkie Collins' *The Woman in White* (1860), Dickens' *Great Expecta-tions* (1860–1), Mary Elizabeth Braddon's *Lady Audley's Secret* (1861–2) and Ellen Wood's *East Lynne* (1861). The notable common denominator in novels diverse in style and attitude was the use of the conventions of the domestic novel – middle-class homes and family relationships – as settings for secrets, mysterious identities, murder, seduction, blackmail and bigamy. This fiction was mainly written to supply the new wave of maga-zines emerging in the 1860s, ranging from the shilling *Macmillan's* and *Cornhill* to cheaper mass-circulation periodicals like *The Sixpenny Magazine*, a serial that first published *Lady Audley's Secret*. The stories' involved plots were particularly suited to making readers rush to buy the next instalment.

This fiction, which was greeted with enthusiasm by the general public, who made *Lady Audley* and *East Lynne* bestsellers, met with an equally strong wave of condemnation from establishment critics. The very appeal to 'sensation' in this fiction was seen as subverting the moral purpose of the novel, and appealing to the lower instincts of its readers. Its use of plots and characters formerly associated with disreputable penny magazines broke down the social boundaries of decency, making 'the reading of the kitchen' the favourite reading of the drawing room. The arbiters of taste were particularly horrified by the stories' moral ambivalence, and their presentation of 'heroines' who contravened all the conventions of women as the embodiment of moral values and the support of husband and children. The sensation novel took emotional excess from melodrama and mystery and menacing settings from the Gothic tradition in order to overturn the ideal of mid-Victorian domesticity, exposing the emotional needs and sexuality repressed by its conventions. The phrase 'every man's home is his castle' took on a new and ominous meaning.

The sensation novel was located in its time, a reaction against the strict mores of the mid-Victorian period, and gave voice to the concern with the rights of women in marriage that culminated in the first Married Woman's Property Act of 1870. It drew on the repressed passions beneath respectability, and the fear of hidden secrets or indiscretions that might bring social disgrace. By the 1870s its impetus was passing, to be revived in the 1890s by the *'new woman' novel. But its significance in the evolution of feminine identity has brought this once neglected genre under increasing critical scrutiny.

Social Problem Novels

It could be argued that all serious Victorian novels in some way explored social problems. But there are three sub-genres that lay particular claim to the title: 'condition-of-England novels'; the novels of 'outcast' London; and novels of social propaganda. The first category goes back to the Radical debates stirred up by the French Revolution, and includes Holcroft's *Anna St Ives* (1782) and Godwin's *Adventures of Caleb Williams* (1794). In the first decades of the nineteenth century, *Harriet Martineau, who was later to translate Comte's *Positive Philosophy* (1853), used fiction to popularize Utilitarian economics for the masses in *Illustrations of Political Economy* (1832–4). The industrial distress of the 1840s created a flurry of novels that drew on investigative journalism and Parliamentary bluebooks, although such fiction tended to see social conflicts in terms of melodrama. Early examples are Charlotte Elizabeth Tonna's *Helen Fleetwood* (1838–40), Frances Trollope's *Michael Armstrong, the Factory Boy* (1840) and Elizabeth Stone's *William Langshaw, the Cotton Lord* (1842).

The novel became a platform for political and religious concepts. Disraeli's *Sybil, or the Two Nations* (1845) was a political call for 'Young England' to redeem an England locked between an effete old order and a leaderless proletariat. Charles Kingsley's *Yeast* (1848) examined contemporary social crises from the perspective of 'muscular Christianity'. Dickens aimed *Hard Times* (1854) at the popular market serializing in the twopenny *Household Words*. He briefly visited Preston to see a strike at first hand, and his fictive picture of Coketown became a *locus classicus* for historians of the industrial city. But the industrial north proved inimical to a Londoner whose *A Christmas Carol* (1843) had equated social reform with Scrooge's change of heart, and the novel's focus shifted to

Utilitarian education and the need for imagination and feeling in a materialist world. The finest industrial novels were written by *Elizabeth Gaskell, who as the wife of a Unitarian minister drew on close and sympathetic experience of Manchester life in her short stories, in *Mary Barton* (1848) and in *North and South* (1854–5). *Charlotte Brontë's novel of the mills, *Shirley* (1849), was set in 1811–12, and of historical rather than industrial interest.

The 'condition-of-England' novel was essentially middle-class speculation on the class divide, and largely disappeared during the prosperity of the mid-century. It was also, with the notable exception of Elizabeth Gaskell, a southern perspective on the north of England. Londoners concerned with social issues in the novel took a more immediate view of class divisions. *Douglas Jerrold's *The History of St Giles and St James* (1845–7) mounted a savage attack on the sufferings of the poor as illustrated by the contrasts between two areas of London; while Kingsley's *Alton Locke* (1850) used the author's journalistic investigations into the London sweated labour trade as a basis for a novel on the Chartist movement. Far outselling both, G. W. M. Reynolds' penny-issue *The Mysteries of London* (1844–6) attacked the wealthy in a heady mix of radical attitudes and melodramatic situation. Reynolds' serial has been credited as an influence on Dickens' novels of divided London society, *Bleak House* (1852–3) and *Our Mutual Friend* (1864–5). Henry Mayhew's *London Labour and the London Poor* (1861–2), which began with a series of articles for *The Morning Chronicle* (1849–50), and the popular journalism of James Greenwood, author of *The Seven Curses of London* (1869) and *The Wilds of London* (1874), intensified interest in the London underworld, while G. R. Sims, whose articles were collected as *The Bitter Cry of Outcast London* (1883), turned the focus of public interest onto the East End. Beginning with *Workers in the Dawn* (1880), *George Gissing wrote five novels of working-class life out of first-hand experience of slum poverty, although he remained temperamentally an outsider. Arthur Morrison also reflects a pessimistic view of working-class life in a very different work, *A Child of the Jago* (1896).

Social work and philanthropy became the subject of fiction. William Gilbert exposed the workings of the Health Inspectorate in the London slums, in *Dives and Lazarus* (1858), and J. E. Jenkins' best-selling *Ginx's Baby* (1870) was a bitter satire on philanthropic childcare agencies. *Ellen Wood's prize-winning first novel, *Danesbury House* (1860), was written to rally the middle classes behind the temperance movement. *Walter Besant's *All Sorts and Conditions of Men* (1882) and *The Children of Gibeon* (1886) made effective pleas for education and self-help in the East End slums. In a very different vein, Anna Sewell's enduringly popular *Black Beauty* (1877), told as the autobiography of a mistreated horse, had a strong influence on the animal welfare movement.

The Supernatural

Shortly before her murder, the terrified Nancy in *Oliver Twist* (1837–8) tells Brownlow she has passed a coffin in the street. 'They have passed me often,' Brownlow replies, surprised. '*Real ones,*' rejoined the girl. 'This was not.' Dickens' novel, in which Fagin is both demonic and a social problem, and in which Sikes is launched to his execution by Nancy's phantom eyes, is an extreme example of the way the Gothic tradition merged with social realism into the Victorian novel. Old-style Gothic tales continued, particularly in penny-issue fiction, where *J. M. Rymer's *Varney the Vampyre* (1847–8) and *G. W. M. Reynolds' *Wagner the Werewolf* (1846–7) were bestsellers. But in the middle-class novel, Gothic elements became modified by social, moral and, increasingly, psychological concerns. In Dickens' Christmas books and stories, tales of ghosts became a seasonal escape from materialistic values.

However, the division between 'natural' and 'supernatural' belief is often uncertain. Writers from *Charles Dickens, *Bulwer Lytton and *William Thackeray early in the century, to *Sir Arthur Conan Doyle, *Rudyard Kipling and *Sir Henry Rider Haggard at its end, shared an intense interest in mesmerism, telepathy, clairvoyance and spiritualism, worlds 'scientifically' explored in such works as D. D. Owen's *The Debatable Land Between this World and the Next* (1872). Ruskin and Lesley Stephen were among the literary co-founders of the Society for Psychical Research in 1880, and Gladstone was an enthusiastic honorary member. Mrs Catharine Crowe claimed the ghostly occurrences in her collection *The Night Side of Nature* (1848) were all true. The power of hypnotism, 'animal magnetism' and second sight was exploited by short stories and fiction. The most celebrated of these was George Du Maurier's *Trilby* (1894). The novel generated a frisson from being set in the carefully sanitized world of the Parisian artist's quarter, where the beautiful, naive artist's model Trilby O'Ferall forms a friendship with three English art students. Tone deaf, but with a magnificent voice, Trilby is taken over by the hypnotic powers of Svengali and turned into a singing star, until the death of her evil genius returns her to nonentity. With its risqué associations, its pathos and the fascination of Trilby's relationship to Svengali intensified by

"'ET MAINTENANT DORS, MA MIGNONNE!'"

Plate 6 George Du Maurier, '"Et maintenant dors, ma mignonne!"', Du Maurier's own illustration to his novel *Trilby* (1894), p. 381.

As a book illustrator of the 1890s, Du Maurier was told to be strictly naturalistic. Nevertheless, his subject allows him a demonic vein within this realistic approach. (Compare Cruikshank's 'THE FIENDS FRYING PAN', p. 157, and see 'Illustrated Novels', pp. 199–201.)

Beerbohm Tree's sensational dramatization on the stage, *Trilby* became one of the most popular novels of its era.

The ghost story came together with historical and domestic interests in the haunted houses of Bulwer Lytton's *The Haunted and the Haunters* (1859), Mrs Riddell's *Weird Stories* (1882) and Mrs Gaskell's *The Old Nurse's Story* (1852). The psychic gained from interest in the 'science' of the super-natural, but it also offered access to issues excluded by realistic fiction. In the last decades of the century, it became associated with decadence and cultural malaise. In *Sheridan Le Fanu's 'Green Tea' (1872), an obscene monkey spirit possesses a bachelor clergyman. In Arthur Machen's *The Great God Pan* (1894), a 'transcendental' experiment leaves a country girl fathering the sinister daughter of the pagan god. The supernatural themes of Stevenson's *The Strange Case of Dr Jekyll and Mr Hyde* (1886), Oscar Wilde's *The Portrait of Dorian Gray* (1891) and Henry James' *The Turn of the Screw* (1898) all reflect the tensions of an era of moral uncertainty.

Working-class Novels

Working-class writers wrote relatively few novels about their own condition. *Godfrey Malvern*, by Lincolnshire 'basket-maker poet' Thomas Miller (see above, pp. 46–8), recorded the difficulties of those outside the class breaking into the dominantly bourgeois novel-writing market. Miller himself, an able, industrious writer, was exploited by predatory publishers and died in extreme poverty. Most working-class novels came out of political struggle: the best Chartist novels, published in such periodicals as *The Northern Star*, include Thomas Cooper's historical romance of the Peasants' Revolt, *Captain Cobler* (1851), Thomas Martin's *Bildungsroman*, *Sunshine and Shadow* (1849–50), and Ernest Jones' exposé of *Women's Wrongs* (1851).

The genre of political working-class novel declined with the dwindling support for the Chartist movement in the 1850s, but did not die away entirely. Ian Haywood has pointed to the massive popularity of the works of Allan Clarke, the son of a Bolton mill-worker, who wrote powerful radical fiction for a range of working-class periodicals towards the end of the century. These included *The Daughter of the Factory* (1898), a passionate plea for the working-class woman. Rose Hilton is the foundling daughter of an unprincipled factory owner brought up by a working-class couple. Employed in her father's cotton mill, she becomes a fearless Radical leader who unintentionally sets off a riot in which the factory owner dies, not before a final reconciliation with his wronged daughter. Another fine industrial novel written entirely from the workers' point of view, W. E. Tirebuck's *Miss Grace of All Souls* (1895), also illustrates the spirit of emergent socialism. But the classic of working-class life, Robert Tressell's *The Ragged Trousered Philanthropists*, only appeared in 1907.

'Working-class fiction' takes on another meaning when applied to *sensational novels that were meant to entertain the rapidly growing mass market. Adam Pae, the son of a Perthshire miller, although shunned by 'respectable' reviewers, had a huge readership in Scotland and the north for his combination of melodrama, religious sentiment and social indignation, and from 1855 pioneered the syndicated publication of fiction in English newspapers that was to be developed by the Tillotsons in the 1870s (see above, p. 208). In London the impoverished hack Thomas Peckett Prest wrote *Ela the Outcast* (1837–8), as well as a mass of sensation novels and plagiarisms, particularly of Dickens, for the pioneer penny-issue publisher Edward Lloyd. But a new generation of more sophisticated writers were turning their talents to exploiting the popular market, including *James Malcolm Rymer, the prolific J. F. Smith, parodied as 'Sigmund Smith' in *Mary Elizabeth Braddon's *The Doctor's Wife* (1865), and, most popular of all, *G. W. M. Reynolds, whose heady mix of radical sentiment with melodramatic sensationalism made him reputedly the most-read novelist of the century.

Further Reading

Background

General

The standard bibliography to the literature of the period is J. Shattock, *Cambridge Bibliography of English Literature, 1800–1900*, 3rd edn, vol. 4 (1999). To trace articles and reviews in major contemporary periodicals see W. Houghton et al., *Wellesley Index to Victorian Periodicals* (1966–89). The many excellent background studies of Victorian literature and society include R. Gilmour, *The Victorian Period: The Intellectual and Cultural Context in English Literature, 1830–1890* (1993); H. F. Tucker, ed., *A Companion to Victorian Literature and Culture* (1999); and P. Davis, *The Oxford English Literary History*, vol. 8, *1830–1880: The Victorians* (2002). J. Sutherland's *Longman Companion to Victorian Fiction* (1999) provides valuable information on authors, novels, themes and publishing background. Useful resources of material are also to be found on Internet sites, including www.victoriandatabase.com; and the *Oxford Dictionary of National Biography*, www.oxforddnb.com.

Criticism of the novel

For Victorian attitudes to the novel, see M. Allott, ed., *Novelists on the Novel* (1959); R. Stang, *The Theory of the Novel in England, 1850–1870* (1959); K. Graham, *English Criticism on the Novel, 1865–1900* (1965); J. C. Olmstead, ed., *A Victorian Art of Fiction: Essays on the Novel in British Periodicals 1870–1900*, 3 vols (1979); H. Orel, *Victorian Literary Critics* (1984); S. Regan, ed., *The Nineteenth-century Novel: A Critical Reader* (2001). A useful survey of post-1901 criticism is F. O'Gorman, *Blackwell Guides to Criticism: The Victorian Novel* (2002), which begins with a discussion of nineteenth-century novel theory. A. Jenkins and J. John, eds, *Rereading Victorian Fiction* (2000) opens stimulating arguments. Other relevant critical texts are cited throughout this bibliography.

General background
C. Matthew, ed., *The Nineteenth Century: The British Isles 1815–1901* (2000) provides an excellent introduction; standard works include W. L. Burns, *The Age of Equipoise* (1964); H. Perkin, *The Origins of Modern English Society 1780–1880* (1969); A. Briggs, *The Age of Improvement, 1783–1867*, rev. edn (1979); J. F. C. Harrison, *Early Victorian Britain 1832–1851* (1971); G. Best, *Mid-Victorian Britain 1851–1870* (1971). See also *Contexts and Topics, below.*

Key Authors

W. H. Ainsworth
W. E. Axon, *William Harrison Ainsworth* (1902); S. M. Ellis, *William Harrison Ainsworth and his Friends* (1911); K. Hollingworth, *The Newgate Novel 1830–1870* (1963); G. J. Worth, ed., *William Harrison Ainsworth* (1972); Topic: Historical Novels.

Walter Besant
W. Besant, *Autobiography* (1902); P. J. Keating, *The Working Classes in Victorian Fiction* (1971). S. Regan, ed., *The Nineteenth-century Novel* (2001) reprints the essays in 'The Art of Fiction' debate. Topic: Working-class Novels.

Mary Elizabeth Braddon
R. L. Wolff, *Sensational Victorian: The Life and Fiction of Mary Elizabeth Braddon* (1979); J. Carnell, *The Literary Lives of Mrs Braddon: A Study of her Life and Work* (2000); M. Tromp, P. K. Gilbert and A. Haynie, eds, *After Sensation: Mary Elizabeth Braddon in Context* (2000); *The Doctor's Wife* and *John Marchmont's Legacy* are reissued in excellent Oxford World's Classics editions. Key Text: *Lady Audley's Secret*. Topic: Sensation Novels.

The Brontë sisters
F. E. Ratchford, *The Brontës' Web of Childhood* (1941); J. H. Miller, *The Disappearance of God: Five Nineteenth-century Writers* (1963); W. Gérin, *Charlotte Brontë* (1967), *Emily Brontë* (1971); M. Allott, ed., *The Brontës: The Critical Heritage* (1974); F. B. Pinion, *A Brontë Companion* (1974); M. Peters, *Unquiet Soul: A Biography of Charlotte Brontë* (1975); H. J. Rosengarten, 'The Brontës', in G. H. Ford, ed., *The Victorians: A Second Guide to Research* (1978); E. Chitham, *A Life of Emily Brontë* (1987); J. Barker, *The Brontës* (1994); S. Shuttleworth, *Charlotte Brontë and Victorian Psychology* (1996); M. Thormählen, *The Brontës and Religion* (2000); C. Alexander and M. Smith, eds, *The Oxford Companion to the Brontës* (2003). Key Texts: Charlotte Brontë, *Jane Eyre*, *Villette*; Emily Brontë, *Wuthering Heights*.

Rhoda Broughton
H. C. Black, *Notable Women Authors of the Day* (1893); M. Wood, *Rhoda Broughton: Profile of a Novelist* (1993).

Wilkie Collins
K. Robinson, *Wilkie Collins: A Biography* (1974); S. Lonoff, *Wilkie Collins and his Victorian Readers* (1982); W. M. Clarke, *The Secret Life of Wilkie Collins* (1988); N. Rance, *Wilkie Collins and Other Sensation Novelists* (1989); T. Heller, *Dead Secrets: Wilkie Collins and the Female Gothic* (1992); C. Peters, *The King of the Inventors: A Life of Wilkie Collins* (1993). Key Text: *The Woman in White*.

Marie Corelli
B. Masters, *Now Barabbas was a Rotter: The Extraordinary Life of Marie Corelli* (1978); T. Ransom, *The Mysterious Miss Marie Corelli* (1999); A. Frederico, *Idol of Suburbia: Marie Corelli and Later Victorian Literary Culture* (2000). Key Text: *The Sorrows of Satan*.

Charles Dickens
Dickens criticism is a massive industry, and any selection is necessarily invidious. Standard biographies include J. Forster, *Life* (1872–4); E. Wilson, 'The Two Scrooges', in *The Wound and the Bow* (1941); E. Johnson, *Charles Dickens: His Tragedy and Triumph*, 2 vols (1952; rev. and abridged, 1977); P. Ackroyd, *Dickens* (1990); G. Smith, *Charles Dickens: A Literary Life* (1996). Michael Slater's forthcoming *Life* promises to be definitive. Both the ongoing Clarendon edition of Dickens' *Letters* (1974–) (various editors) and the Dent volumes of Dickens' *Journalism* (1994–), ed. M. Slater, contain invaluable material. Background studies include H. House, *The Dickens World* (1941); G. Ford, *Dickens and his Readers* (1955); J. Butt and K. Tillotson, *Dickens at Work* (1957); H. J. Miller, *Charles Dickens, the World of his Novels* (1958); P. Collins, *Dickens and Crime* (1962) and *Dickens and Education* (1971); Collins, ed., *Charles Dickens: The Public Readings* (1975); D. Walder, *Dickens and Religion* (1981); M. Slater, *Dickens and Women* (1983); M. Andrews, *Dickens and the Grown-up Child* (1994). Anthologies of criticism include J. Gross and G. Pearson, eds, *Dickens in the Twentieth Century* (1962) and S. Wall, *Penguin Critical Anthology* (1970); see also the survey essay 'Criticism and Scholarship', in P. Schlicke, ed., *Oxford Reader's Companion to Dickens* (1999). Key Texts: *Oliver Twist*, *Bleak House*, *Great Expectations*.

Benjamin Disraeli
R. Blake, *Disraeli* (1966) (biography); D. R. Schwartz, *Disraeli's Fiction* (1979).

Sir Arthur Conan Doyle

H. Pearson, *Conan Doyle: His Life and Art* (1943); I. Ousby, *Bloodhounds of Heaven: The Detective in English Fiction from Godwin to Doyle* (1976); R. D. Cox, *Arthur Conan Doyle* (1985); H. Orel, ed., *Critical Essays on Sir Arthur Conan Doyle* (1992). See Context 2: Detectives, p. 64.

George Eliot

Outstanding among many good biographies are G. Haight, *George Eliot: A Biography* (1968), which is supplemented by Haight's edition of *The George Eliot Letters*, 9 vols (1954–78); M. Laski, *George Eliot and Her World* (1973); J. Uglow, *George Eliot* (1987); R. Bodenheimer, *The Real Life of Mary Ann Evans* (1994). Critical studies include: J. Bennett, *George Eliot: Her Mind and Her Art* (1948); B. Hardy, *The Novels of George Eliot* (1959); W. J. Harvey, *The Art of George Eliot* (1961); G. Beer, *George Eliot* (1968); G. Haight, ed., *A Century of George Eliot Criticism* (1986); G. Handley, *State of the Art: George Eliot, a Guide through the Critical Maze* (1990); D. Carroll, *George Eliot and the Conflict of Interpretations* (1992); J. Rignall, ed., *Oxford Reader's Companion to George Eliot* (2000). Key Texts: *Adam Bede, Middlemarch*.

Elizabeth Gaskell

W. A. Craik, *Mrs Gaskell and the English Provincial Novel* (1975); W. Gérin, *Elizabeth Gaskell* (1976); A. Easson, *Elizabeth Gaskell* (1979); J. Uglow, *Elizabeth Gaskell: A Habit of Stories* (1993). Gaskell's *Letters*, ed. J. A. V. Chapple and Arthur Pollard (1966), and *Further Letters*, ed. J. A. V. Chapple and A. Shelston (2000), provide an invaluable background to her life and fiction. Key Text: *North and South*.

George Gissing

J. Korg, *George Gissing: A Critical Biography* (1963); P. Coustillas, ed., *Collected Articles on George Gissing* (1968); Coustillas and C. Partridge, eds, *George Gissing: The Critical Heritage* (1968); J. Goode, *George Gissing: Ideology and Fiction* (1978); R. Selig, *George Gissing* (1983); M. Collie, *George Gissing: A Bibliographical Study* (1985). Key Text: *New Grub Street*.

Sir Henry Rider Haggard

D. S. Higgins, *Rider Haggard: The Great Storyteller* (1981); W. R. Katz, *Rider Haggard and the Fiction of Empire* (1987). Key Text: *She*. Topic: Colonial Novels.

Thomas Hardy

N. Page, ed., *Oxford Reader's Companion to Hardy* (2000) is a useful survey, with bibliography. The standard biography is M. Millgate, *Thomas Hardy: A Biography*

Revisited (2005). On criticism: D. H. Lawrence, 'A Study of Thomas Hardy', in *Phoenix* (1936); R. L. Purdy, *Thomas Hardy: A Bibliographical Study* (1954, rev. 1968); J. Hillis Miller, *Thomas Hardy: Distance and Desire* (1970); M. Williams, *Thomas Hardy and Rural England* (1972); I. Gregor, *The Great Web: The Form of Hardy's Major Fiction* (1974); P. Boumelha, *Thomas Hardy and Women* (1982). Key Text: *Tess of the D'Urbervilles.*

G. P. R. James
S. M. Ellis, *The Solitary Horseman: Or the Life and Adventures of G. P. R. James* (1927).

Henry James
The standard biography is still L. Edel, *Life of Henry James* (1977), supplemented by J. Tambling, *Henry James* (2000). Selections of James' critical essays include Edel, ed., *The House of Fiction* (1957) and R. Gard, ed., *Henry James, The Critical Muse: Selected Literary Criticism* (1987). See also F. O. Matthiessen, *Henry James: The Major Phase* (1944; with new appendix, 1963); T. Tanner, ed., *Henry James: Modern Judgement* (1968); K. Graham, *Henry James: The Dream of Fulfilment* (1975). A useful guide through the mass of criticism on James is J. Freedman, ed., *Cambridge Companion to Henry James* (1998). Key Text: *Portrait of a Lady.*

Douglas Jerrold
M. Slater, *Douglas Jerrold, 1803–1857* (2002).

Geraldine Jewsbury
S. Howe, *Geraldine Jewsbury* (1935); J. R. Fahnstock, 'Geraldine Jewsbury: The Power of the Publisher's Reader', *Nineteenth-century Fiction*, 28 (1973), pp. 253–72. Key Text: *Zoe*, reprinted by Virago Classics (1986).

Charles Kingsley
R. B. Martin, *The Dust of Combat* (1959); S. Chitty, *The Beast and the Monk: A Life of Charles Kingsley* (1975); B. Colloms, *Charles Kingsley* (1975); G. Kendall, *Charles Kingsley and His Ideas* (1975). Key Text: *The Water-Babies.* Topic: Religious Novels.

Rudyard Kipling
C. Carrington, *Rudyard Kipling, his Life and Work* (1955, rev. 1976); J. M. S. Tomkins, *The Art of Rudyard Kipling* (1959); A. Rutherford, ed., *Kipling's Mind and Art* (1964); R. E. Harbord, *The Reader's Guide to Rudyard Kipling's Work*, 8 vols (1962–72).

Sheridan Le Fanu
N. Browne, *Sheridan Le Fanu* (1951); S. M. Ellis, *Wilkie Collins, Le Fanu and Others* (1951); W. J. MacCormack, *Sheridan Le Fanu and Victorian Ireland* (1980). Topic: The Supernatural.

Edward Bulwer-Lytton
M. Sadlier, *Bulwer: A Panorama* (1931); A. C. Christensen, *Edward Bulwer-Lytton: The Fiction of New Regions* (1976); J. L. Campbell, *Edward Bulwer-Lytton* (1986); A. C. Christensen, ed., *The Subverting Vision of Bulwer-Lytton* (2004). Topic: Science, Utopias and Dystopias.

George Macdonald
A. Freemantle, *The Visionary Novels of George Macdonald* (1954); R. L. Woolf, *The Golden Key: A Study of the Novels of George Macdonald* (1961); R. Robb, *George Macdonald* (1988).

Frederick Marryat
F. Marryat, *The Life and Letters of Captain Marryat*, 2 vols (1872); D. Hannay, *Captain Marryat* (1889); O. Warner, *Captain Marryat: A Rediscovery* (1953).

Harriet Martineau
R. K. Webb, *Harriet Martineau, a Radical Victorian* (1960); V. Sanders, *Reason over Passion: Harriet Martineau and the Victorian Novel* (1986).

George Meredith
L. Stevenson, *The Ordeal of George Meredith* (1953) (standard biography); W. F. Wright, *Art and Substance in George Meredith* (1953); G. Beer, *Meredith: A Change of Masks* (1970) (analyses six novels); I. Fletcher, ed., *Meredith Now* (1971). Key Text: *The Egoist*.

George Moore
J. Hone, *The Life of George Moore* (1936); M. J. Brown, *George Moore: A Reconsideration* (1955); J. E. Dunleavy, *George Moore: The Artist's Vision, the Story-teller's Art* (1973); R. A. Cave, *A Study of the Novels of George Moore* (1978); J. E. Dunleavy, ed., *George Moore in Perspective* (1983); T. Gray, *A Peculiar Man: A Life of George Moore* (1996). Key Text: *Esther Waters*.

Margaret Oliphant
E. Jay, ed., *The Autobiography of Margaret Oliphant: The Complete Text* (1990); Jay, *Mrs Oliphant: A Fiction to Herself* (1995).

Ouida (Marie Louise de la Ramée)

E. Bigland, *Ouida, the Passionate Victorian* (1950); M. Stirling, *The Fine and the Wicked: The Life and Times of Ouida* (1957). Key Text: *Under Two Flags*.

Charles Reade

A. M. Turner, *The Making of the Cloister and the Hearth* (1938); W. Burns, *Charles Reade: A Study in Victorian Authorship* (1961); E. E. Smith, *Charles Reade* (1976). See Context 3: The Modality of Melodrama, p. 88.

G. W. M. Reynolds

'G. W. M. Reynolds', *Bookseller* (1879) (obituary); R. C. Maxwell, 'G. W. M. Reynolds, Dickens, and "The Mysteries of London"', *Nineteenth-century Fiction*, 32 (1977), pp. 188–213; A. Humpherys, 'The Geometry of the Modern City: G. W. M. Reynolds and "The Mysteries of London"', *Browning Institute Studies*, 34, 4 (Summer 1991), pp. 69–80; T. Thomas, 'Introduction' to his selection, *G. W. M. Reynolds, 'The Mysteries of London'* (1996); Thomas, 'Rereading G. W. M. Reynolds's "The Mysteries of London"', in A. Jenkins and J. John, eds, *Rereading Victorian Fiction* (2000), pp. 59–80. Key Text: *The Mysteries of London*.

J. M. Rymer

M. Dalziel, *Popular Fiction a 100 Years Ago* (1957); L. James, *Fiction for the Working Man, 1830–1850* (1963; rev. 1974); E. F. Beiler, 'Introduction' to J. M. Rymer, *Varney the Vampyre* (1972), pp. v–xviii; L. James, 'James Malcolm Rymer', in *Oxford DNB* (2004).

Robert Louis Stevenson

R. L. Stevenson, 'A Humble Remonstrance', *Longman's Magazine* (1884); D. Daiches, *Robert Louis Stevenson and His World* (1946); R. L. Stevenson, *Essays*, ed. M. Elwin (1950); D. Daiches, *Stevenson and the Art of Fiction* (1951); J. C. Furnas, *Voyage to Windward: The Life of Robert Louis Stevenson* (1952); R. Kiely, *Robert Louis Stevenson and the Fiction of Adventure* (1964); P. Maixner, ed., *Robert Louis Stevenson: The Critical Heritage* (1981). Key Text: *The Strange Case of Dr Jekyll and Mr Hyde*.

Robert Surtees

J. Welcome, *The Sporting World of J. S. Surtees* (1982); N. Gash, *Robert Surtees and Early Victorian Life* (1993).

W. M. Thackeray

G. N. Ray, ed., *Letters and Private Papers*, 4 vols (1945–6); Ray, *Thackeray: The Uses of Adversity, 1811–46* (1955); Ray, *Thackeray: The Age of Wisdom, 1847–63* (1958) (the standard biography); G. Tillotson, *Thackeray the Novelist* (1954); G. Tillotson and D. Hawes, eds, *Thackeray: The Critical Heritage* (1968); B. Hardy, *The Exposure of Luxury: Radical Themes in Thackeray* (1972); J. A. Sutherland, *Thackeray at Work* (1974); J. Carey, *Thackeray: Prodigious Genius* (1978); R. A. Colby, *Thackeray's Canvass of Humanity* (1979); C. Peters, *Thackeray's Universe: Shifting Worlds of Imagination and Reality* (1987). Key Texts: *Vanity Fair, Pendennis*.

Anthony Trollope

A. Trollope, *An Autobiography* (1883); N. J. Hall, ed., *The Letters of Anthony Trollope*, 2 vols (1983); R. Mullen, *Anthony Trollope: A Victorian in His World* (1990); V. Glendenning, *Trollope* (1992). On criticism see R. Kincaid, *The Novels of Anthony Trollope* (1977); D. Skilton, *Anthony Trollope and His Contemporaries* (1972, 1996); S. Wall, *Trollope and Character* (1988); L. J. Swingle, *Romanticism and Anthony Trollope: A Study of Continuities in Nineteenth-century Literary Thought* (1990). Surveys include N. J. Hall, ed., *The Trollope Critics* (1981); R. C. Terry, *Oxford Reader's Companion to Trollope* (1999). Key Texts: *Barchester Towers, The Way We Live Now*.

Mrs Humphry Ward

E. H. Ward, *Mrs Humphry Ward* (1973); W. S. Paterson, *Victorian Heretic: Mrs Humphry Ward's 'Robert Elsmere'* (1973); E. M. G. Smith, *Mrs Humphry Ward* (1980); J. Sutherland, *Mrs Humphry Ward: Eminent Victorian, Pre-eminent Edwardian* (1990).

H. G. Wells

H. G. Wells, 'Preface' to *Seven Famous Novels* (1934), reprinted as *The Complete Science Fiction . . .* (1978); B. Bregonzi, *The Early H. G. Wells* (1961); R. Hillegas, *The Future as Nightmare: H. G. Wells and the Anti-Utopians* (1967); M. Rose, ed., *Science Fiction* (1976); J. Huntingdon, *The Logic of Fantasy: H. G. Wells and Science Fiction* (1982). Key Text: *The Time Machine*. Topic: Science, Utopias and Dystopias.

[William Hale White] Mark Rutherford

C. M. Maclean, *Mark Rutherford: A Biography of William Hale White* (1955); I. Stock, *William Hale White: A Critical Study* (1956); V. Cunningham, *Everywhere Spoken Against: Dissent in the Victorian Novel* (1975); J. Lucas, *The Literature of Change*, 2nd edn (1980), ch. 3.

Mrs Henry [Ellen] Wood

C. W. Wood, *Memorials of Mrs Henry Wood* (1894); W. Hughes, *The Maniac in the Cellar: Sensation Novels of the 1860s* (1980); N. Auerbach, *The Woman and the Demon: The Life of a Victorian Myth* (1982). Key Text: *East Lynne*. Topic: Sensation Novels.

Charlotte Mary Yonge
G. Battiscombe, *Charlotte Mary Yonge* (1943); Battiscombe and M. Laski, eds, *A Chaplet for Charlotte Yonge* (1965) (good critical essays, bibliographies); R. L. Woolf, *Gains and Losses: Novels of Faith and Doubt in Victorian England* (1977) (context); B. Dennis, *Charlotte Yonge: Novelist of the Oxford Movement* (1992); J. Sturrock, *Heaven and Home: Charlotte Yonge's Domestic Fiction* (1995).

Key Texts

Mary Shelley, Frankenstein
The 1818 version of *Frankenstein* was published as a Broadview Literary Text, ed. D. L. Macdonald and K. Scherf (1994); see also G. Levine and U. C. Knoepflmacher, *The Endurance of Frankenstein: Essays on Mary Shelley's Novel* (1979); Levine, *The Realistic Imagination: English Fiction from Frankenstein to Lady Chatterley* (1981); F. Moretti, *Signs Taken as Wonders* (1983), ch. 3; C. Baldick, *In Frankenstein's Shadow* (1987); F. Botting, *Making Monstrous* (1991) (extensive bibliography).

Pierce Egan, Sr, Life in London
J. Franklin, *The Cockney* (1953) (on Egan's speech idioms); J. C. Reid, *Bucks and Bruisers: Pierce Egan and Regency England* (1971); J. Marriott, 'Introduction' to *Unknown London: Early Modernist Visions of the Metropolis, 1815–1845* (2000), vol. 1 (this volume reprints Egan's text).

Charles Dickens, Oliver Twist
K. Tillotson's Clarendon edition of *Oliver Twist* (1966) prints Dickens' textual revisions. Important essays include A. Kettle, in *An Introduction to the English Novel* (1951); J. Bayley, 'Oliver Twist: Things as They Really Are', in J. Gross and G. Pearson, eds, *Dickens and the Twentieth Century* (1962). Dickens' famous reading, 'Sikes and Nancy', is transcribed in P. Collins, ed., *Dickens: The Public Readings* (1975).

G. W. M. Reynolds, The Mysteries of London
R. C. Maxwell, 'G. W. M. Reynolds, Dickens, and "The Mysteries of London"', *Nineteenth-century Fiction*, 32 (1977), pp. 188–213; L. James, 'The View from Brick Lane', *Yearbook of English Studies*, 11 (1981), pp. 87–101; Anne Humpherys, 'The Geometry of the Modern City: G. W. M. Reynolds and "The Mysteries of London"', *Browning Institute Studies*, 34, 4 (Summer 1991), pp. 69–80; Reynolds, *The Mysteries of London*, abridged with introduction and bibliography by T. Thomas (1996); R. Mighall, *A Geography of Victorian Gothic Fiction* (1999).

Charlotte Brontë, Jane Eyre
S. M. Gilbert and S. Gubar, *The Madwoman in the Attic* (1979); P. Nestor, *Charlotte Brontë's Jane Eyre* (1992). There is a useful *Casebook*, ed. M. Allott (1973), and a Norton edition, ed. R. J. Dunn (1987).

Emily Brontë, Wuthering Heights
D. van Ghent, in *The English Novel: Form and Function* (1953); T. Eagleton, *Myths of Power* (1975). There are anthologies of criticism on the novel edited by A. Everitt (1967) and P. Stoneman (1993), and a Norton anthology edited by W. M. Sale, Jr and R. J. Dunn (1990).

W. M. Thackeray, Vanity Fair
G. and K. Tillotson, 'Introduction' to the Riverside edition (1963). The Oxford World's Classics edition, ed. J. Sutherland (1983), reproduces the original text, and has excellent introduction and notes.

W. M. Thackeray, Pendennis
R. A. Colby, in *Thackeray's Canvass of Humanity* (1979).

Charles Dickens, Bleak House
J. Butt and K. Tillotson, in *Dickens at Work* (1957); H. Miller, in *Charles Dickens: The World of His Novels* (1958); W. J. Harvey, in J. Gross and G. Pearson, eds, *Dickens and the Twentieth Century* (1962); D. A. Miller, in *The Novel and the Police* (1988). Both A. E. Dyson (1969) and H. Bloom (1987) have edited collections of essays on the novel.

Charlotte Brontë, Villette
M. Allott, ed., *Charlotte Brontë, Jane Eyre and Villette: A Casebook* (1973); S. Shuttleworth, *Charlotte Brontë and Victorian Psychology* (1996).

Elizabeth Gaskell, North and South
W. A. Craik, *Elizabeth Gaskell and the English Provincial Novel* (1975); D. David, *Fictions of Resolution in Three Victorian Novels: North and South, Our Mutual Friend, Daniel Deronda* (1981).

George Eliot, Adam Bede
D. van Ghent, 'Adam Bede', in *The English Novel: Form and Function* (1953); R. Williams, *The Country and the City* (1973), ch. 16; J. Sutherland, 'Why Doesn't the Reverend Irwine Speak Up for Hetty?' in *Can Jane Eyre Be Happy?* (1997).

Wilkie Collins, The Woman in White
W. Collins, 'How I Write My Books', *The Globe*, 26 November (1887); W. Hughes, in *The Maniac in the Cellar: Sensation Novels of the 1860s* (1980); J. B. Taylor, *In the Secret Theatre of the Home: Wilkie Collins, Sensation Narrative and Nineteenth-century Psychology* (1988). See also 'Sensation novels', below.

Charles Dickens, Great Expectations
J. Moynahan, 'The Hero's Guilt: The Case of *Great Expectations*', *Essays in Criticism*, 10 (1960); R. Gilmour, *The Idea of the Gentleman in the Victorian Novel* (1981). The fullest of several good editions is the Norton critical edition (1999), ed. E. Rosenberg.

Mrs Henry [Ellen] Wood, East Lynne
W. Hughes, in *The Maniac in the Cellar: Sensation Novels of the 1860s* (1980).

Mary Elizabeth Braddon, Lady Audley's Secret
C. Briganti, 'Gothic Maidens and Sensation Women: Lady Audley's Journey from the Ruined Mansion to the Madhouse', *Victorian Literature and Culture*, 19 (1991), pp. 189–211; J. B. Taylor and R. Crofts, eds, *Lady Audley's Secret*, Penguin Classics (1998).

Lewis Carroll, the Alice books
A. L. Taylor, *The White Knight: A Study of C. L. Dodson (Lewis Carroll)* (1952); M. Gardner, ed., *The Annotated Alice*, rev. edn (1970); R. Phillips, ed., *Aspects of Alice* (1971); D. Hudson, *Lewis Carroll: An Illustrated Biography* (1976); R. Fordyce, *Lewis Carroll: A Reference Guide* (1988).

R. D. Blackmore, Lorna Doone
W. H. Dunn, *R. D. Blackmore: The Author of Lorna Doone* (1956); W. J. Keith, *Regions of the Imagination: The Development of Rural Fiction* (1988).

George Eliot, Middlemarch
J. Beaty, ed., *Middlemarch from Notebook to Novel: A Study of George Eliot's Critical Method* (1960); B. Hardy, ed., *Middlemarch: Critical Approaches to the Novel* (1967); K. McSweeney, *Middlemarch* (1984).

Anthony Trollope, The Way We Live Now
T. Tanner, 'Trollope's *The Way We Live Now*, its Modern Significance', *Critical Quarterly*, 9.3 (1967), pp. 256–73; R. Tracy, *Trollope's Later Novels* (1978).

George Meredith, The Egoist
V. Woolf, 'The Novels of George Meredith', in *The Second Common Reader* (1932); D. van Ghent, in *The English Novel: Form and Function* (1953); G. Beer, *Meredith: A Change of Masks* (1970), pp. 114–19.

Henry James, The Portrait of a Lady
P. Buitenhuis, ed., *Twentieth-century Interpretations of The Portrait of a Lady* (1968); J. Porter, ed., *New Essays on James's The Portrait of a Lady* (1990).

[Olive Schreiner] Ralph Iron, The Story of an African Farm
J. A. Berman, *The Healing Imagination of Olive Schreiner* (1989); E. Showalter, *Sexual Anarchy: Gender and Culture in the Fin-de-siècle* (1991); J. Bristow, 'Introduction' and 'Bibliography' to the Oxford World's Classics edition (1998).

Sir Henry Rider Haggard, She
S. M. Gilbert and S. Gubar, in *No Man's Land*, vol. 2 (1989); D. Karlin, 'Preface' to Oxford World's Classics edition (1991).

Thomas Hardy, Tess of the D'Urbervilles
A. Kettle, in *An Introduction to the English Novel* (1951), vol. 2, pp. 49–62; D. van Ghent, in *The English Novel: Form and Function* (1953), pp. 195–209; the Norton critical edition of *Tess*, 2nd edn, ed. S. Elledge (1965); W. E. Davis, 'Tess of the D'Urbervilles', *Nineteenth-century Fiction*, 22 (1968), pp. 397–401; J. S. Miller, in *Forms of Modern English Fiction* (1975), pp. 43–71.

Marie Corelli, The Sorrows of Satan
P. Keating, 'Introduction' to the Oxford World's Classics edition (1998).

H. G. Wells, The Time Machine
H. M. Geduld, ed., *The Definitive Time Machine: A Critical Edition* (1987); P. Parrinder, *Shadows of the Future: H .G. Wells, Science Fiction and Prophecy* (1995).

Arthur Morrison, A Child of the Jago
P. Keating, *The Working Classes in Victorian Fiction* (1971). The Everyman edition, ed. P. Miles (1996), has good notes and an extensive bibliography.

Bram Stoker, Dracula
L. Wolf, ed., *The Annotated Dracula* (1975); F. Moretti, *Signs Taken for Wonders* (1983); M. L. Carter, ed., *Dracula, the Vampire and the Critics* (1988); *Bram Stoker's Dracula: A Centennial Exhibition* (1997).

Contexts and Topics

Biography
G. P. Landow, ed., *Approaches to Victorian Autobiography* (1979); D. Vincent, *Bread, Knowledge and Freedom* (1981); V. Sanders, *The Private Lives of Victorian Women* (1989); C. Ricks, 'Victorian Lives', in *Essays in Appreciation* (1996).

Childhood and the family
A still useful summary is W. E. Houghton, *The Victorian Frame of Mind, 1830–1870* (1973), pp. 341–8. See also C. Stedman, *Strange Dislocations: Childhood and the Idea of Human Interiority, 1830–1930* (1959); P. Ariès, *Centuries of Childhood*, trans. R. Baldick (1962); E. Shorter, *The Making of the Modern Family* (1975); L. Stone, *The Family, Sex and Marriage in England, 1500–1800* (1977); N. Armstrong, *Desire and Victorian Fiction* (1987); A. Davin, *Growing Up Poor: Home, School and Street in London, 1870–1914* (1996).

Children's novels
H. Carpenter, *Secret Gardens: A Study of the Golden Age of Children's Literature* (1985); P. Hunt, ed., *Children's Literature: An Anthology, 1801–1902* (2001).

Colonial novels
A. Sandison, *The Wheel of Empire* (1967); K. Carpenter, *Desert Isles and Pirate Islands: The Island Theme in Nineteenth-century Juvenile Fiction* (1984); P. Brantlinger, *Rule of Darkness: British Literature and Imperialism, 1830–1914* (1988); B. Moore-Gilbert, G. Santon and W. Marley, eds, *Postcolonial Criticism* (1997).

Detective stories
T. S. Eliot, 'Wilkie Collins and Dickens', in *Collected Essays* (1960); W. H. Auden, 'The Guilty Vicarage', in *The Dyer's Hand* (1963); J. G. Cawelti, *Adventure, Mystery and Romance* (1976); I. Ousby, *Bloodhounds of Heaven: The Detective in English Fiction from Godwin to Doyle* (1976); R. R. Thomas, *Detective Fiction and the Rise of Forensic Science* (1999).

Evolution
L. J. Henkin, *Darwinism in the English Novel, 1860–1910* (1940, reissued 1963); W. Irvine, *Apes, Angels and Victorians: The Story of Darwin, Huxley and Evolution* (1955); T. Cosslett, ed., *The 'Scientific Movement' in Victorian Literature* (1984); R. M. Young, *Darwin's Metaphor: Nature's Place in Victorian Culture* (1985); G. Levine, *Darwin and the Novelists: Patterns of Science in Victorian Fiction* (1988); G. Beer, *Darwin's Plots: Evolutionary Narrative in Darwin, George Eliot and Nineteenth-century Fiction* (1983); S. Shuttleworth, *George Eliot and Nineteenth-century Science* (1984).

Historical novels
G. Lukács, *The Historical Novel*, trans. H. and S. Mitchell (1962); A. Fleishman, *The English Historical Novel* (1971); A. Sanders, *The Victorian Historical Novel, 1840–1880* (1978).

Illustrated novels
J. H. Harvey, *Victorian Novelists and Their Illustrators* (1970); G. N. Ray, *The Illustrator and the Book in England from 1790 to 1914* (1976); F. Reid, *Illustrators of the 1860s* (1995); S. Sillars, *Visualization and Popular Fiction, 1860–1960: Graphic Narratives, Fictional Images* (1995).

Irish novels
M. Harmon, *Modern Irish Literature, 1800–1967: A Reader's Guide* (1967); R. McHugh and M. Harmon, *A Short History of Anglo-Irish Literature* (1982).

Melodrama
M. R. Booth, *English Melodrama* (1965); F. Rahill, *The World of Melodrama* (1967); J. L. Smith, *Melodrama* (1973); P. Brooks, *The Melodramatic Imagination* (1976); J. Redmond, ed., *Melodrama* (1992); J. Bratton, J. Cook and C. Gledhill, eds, *Melodrama: Stage, Picture, Screen* (1994).

'New woman' novels
E. Showalter, *A Literature of Their Own* (1977); G. Cunningham, *The New Woman and the Victorian Woman* (1978); L. Pykett, *The Improper Feminine: The Woman's Sensation Novel and the New Woman Writing* (1992).

Publishing formats, journalism, audiences
J. Butt and K. Tillotson, *Dickens at Work* (1957); J. A. Sutherland, *Victorian Novelists and Publishers* (1976); N. N. Feltes, *Modes of Production of Victorian Novels* (1986); K. Flint, *The Woman Reader, 1837–1914* (1993); L. Brake, *Subjugated Knowledges: Journalism, Gender and Literature in the Nineteenth Century* (1994); J. Sutherland, *Victorian Fiction: Writers, Publishers, Readers* (1995); M. Beetham, *A Magazine of Their Own? Domesticity and Desire in the Woman's Magazine, 1800–1914* (1996); G. Law, *Serializing Fiction in the Victorian Press* (2000); A. King, *The London Journal, 1843–1883: Periodicals, Production and Gender* (2004).

Regional novels
J. Lucas, *The Literature of Change: Studies in the Nineteenth-century Provincial Novel* (1977).

Religion, literature and society
O. Chadwick, *The Victorian Church*, 2 vols (1966, 1970); J. Coulson, *Religion and Imagination* (1981); H. Fraser, *Beauty and Belief* (1986); B. Hilton, *The Age of Atonement: The Influence of Evangelicalism on Social and Economic Thought, 1785–1865* (1988); M. Wheeler, *Death and the Future Life in Victorian Literature and Theology* (1990).

Religious novels
M. Maison, *Search Your Soul, Eustace* (1961); V. Cunningham, *Everywhere Spoken Against* (1975); R. L. Woolf, *Gains and Losses: Novels of Faith and Doubt in Victorian England* (1977); E. Jay, *The Religion of the Heart: Anglican Evangelicalism and the Nineteenth-century Novel* (1979).

Sensation novels
W. C. Phillips, *Dickens, Reade and Collins: Sensation Novelists* (1969); K. Tillotson, 'The Lighter Reading of the Eighteen-sixties', in W. Collins, *The Woman in White*, Riverside edition (1969), pp. ix–xvii; W. Hughes, *The Maniac in the Cellar: Sensation Novels of the 1860s* (1980); L. Pykett, *The Improper Feminine: The Woman's Sensation Novel and the New Woman* (1992); D. Wynne, *The Sensation Novel and the Victorian Family Magazine* (2001).

Social problem novels
L. Cazamian, *The Social Novel in England, 1830–1850*, trans. M. Fido (1973; original text, 1903); R. Williams, *Culture and Society, 1980–1950* (1958); R. Colby, *Fiction with a Purpose* (1967); R. Williams, *The Country and the City* (1973); S. Smith, *The Other Nation: The Poor in English Novels of the 1840s and 1850s* (1980); G. Himmelfarb, *The Idea of Poverty: England in the Early Industrial Age* (1984); C. Gallagher, *The Industrial Reformation of English Fiction, 1832–1867* (1985).

The supernatural
J. Briggs, *The Night Visitors: The Rise and Fall of the Ghost Story* (1977); E. M. Eigner, *The Metaphysical Novel in England* (1978); N. Royle, *Telepathy and Literature* (1991).

Town and country
H. J. Dyos and M. Wolff, eds, *The Victorian City: Images and Realities* (1973); G. E. Mingay, ed., *The Victorian Countryside* (1981).

Ways of seeing
S. Sitwell, *Narrative Pictures* (1937); C. Wood, *Victorian Panorama* (1976); A. Thomas, *The Expanding Eye: Photography and the Nineteenth-century Mind* (1978);

R. Southern, *The Victorian Theatre* (1979); M. Booth, *Victorian Spectacular Theatre* (1980); R. Hyde, *Panorama!* (1988); L. Nead, *Victorian Babylon: People, Streets and Images in Nineteenth-century London* (2000) (extensive bibliography).

Working-class novels
R. D. Altick, *The English Common Reader: A Social History of the Mass Reading Public, 1800–1900* (1957); M. Dalziel, *Popular Fiction 100 Years Ago* (1957); L. James, *Fiction for the Working Man, 1830–1850* (1963; rev. 1974); P. Keating, *The Working Classes in Victorian Fiction* (1971); I. Haywood, *Working-class Fiction: From Chartism to Trainspotting* (1977); D. Vincent, *Bread, Knowledge and Freedom* (1981); H. Gustav Klaus, ed., *The Socialist Novel in Britain* (1982); I. Haywood, ed., *Chartist Fiction*, 3 vols (1995–2001); G. Law, *Serializing Fiction in the Victorian Press* (2000); J. Rose, *The Intellectual Life of the British Working Classes* (2001); A. King, *The London Journal, 1845–83* (2004).

Index

Main entries are indicated in **bold**.

Autobiography of Mark Rutherford, 145; *Clara Hopwood*, 145; *Mark Rutherford's Deliverance*, 51; *Revolution in Tanner's Lane*, 145
Wilde, Oscar, *Portrait of Dorian Gray*, 96
Wood, Ellen, **145–6**
  The Channings, 146; *Danesbury House*, 218; *East Lynne*, **171–2**, 216; *Mrs Haliburton's Troubles*, 146

Wordsworth, William, 17, 68
working-class novels, **223–4**

Yonge, Charlotte Mary, **146–7**
  Daisy Chain, 78, 146–7; *A Dove in the Eagle's Nest*, 147, 211; *The Heir of Redcliffe*, 20, 146; *The Lances of Lynwood*, 39–40, 147

Zangwill, Israel, *Children of the Ghetto*, 212
Zola, Emile, 33